TIMELESS SECRETS

VOLUME 1

Love My People

*Dearest
Larry + Lody Cynthia
Ruth 2:12*

*for this Glorious
Kingdom*

Jay + Meridel

DRS JAY AND MERIDEL RAWLINGS

Unless otherwise noted, all Scripture quotations are taken from the
Tanach - The Holy Scriptures, The New JPS Translation According to the
Traditional Hebrew Text, The Jewish Publication Society, Philadelphia,
New York, Jerusalem. 5748 - 1988 used by permission. Holy Bible, New
King James Version, copyright 1982 by Thomas Nelson Inc, Nashville,
Tenn., and are used by permission. Scripture quotations marked NKJ are
taken from the New King James Version of the Bible. Scripture quotations
marked KJV are taken from the King James Version of the Bible. Scripture
quotations marked MSG, are taken from The Message Version of the Bible. By Eugene Peterson, and are used by permission.

Timeless Secrets - Volume 1 - *Love My People*

ISBN 978-965-7542-35-4

Editing and Lay-out:
Petra van der Zande, Tsur Tsina Publications, Jerusalem, Israel.

Photo Credits:
Cover: David Rawlings, Back cover: Reynold Mainse, Illustrations: Victor
Rawlings (deceased); India Photos: Meridel Fowler Rawlings; Canada
Photos, Sheila Haslam, (deceased); Holland cemetery photo: Meridel
Rawlings.

Order information:
P O Box 84156, Mevasseret Zion, 9079097, Israel
www.israelvisiontv.blogspot.com
www.stillsmallvoice.tv

Revised: March 2018

Dedication 1

This book is dedicated to our sons David, Chris, Josh and Daniel. You inspired us to write by asking, "Dad, tell us a 'faith' story about the early days when you and Mom left Canada for Israel?" Each of you has blessed us by your lives, your dedication to your families and zeal to excel in the media. Collectively and individually you have caused me to change my approach to TV production and writing when you said, "Dad, your ways are old fashioned! Come on, here is the new technology. Now let's get up to speed!" Thanks guys.

To our grandchildren, Noam, Maya, Amitai, Sophia, Liyah, Cecilie, Youni and Liam, (and to those on the way) you are also a delightful inspiration to our writing. We are so enriched by your presence in our hearts, home and garden! I loved it when, very early one morning, sleepy eyed Noam, in pajamas, traipsed down the stairs into the family room where I was up early writing this book. He came over and stood quietly at my side before venturing, "Grandpa, can you read me what you wrote today?" Thanks kids.

To my mother Sheila - "Sheena" who loved to laugh! Her life was a joy to so many. She spent countless hours with Meridel and me sharing her deepest and most intimate thoughts concerning our family history. I dedicate this book to your memory. Thanks Mom.

To my father, Victor Alloway Rawlings, who fell in battle seventy years to the day that I penned these words: Dad you are the first person I long to meet in heaven. To Billy, my 'appointed' Dad, I thank you for all that you put into my life. I bless the memory of you both. Thanks.

Jay Rawlings

Dedication 2

I Meridel, dedicate this book to my godly grandmother, Neva Smith, who confirmed my Jewish heritage. I respected her life of prayer and service, the distillate of suffering. She proved to me *"...all things work together for good to those who love God, to those who are the called according to His purpose."* Romans 8:28

To my pioneer Scots grandfather, Rob Scoular: "do you have any idea how I drank in the loving kindness shown me by your sweet smile and laughing blue eyes? 'Take mine hand granddaddy' was my four year old request of you." You always made me feel safe.

I will never forget when you put us kiddies in your horse drawn sleigh and off we glided over snow covered field and dale. Bells on the horses harness rang sweetly out over the quiet winter landscape. Those bells jingle in my heart to this day.

To Euretta, known affectionately as "Mini," (my diminutive grandma Scoular) you gave me 'space to grow'. Your imagination became mine. I am still warmed by the memories of running barefoot among the rows of flowers and vegetables in your garden at the farm.

Such cherished memories are forever alive within me. The warmth and beauty of your gracious farm home still reach me. It was another world of violin music, poetry, canary song, dreams and prayers. Fragrant gardens surround these memories. You were a champion for the environment way back then. Your children's radio programs taught us about the amazing world of our feathered friends. As an inheritance my mother gave me one of your diaries. Back in 1904, your hand writing recorded the flocks of migrating birds and herds of red deer and elk that roamed over the vast, verdant rolling hills of central Alberta, Canada.

To my mom: You are the joy of my life. Perfectly named 'Joy' you proved to me that with God all things are possible. You encouraged me to believe that I could do what was in my heart. What a heritage I now have in years filled with exploits that have taken me many times around the world, now shared in my marriage, with our children and grandchildren all centered in Jerusalem.

To dad: Thank you. Your effect upon my life was more profound than could ever have been imagined! From you, Edward Donovan, I received wisdom and discernment. You were so gifted and yet so compromised. Leonard Cohen expresses it so well in his song: "Ring the bells that still can ring, forget your perfect offering, there is a crack in everything, that's how the light gets in..."

Each one of you changed the course of history for me. Your lives of loving kindness inspired me from childhood. Because of you, I learned to 'see' how the spiritual and natural worlds are interwoven. For this I am ever grateful.

Meridel Joy Rawlings

Acknowledgements

My thanks to Sara Thiessen, who faithfully typed out my hard to read, hand written words in smudged pencil, on scores of yellow pads.

Thanks to our precious friend and faithful co-worker who runs the Israel Vision office in Israel. We could not have done this creative writing without someone there to "pick up the pieces."

Heartfelt thanks to Petra van der Zande for her excellent work on this book. Her professional advice coupled with her publishing and layout skills in both English and German have added much to this project.

My appreciation also goes to our sons, David, Chris, Josh and Daniel Rawlings for their media expertise during the creative process of this book. Hearty thanks to Dr. James and Helen Lunney for their wise and timely suggestions.

Next I want to honor our faithful partners who have stood with us over a lifetime. Only the Lord will adequately reward you. We could not have accomplished all that we have without each and every one of you!

My total appreciation goes to my wife Meridel, who has stood with me all along the way. Her expertise as a writer, sensitive critic and editor has been vital in this story, our story. Thanks for being a "woman of valor" during our first forty-seven years together. You are my best gift.

Having said all of that, what would have been accomplished without my Creator, the Lover of my soul making Himself known to me? He is my inspiration, my creativity, my strength and hope. He has been extending His loving mercy to me always. To Him, I am forever grateful.

Jay Rawlings, Mevasseret Zion
Israel

Endorsement

I have had the privilege of reading *Timeless Secrets* - Volume 1, *"Love My People,"* the first in a series of books authored by Jay and Meridel Rawlings.

Two gifted writers have produced *"Love My People"*, the first volume of the gripping, true account of a modern Abraham and Sarah singularly called out of their comfortable Canadian "Ur of the Chaldeans" to abandon their affluent lifestyle and to embark on an extraordinary lifetime journey of faith and devotedness to God's ancient chosen people, the Jews. To read this book is to realize afresh that indeed "truth is stranger than fiction."
Beautifully and transparently written, and peppered with deep and abiding spiritual insights learned in the furnace of sometimes hard and painful experience, this is a book which I am convinced cannot fail to bring rich blessing to very many.

John Stone
Pastor Emeritus
Victoria, BC, Canada

Foreword

There are those who simply believe that the Bible is a record of God's dealing with mankind from the beginning of time and live their lives as though it were true.

It has been my privilege to know Drs Jay and Meridel Rawlings for nearly 35 years. The Rawlings are true, if unofficial, ambassadors for Canada. They went out to nations with no embassy and to villages with no consulate. They also represented a Kingdom not made with hands.

Jay and Meridel Rawlings write this timely account from the annals of their own lives lived by faith. If God is real and Eternity is our destination, we all face the imperative: "how then shall we live?"

Timeless Secrets challenges the reader to trust and obey or not! It provides insights to the dynamics of listening for that Still Small Voice, when faith seeks a door that can't normally be 'seen'! Read the amazing possibilities that opened through impossible circumstances.

To each who has embarked upon their own pilgrimage of faith comes the call: "follow me!" Of them it is written: "they overcame by the blood of the Lamb and the word of their testimony."

To God be the glory!

Dr James Lunney, MP

Note: James is a doctor of Chiropractic who practiced for 24 years in two provinces of Canada. He has also led numerous tours to Israel and the Middle East. For the past fifteen years he has served as a member of the Canadian Parliament, and as a member of the Standing Committees on Health, National Defense and Foreign Affairs. He is past chair of the Canada-Israel Inter-parliamentary Group.

Table of Contents

Preface

Shalom and welcome dear reader!

As Meridel and I write the first volume of the Timeless Secrets series, we will highlight our first decades. We move from being quiet Canadians to world travelers and lovers of Israel. Questions immediately arise. Where to start? What to include? How do we tell the difficult things about our lives; some challenges in pulling up our Canadian roots, going against the status quo and following our dreams into the volatile Middle East. Israel has been the focal point of our lives for the last 46 years. We could not shake the reality that the nation of Israel, reborn after nearly two thousand years, has a significant place in the present and future of the world, out of all proportion to its size and population.

Wouldn't it be easier for me to push back my chair, put away my pencil, yellow pads and trusted eraser? Perhaps I should take seriously my grandson, Noam's, advice when he observed me perspiring one hot day as I worked in our garden in Mevasseret Zion, a western municipality near Jerusalem. "Take it easy, Grandpa!" He spoke emphatically. That would be the most logical thing to do at my age, put my feet up and retire! However, my family members have always been a great encouragement and inspiration to me to proceed by faith. On numerous occasions the boys asked, "Dad, Mom, tell us a faith story? We want to hear about your early days and how we got to Israel." So this writing is really for our sons, grandchildren and great grandchildren and to future generations. This is the true inheritance that we have to leave them and hopefully our saga will be an encouragement to you as well.

What I have discovered, living in Israel, is that everyone needs their own "private set" of miracles. That's what these stories are all about. In this first volume *Love My People*, Meridel and I relate a series of miracles telling our love story which includes leaving Canada for Israel as well as key events in my life growing up. At the end of this book you can read more about the contents of Volumes 2—8.

Eventually, we practiced what we preached by going 'home' to live in Zion. Over these last four decades, I have learned much about God, the Bible, our own Jewish heritage, Israel and how to survive. It's simple. We all need to trust in the Word of the Almighty and expect amazing results; this is the privilege of anyone who believes! Today everyone everywhere needs miracles!

Most people today want to know what is going to happen tomorrow, next month, next year. A recent poll taken in the USA asked the question, "What type of television shows are you interested in watching?" The overwhelming response from people of all walks of life was unanimous. Everyone wanted to know, "what is going to happen in the future and how are we going to cope?" In this regard we have included at the end of each chapter something called, *"Timeless Secrets"*. These short summaries of the lessons learned along the way are offered as suggestions to help you, especially in these difficult times. Where appropriate I have included promises from the Bible that have strengthened and inspired us as a family over the years.

As you read on I trust that our stories and the truths gleaned will empower you and your family, to prosper and make you a blessing in the lives of those around you in spite of looming uncertainty. Some would even say, "dark clouds arising on the horizon"! That's the "bad news"!

Now, here's the "good news"! We have been privileged to live out amazing, eternal promises on an almost daily basis among the nations and here in Israel. For me there is nothing more exciting or fulfilling than seeing "The Eternal" present in the everyday. May this book strengthen, encourage, inspire and bless you by pointing to the Owner's Manual. Yes, the Book of Books - The Bible, is full of eternal treasures and one of the greatest of them is when you begin to see that many of His Timeless Secrets have your name on them.

Jay Rawlings

Our first family picture in Hamilton, Ontario
May-June 1969

CHAPTER 1

"Lech Lecha" - Go![1]

"Now, the Lord said to Abram: "Get out of your country, from your family and from your father's house, and go to a land that I will show you." Genesis 12:1

Our personal journey with the nation of Israel began in quite a unique manner. One day, I was driving home after work to our country home in Dundas, Ontario, Canada, about eighty kilometers southwest of Toronto. Tired, after a hard week as the Assistant Administrator at the Hamilton General Hospital I was looking forward to a quiet weekend.

That Friday afternoon, September 1969, the trees in southern Ontario displayed a riot of color. Their spectacular orange, yellow, burgundy, golden brown and fiery red colors were inspiring. I drove into the circular driveway, passed the swimming pool, Shetland ponies in their paddock and stopped in front of the bungalow. The tires crunched on the gravel. Meridel, my young wife, was there on the steps waiting to greet me with eight month old David bouncing on her hip. It was an idyllic setting. Climbing out of my Corvette sports car, I pulled off my driving gloves and gave Meridel and David a hug and a kiss. Little did I know that all of this was about to change in an instant.

Arm in arm, we walked into the house. A mouth watering aroma of freshly baked bread and a roast of Canadian beef simmering in the oven made me smile. Meridel had learned from her mother that the way to a man's heart is through his stomach... well partly! I was hungry and ready to sit down to dinner. But as Meridel put David in his high chair and got him ready to eat, she just couldn't hold back.

---

[1] *"Lech Lecha"* is Hebrew for "get up and go!"

Bursting with her excited discovery of that day, she began, "Jay, today while writing letters at the picnic table, I heard a still small voice. I think the Lord spoke to me."

Sitting at the head of the table, I responded, rather matter-of-factly, "Well that's great. What did He say? But can we eat, I'm hungry?"

Looking full into my face, she took a deep breath. "He said, 'If you love Me, love My People.'"

"Well, that's interesting but what does it really mean to us?"

Are those few amazing words somehow going to change our lives? I wondered, suddenly feeling anxious. Part of me hoped to maintain our lifestyle...forever. After all, I had studied six long years at two universities to obtain my current career, and now it was just beginning to take off. I had been given a choice executive position right out of graduate school from the University of Toronto's Health Care Administration program, in the Faculty of Medicine.

Busy with my own thoughts, I didn't hear what else she said. I had completed my final year residency in hospital administration at the prestigious Hamilton Civic Hospitals Center, Canada's largest multiunit hospital complex at the time with 1,800 beds. It was a distinct honor to be mentored by well known executives of the overall operation as well as being part of the top administrative team at the Hamilton General. At age 24, I found myself in charge of six departments with a combined annual budget of over eighty million dollars. I loved my work. Was what Meridel saying going to change all of this? Becoming nervous, I **tuned her out.**

She knew when I wasn't listening and so she repeated, "'If you love Me, love My People'! You know, that means the Jews!"

"Well, if God speaks so directly to you, I wonder why He didn't speak to me?" I coolly responded rather insensitively because of my fear and uncertainty. *Am I so afraid of change?* Change was (and still is) hard for me. But I believe, if we're honest, this phobia affects most of us.

Meridel's response was full of wisdom and love. While taking the roast out of the oven she said over her shoulder, "Darling, you are so busy it's hard for the Lord to get your attention."

I was glad her back was turned so she couldn't see my reaction. Like an arrow, her words 'hit their mark' of not only my head, but also my heart.

Instantly I knew that she was right. I was far too involved with all of my activities at work, at home, with my car and a group of teens. It was true that my Creator wanted my attention. I knew His desire for me was to hear His 'still small voice'. Wisely she dropped the subject over dinner and moved into a relaxed Friday evening weekend mode but internally I was still on full alert.

The following morning just before dawn, tiptoeing around the bedroom I accidentally awakened Meridel. "What are you up to?" she whispered, lifting heavy eyelids as it was our day to sleep in. "I'm going to the woods with my Bible," I whispered, "And I am not coming back until the Lord speaks to me!" I think my determined response came as a total surprise to her.
It was a cool, clear fall day as I stepped out of the house and walked up into the nearby hills, for my 'appointment with destiny'.

Now here is Meridel's take on the situation:
The previous afternoon, while David was napping I sat at our picnic table under the maple trees. Nature had opened her paint box, everything was alive with color and the sunshine was still very warm by mid-afternoon. Writing letters to loved ones had become a way of life for me. Jay and I had been engaged for twenty months while he completed graduate school and I nursed with CUSO[2] in India. So, writing and receiving letters was one of the 'joys' of my life.

Suddenly, completely unexpected, I heard silent words as clearly as if they had come through a loud speaker. "Meridel, IF you love Me, love MY People!" Shaken, instantly I listened to what I now recognize as the 'still small voice'.[3] Strangely, those words unsettled me. Nearly all my life I have lived securely in the knowledge of God's love for me, yet, that word 'IF' troubled me. My self-justified thoughts ran something like: 'Lord you know that I love you...' but those words seemed to bounce back in my face. On the other hand, why was I so surprised because, for months I had been longing and praying to go to Israel?

---

[2] CUSO—Canadian University Service Overseas
[3] 1 Kings 19:12

Yes, it is true that Jay and I enjoyed marriage along with every material blessing. But I knew I was not cut out to live the rest of my life in suburbia! I had said very little to Jay about these feelings. During a moment of intense 'asking' just a month prior to this afternoon, I heard the Lord caution me, "Don't force the door; I will open it My way and in My time." Since then I had been working at waiting...patiently!

Jay:

The pure autumn fragrance of the woods cleared my head. Sitting on a log a penetrating stillness settled into me. I traced the path of a single golden maple leaf as it gently wafted its way down to the mossy bank near my boot. The season was changing and I acknowledged that it was much the same for my life. I also felt somewhat disconnected and alone as I spied that leaf lying at my feet. I was anxious about 'my meeting' with the Lord. Trying to unwind and get a hold of my thoughts the day passed ever so slowly and the longer I heard nothing, the more my anxiety grew. Walking along a chattering stream, I pleaded with Him out loud, sure that no one could hear me. "What do you want for me and my family? Please speak to me! Please Lord?" Still I heard nothing. Meridel could easily hear His voice. What was wrong with me?

As the sun began to set, I got down on my knees and repented of everything I could think of. Looking back now, I realized that it was that time of year in the Jewish calendar when we observe a day of fasting and prayer, called *Yom Kippur* or The Day of Atonement. Bringing everything before the One who sees and understands all I felt naked and wanting, pleading for an audience with the King of the Universe. Still, this silence unnerved me.

A deep loneliness moved from within me, surfacing in my mind. Conflicting thoughts troubled me. The day melted away and it was getting dark. For the first time I realized that I was hungry, thirsty and cold. Desperation rose up in my chest. Then in the waning light I simply opened my Bible asking Him to speak to me from His Word.
Suddenly it happened! My eyes fell on a verse in the Book of Jeremiah and instantly I sensed His Presence with me.
How did I know this Presence?

I was electrified and had goose bumps all over my head and shoulders. Getting warm and excited I knew that I was getting closer to an answer. The ancient words of Jeremiah 50: 2a jumped off the page, captivating me. The Message translation is my favorite, *"Get the word out to the nations. Go public with this; broadcast it far and wide."*

That was it! This time, His direct way of speaking into my life was through His Word. It all became clear in an instant. At that moment, many familiar thoughts that I had tried to ignore now ran unhindered through my mind. Yes, we were to go to Israel. Yes, we were called to stand with the Jewish people. Yes, we were called to also publish the Good News about Israel among the nations, to all peoples. And yes, I was to resign my position... now! A twinge of fear hit me in the pit of my stomach.

The truth of it all came rushing through my mind. This scripture somehow brought a confirmation of the coming change, I sensed stirring within. I filled my lungs with the damp evening air, exhaling slowly. Trying to relax, I was happy that now, I could actually feel my trust level rising. I received this 'understanding' in a matter of seconds.

No, of course, I could not see all that it entailed. But a sense of quiet assurance filled my mind with unmistakable peace. Did I understand this? Absolutely not! Did I sense that I had received the answer I was seeking? Absolutely! I held onto the comforting quiet peace settling way down deep inside of the core of my being. Over the years, I have discovered that this is the "peace that passes ALL understanding." [4]
Carefully, I thought out my plan of action. We had been invited to join a tour group going to Israel on October 20, 1969 from New York's JFK Airport. Why wouldn't we be with them to spy out the land, like Joshua and Caleb of old? However, this was exactly thirty days away and I knew I had to act swiftly. The first thing was to write out a letter of resignation and hand it in that night. Next I must call, John, my boss at the Hamilton General Hospital and deliver it to him immediately.

---

[4] Philippians 4:7 and Numbers 6:26

I tramped through the dark woods back into our warm and comfy home, tastefully lit with candles and soft lamps. Before even stopping to explain to Meridel what had transpired, I called John and got permission to see him shortly. I then sat down at my desk to write out my resignation. Sensing my need to focus, Meridel busied herself and tucked David into bed.

Meridel:

I had tried to content myself all day long by caring for David, the ponies and our Siamese cats. By mid-morning I expected Jay would come bounding in for coffee. But morning came and soon it was lunch, which blended into mid afternoon and tea time. I knew that when he didn't show up for dinner he was having a very serious day.

Then, he silently slipped in through the back door about eight pm. One quick glance at his face and instinctively I knew to 'be still.' His body language said it all. He was quietly determined, looking neither to the right or left, not even greeting me, while calling his boss. It seemed he was a man with a mission, and no one was going to persuade him otherwise. After a muffled phone call he went straight to his writing desk and taking out his fountain pen and stationery, silently, he began to write. "What are you doing?" I softly asked. "Give me a few minutes," he responded, clearly deep in thought.

Jay:

Meridel was really puzzled when less than half an hour later I said, "Quick, get David up. We are going over to John's house to hand in my resignation. We are leaving for Israel in one month." She looked stunned and I know she was shocked!

Meridel:

You can say that again! The order had been issued. Now I was lost for words and moved silently. Gently, I got David out of bed and wrapped him into a warm blanket. He hardly bothered to open his sleepy blue eyes. I threw on my coat, and by that time Jay had the letter in his breast pocket and the car warmed up at the door. The tension between us was building. I remained quiet and prayed.

Jay:

It was just a twenty minute drive to Burlington where my boss lived. As soon I drove up the ramp unto the QEW, or Queen Elizabeth Way, the full impact of my decision began to dawn upon me. I staggered in my mind... at the enormity of it. Glancing over at Meridel, I slammed the heel of my hand onto the steering wheel and in pain and dismay shouted, "What am I doing? I'm throwing away everything that I have worked so hard for!" Fighting tears, I thought, *I'm throwing away everything that I have worked for.*

Meridel remained completely still. All that could be heard was the steady swishing of the windshield wipers and pounding rain on the car. Upon arrival, I switched off the engine and rested my head on my arms over the steering wheel for a moment to regain my composure.

Meridel:

I knew that what he was saying was absolutely right. He was pained, but how could I respond when I had no idea what Jay had experienced earlier that day in the woods. I held my peace. David was asleep on my lap, so I remained in the car. Jay got out. I felt shivery and alone. It was a bit scary.

Jay:

My heart pounded as I rang the doorbell. John was right there, opening the door. Warm light reflected the driving rain bouncing off of the stone steps. His greeting was kind, "Man, come in, out of the weather."

Feeling exposed and weak, his firm grip on my shoulder was reassuring. I stooped to take off my shoes, before entering their living room. Stepping onto their white Chinese carpet and glancing into the hall mirror, a pale drawn face with sad eyes stared back at me.

Meekly, I followed my boss over to a light yellow brocade chair and collapsed into silk cushions. Taking a deep breath, I cleared my throat and said, "John, this may seem strange to you but I am resigning from my position at the Hospital because I believe that the Lord is calling us to Israel." After I said it I blinked several times.

His mouth fell open in surprise. After the initial shock, he sat back on the sofa, lit a cigarette, took a long draw and exhaled before saying,

"Well Jay, we are going to miss you from the team at work. Although your decision is, frankly, quite strange to me, I must respect your judgment in the matter. I honestly don't know anything about such spiritual things."

I was grateful for his honesty at not understanding and tried to further explain what had happened to me just a few hours earlier at my 'encounter in the woods.' As I spoke I felt very much alone and wondered if I sounded 'strange'? I thought to myself, 'Am I proceeding along the right pathway'? All I knew for sure was that the Executive Director of the universe gave me a peek into His plans for my life. With my resignation now safely in John's hands, I stared into his face realizing that now there was no turning back.' It became clear. This short meeting was to have life long consequences.

Back at the car I felt greatly relieved by following through on what I felt I had to do. Breathing a sigh, I looked directly into Meridel's eyes for the first time that day. Apologetically I said, "This is crazy! But if we are together in this venture, somehow I know, it will be OK?"
"Jay, I wish you would explain to me what happened to you out there in the woods?" she said.
I had been so set on accomplishing my task of 'resigning' that I had completely ignored my wife. Abashed, I said, "Oh honey, I'm sorry." Hanging my head I took a deep breath. "In my haste I could think of nothing other than getting the resignation written and delivered because of the shortness of time. Turning to her I looked directly into her eyes, which showed me she was hurt. "Forgive me sweetheart, this is not an excuse, but the Lord spoke to me out there in the woods from Jeremiah 50 verse 2, the first part. This word became alive to me, like a fire in my bones."

Meridel:
"Jay," my voice was soft, "I knew it had to be something very important," I said, trying to reassure us both, "and I want you to know that I was praying for you throughout the entire day. Well let's read this important verse together." I handed Jay my small Bible.

Jay:

Switching on the light I read aloud: *"Declare among the nations, proclaim (publish) speak out and set up a standard; (lift up a banner or flag) and proclaim (publish) and do not conceal it. (or broadcast it)"* [5]
Excitedly I went on, "Meridel, I think this is the only time in scripture that "publish" is written three times in one verse. I don't pretend to understand this but I know Israel is central to it all." I put the key into the ignition, pulled out into the street and turned toward home.

Meridel was very quiet on the return journey. I have learned that when my 'chatter-box' gets 'quiet', there is a very good reason. Only when we got back home did the tension between us begin to ease.

Meridel:

Jay got a roaring fire going. I laid our sleeping baby into his crib, and went to the kitchen to make hot chocolate for us. My mind was racing. Part of me was exhilarated. For the last months, I had consistently prayed for us to go to Israel. But now, that I was seeing the beginning of the answer I was terrified. We were pulling up anchor, unfurling our sails, and pointing our frail craft out into unknown waters. Would we be guided by mighty unseen currents and moved by the wind of God's Spirit? The more I thought about it the weaker I felt.

I walked into the living room, now warm and aglow with the crackling fire in the hearth dispersing the chilly dampness brought on by fall rain. I set the hot drinks down on the coffee table. Sinking heavily into the sofa, I buried my stocking feet deep into the sheepskin rug and threw a woolen blanket around our shoulders. Jay moved toward me, and pulled me into his strong arms. I sighed deeply, relaxing.
The uniqueness of the moment began to sink in. This was our first private moment of a weekend, that was highlighted by extraordinary life changing events and we both needed each other as well as the warmth of the fire.
"It takes men longer than women to open up to spiritual things," I told Jay, "but when they begin to move, they take the lead.
I was raised to believe that our men are ordained to lead. However,

---

[5] Jeremiah 50:2a NKJ (my clarification in brackets)

I could never have guessed that you would have made such a far reaching, life changing decision so quickly. It is actually amazing, my darling." My voice trembled with conviction. "Please tell me everything."

Jay:
"I just somehow knew that I had to make this move. It was now or never." We snuggled closer, Meridel, I don't understand this, but..." my voice was filled with emotion, I paused and swallowed hard before going on; "I believe we are onto something here that is so profound, it is breathtaking. We'll be doing something for the good of Israel and the Jews worldwide at just the right time. Frankly at this point it is all a mystery to me, but I am willing to learn. How about you, Darling?"

Meridel:
My answer to him was a tender, sweet kiss. Lingering in each other's arms I whispered part of my wedding vows spoken just eighteen months earlier. The words from Ruth 1:16,17 now seemed amazingly prophetic.
> *"Entreat me not to leave you, or to turn back from following after you; for wherever you go, I will go; and wherever you lodge, I will lodge. Your nation (or people) shall be my nation and your God my God. Where you die, I will die, and there will I be buried. The LORD do to me and more also, if anything but death parts you and me."*

Shivering with anticipation a feeling of profound gratefulness flooded my whole being. I was thankful and felt a surge of respect. Jay had made this decision and would lead us out. The ornamental clock ticking on the mantel piece of the stone fireplace sounded 'midnight'.

Timeless Secrets

Over the years we have shared the above story along with the following 'timeless and foundational secrets' with our four sons when they asked us one by one. "What shall I do with my life"? It seems that this universal question comes to all of us at some point or another as we mature. I tried to make my answers personal,

1.   First, give your life completely to your Maker. Then be ready for the adventure of a lifetime!

"You shall have no other gods before me." Exodus 20:3.

2. Second, find out what <u>He</u> wants you to do with your life, and then move toward that goal. Don't worry if you have a few detours along the way.

"Who is the man that fears [respects] the Lord? Him shall He teach in the way He chooses. He himself shall dwell in prosperity and his descendants shall inherit the earth. The secret of the Lord is with those who fear Him." Psalm 25: 12, 13, 14a

"If they obey and serve Him, They shall spend their days in prosperity and their years in pleasures." Job 36:11 NKJ

3. Third, find out who He wants you to marry. Learn to wait, and marry only that person. Life with the right marriage partner is heaven on earth while life with the wrong marriage partner is the opposite!

"He who finds a wife finds a good thing, and obtains favor from the Lord." Proverbs 18:22 NKJ

**Our Triumph TR3 would start in any weather.
January 1969**

CHAPTER 2

Countdown

**"It was a hectic time preparing to leave Canada...
We had many fears..."**

First thing on Monday morning I met with Dr. Bill Noonan, the Executive Director/ CEO of both hospitals. He too was surprised. "Jay, you realize that we created this position for you after your residency with us." I thanked him. Then he said something I will never forget, "Jay, you know I am not a religious man but may I offer you this one piece of advice?" He waited for my response, searching my face. I nodded. He continued, "You have done a good job for us at the hospital, now go out and do a good job for God."
Looking back over the last forty years, I have often thought about his wise words and respect for my calling. Both continue to be an encouragement to me.

It was a hectic time preparing to leave Canada. The proposed journey would take us around the world over a period of one year. From Israel we were booked to visit India and the Far East. With the tickets ordered, I turned my attention to the multitude of issues needing resolution within the remaining twenty eight days before departure. As a young mother, Meridel's major concerns were first and foremost for our first born who would be nine months old the day of our departure.

Meridel:
While living and working as a nurse in India I had become deathly ill. Thanks to medical and divine intervention I survived but had to work through many fears concerning my baby's health. I did not verbalize them to Jay but battled it out on my own. Now I was being challenged to trust my child to the ONE who was calling us away from the very high standard of Canadian health care. I realized that I needed a new level of faith in this matter. The other factor was, how to break this news to our families?

When I telephoned my parents outlining our planned departure, they were open and supportive. Mother had raised all six of us to believe that we could accomplish what ever was in our heart. Thanks to her wisdom all of her offspring are making notable contributions in their areas of expertise. We didn't hear a negative word from any family members which, when I look back and consider the magnitude of all that transpired, is absolutely amazing. I bless each of our parents for being willing to hold their peace, and trust that God was with us, especially with their little grandson David. But, as parents today of adult sons, I am sure they kept us all continually in prayer.

Jay:

As we prepared to leave our comfort zone, one issue foremost on my mind was finding someone to buy our expensive Corvette sports car. We completely emptied our home, sold the living room furniture, and the rest of our belongings we gave away. We also packed up our wedding presents and sent them in a crate for storage in my folk's dry basement. During those last weeks, our dear family were wonderful to call us regularly with encouraging words. Friends and neighbors probably wondered secretly about our future.

We found sympathetic hearts and listening ears in David and Norma Jean Mainse. At that time David was the host of Canada's first national Christian TV program, Crossroads, the precursor of 100 Huntley Street, which back then was just 15 minutes a week. David was also pastor of a large church on the Hamilton Mountain called Bethel Tabernacle. When we explained to them our decision they immediately began to pray for us. Afterwards, David was refreshingly honest with us, "Frankly, I acknowledge that you both are called of God, that's for sure, but I can't say that I understand this calling!" He then prayed 'blessing' upon us and told us, "My father was called to Egypt when I was a lad, so I have a real soft spot in my heart for the Middle East. We will certainly be standing behind you in prayer."

As I look back all I can say is, "Thank you, David and Norma Jean. For you had eyes to see that we were truly being 'set apart' to do a very special work in the earth. That takes faith as well. You cheered us on our way.

Your encouragement has meant much to us as a family over the years."

In subtle and not so subtle ways people reminded us that we were launching out 'by faith' with no assured regular income. For me, this was the single most difficult hurdle. All my life I had been trained to work hard and to be a good provider, especially now, for my new family. This venture really went against the grain of all that I had known. Talk about walking by faith and not by sight!

As if on cue, the Chief of Surgery came into my office wearing his OR greens with a mask dangling around his neck. His carefully trimmed white mustache and hair graying at the temples smoothed back under his OR cap, showed him to be the epitome of success. He had made it 'big', as the head of a very busy surgical department and the esteemed mentor of many young resident doctors in various surgical disciplines. Standing before my desk he peered down at me over his half frame gold rimmed spectacles.

When I looked up he said, "So, you have made it into the hospital 'grapevine', Rawlings. I hear that you are leaving us for overseas. Is that right?"

I drew in my breath and smiled, "Yes," trying to sound confident. Before I could say more he folded his arms across his chest and challenged, "So, when you are in Timbuktu with your family, who then is going to pay your bills?"

He had struck at my 'Achilles heel,' my weakest spot. Mustering my courage I replied, "Well, of course, the Lord is going to pay our bills." He gave me a sardonic smile and turned to leave my office. "We will see if the Lord will provide won't we?"

I must say his words bothered me all day long and I arrived home that evening. I said to Meridel rather abruptly, "When we get to Israel, who is going to pay the bills?" So much for my great confidence and 'unwavering' faith!

Knowing me well, she smiled. "Oh darling! The Lord, of course!" She had ample faith for the three of us.

In contrast to the Chief of Surgery, there were two senior executives at the hospital who really comforted me during those last days at work. The first was Dr George Woodward, the Associate Director of the Hamilton General, and the second was Miss Margaret Charters, the Director of Nursing. One day in mid-October, George summoned me into his office. Marge was there sitting on the edge of her chair. They had obviously been talking about my situation because the first thing George asked was, "Well Jay, how are your preparations to leave us coming along?"

"Pretty good... I suppose!," I said rather sheepishly. "But there certainly are a lot of last minute details to cover."

"Marg and I have been discussing your career move." he said, "and want you to know that we have decided that if things don't work out for you and Meridel, then you are always welcome to come back here."

I was deeply touched by his fatherly concern. George was a single parent raising two teenage sons and Marg had never married yet they both made me feel like family. It was a moment where I found myself fighting to hold back tears. I will never ever forget it.

With all due respect though, I decided to cling to the Bible promise from Philippians 4:19, that says, *"My God will supply all your needs according to His riches in glory."* I chose to believe we wouldn't need to come back. Later, at home that night, I apologized to the Lord and to Meridel for my lack of faith.

With only a short time left, I still hadn't sold my dream car, the Corvette. The Mainse's called the prayer chain at their church to pray for a sale. I had always liked sports cars, having purchased an Austin Healy while studying in Victoria, B.C. and later a Triumph TR3 when finishing my degree at the University of Toronto.

Meridel had encouraged me to buy the Corvette after we had been married only a few months. I was surprised at her attitude because I thought she might think it rather frivolous to have such a powerful and fancy vehicle. She had just spent two years nursing the poorest of the poor in India. There her salary was $9 a month as a volunteer. I always say that I married Meridel for her money!

When considering a new car, she had encouraged me by saying, "Go for it!" and that's how we purchased the "Vette".

Now, all I wanted to do was sell it and fast. Over the next three weeks we had a few nibbles but three days before our planned departure we still had not sold the car. The next day was Friday, and my last day at work. We had announced that we would depart for New York that Saturday to catch the flight on the following Monday to Israel. So we were right down to the wire. During our morning coffee break in the hospital cafeteria, in walked Dr. Herb Cohen[6], the Chief of Urology. Smugly he asked, "Well Rawlings, what's this I hear about you leaving us for Israel?"

"Yes, that's right, Dr. Cohen, I feel it's time to go to our 'Promised Land'. As they say, it's now or never!"

"Well, what about your car? I heard that you are trying to sell it?"

Looking him in the eye I said, "That's right, I am!"

"How much do you want for it?"

I told him my final price, knocking off $100. I also mentioned that I had just put on it a $1000 paint job.

"What color is it?" he wanted to know.

"Metallic burgundy." I replied.

"I loathe that color! Is it an automatic?"

Trying to sound positive I said, "No, it's a three speed stick shift with a 327 cubic inch engine."

"I detest having to change gears!" He groaned.

My heart began to fall with all of his negative comments.

"And it must be a real gas guzzler eh!"

But just as I was about to answer, suddenly he said, "I tell you what; let's take it out for a spin."

"Okay, here, try it out," I offered him the keys.

We went out to the parking lot. It was a rainy day and as we bent down to get into the bucket seats, he grumbled, "Well, I really don't like sports cars, especially in this kind of weather."

We drove around the block several times as he got used to the clutch, instant power and quick response steering. As we pulled back into the hospital parking lot he said, "I really don't want the car, but what is your last price?"

---

[6] Not his real name

I gave him the price once again and he pulled out his cheque-book muttering to himself, "I don't know why I'm doing this. Here's your money." He handed me his cheque.

Immediately, we drove to the motor vehicle branch and transferred the car into his name. All I could say was, "Whew, thank you Lord! But in the future could it please be a little less stressful?"

That afternoon, I went to the bank and paid off the balance owing on the car. With my final salary, I took care of our other financial obligations. The following day was Saturday, and thanks to Dr Cohen's willingness to purchase our car, we were able to leave Canada as planned. Praise God for that dear Jewish man.

After twenty eight days we were now ready to go to the airport in New York. The only problem was that after paying all of our bills we had only enough money for one round the world air ticket. There was nothing left for Meridel and baby David. Nevertheless, we started out by faith to the JFK International Airport, 750 km or nearly 500 miles away.

If you keep reading you will find out what happened to us when we got there. Just hours before we left New York, at the very last minute in obedience, I gave away my few remaining dollars. You will then find out how the Lord amazingly 'moved mountains' for us.

In the next chapters we will take you back in time, giving you some of our family history. You will discover how Meridel and I met each other; our 'wake-up call' and our separate instructions on how to begin the adventure of a lifetime. Stay tuned, some of it is stranger than fiction. Now, let's consider some vitally important things that we have learned so far.

Timeless Secrets

"Behold how good and how pleasant it is for brethren to dwell together in unity! It is like the dew of Hermon, descending upon the mountains of Zion; for there (in unity) the Lord commanded the blessing - Life forever more." Psalm 133: 1, 3.

Unity or connecting with the Almighty, then with yourself and of course your marriage partner has to be the greatest challenge and yes... blessing in life. That old saying about unity goes, 'it's hard to say what it is, but you sure know what it isn't.' May I ask, where are you in this quest for unity or wholeness... right now?

Forced or artificial unity can be the result of any controlling relationship. Most people understand something of this kind of disunity. The majority of us have never experienced or lived with a true sense of 'unity' as spoken of in Psalm 133: *"How good and pleasant it is for brothers to live together in unity...for there the Lord commands the blessing. "*

The first thing we learn about the God of Israel is that "He is One" and cannot be divided. His call to us is "to hear" or "to take in" or "to live" His words. This is the foundational statement of the Jewish faith called the Shema; as follows, *"Hear, O Israel; The LORD our God, The LORD is One."* Deuteronomy 6:4

Our Creator is a unified 'whole' and you and I are created in His image. Jesus also referred to this fundamental need for unity and spoke out about the consequences of division, *"If a house is divided against itself, that house cannot stand."* Mark 3:25

When, Jay and I, first as individuals, came into the Presence of 'The Source of Life,' only then was our personal disconnectedness challenged. After our separate encounters of being "born by the Spirit" we began to change from the inside out. Experiencing and accepting the 'all encompassing Love of God' is what gave us the hope and power to live life to the full.

This Love from above has and continues to initiate ongoing change in each of us. If we allow it! Honestly, as hard as it is to do, we try to be yielded to positive change every day. Easier said than done!

God is a complete unity. I am not speaking here of any kind of 'cultish' idea. When you open your life to God's heart and Word, you begin to grow in unity with your Creator. I discovered that this unity grows in me when I acknowledge that I am found in God. When my spirit and soul are on favorable terms with God and with each other, 'unity' comes into my life. My mind and soul pay attention to my body and my body is sensitive to my soul. Then it is possible to sense "peace that passes understanding."

As you seek to incorporate harmony into your marriage, or any other relationship, the fruit will be gradually life-giving as well as sweet. You will have the ability to honestly agree or disagree until you are able to work out an agreement. Then you will know what true agreement is as Psalm 133 suggests. This work of 'agreeing' with God, self, and each other has been the call of our lives. Marriage demands the commitment of both partners. That means deep honesty and transparency with your partner. Ask for patience, long suffering, endurance, hope and the determination to overcome. The challenge in marriage is to keep growing. Hey, then anything is possible!

CHAPTER 3

New Beginnings

"Blaring sirens and red lights flashing told everyone that there was an emergency. Sheila, weak and pale because of her blood loss, was lifted onto the stretcher ..."

Meridel:

In this first volume of the *Timeless Secrets* series, you will read several chapters about Jay's family going back to his Scots grandparents and even touching upon his French great grandparents. Boring? Maybe! It was suggested that we skip 'all of that' and 'cut' to the real gold nuggets of our present lives.

How typical of our modern age, I thought. We want the best of someone's life experiences in a thirty second TV sound-bite between commercials! We want it all done up in a sweet little package, in as short a time as possible, with no thought given to the importance of the often precious, painstaking, even precarious process it took to get there.

We have nothing to say about which family we were born into, or about the design, coloring or packaging that we arrived in on planet earth. Was this 'genetics' or a Divine Plan or perhaps both? We find in North America, speaking generally, a noticeable lack of interest in spending time nurturing relationships between the generations. There are those who act as if 'it' all began with 'us', and 'we' are the sum total of our being. How short sighted and untrue that kind of thinking is. Sadly, others are made to feel 'old' and redundant at age fifty five.

Jay and I spend time now describing "family" because it was in the home where we learned all the basics that carried us through life to this point. Living now in Israel and being from Canada, we have had to climb over our careful and non confrontational Canadian ways.

The idea of minding our own business, and being politically correct and 'nice' were attitudes we had to deal with, while living in the vibrancy, pressure and stark openness of some cultures we were about to experience.

Our neighbors and friends in Israel think nothing of asking us the most personal of questions. For example, where did your children go to school? How much did it cost? How long did it take to build your home? Where did your ancestors come from? Why are you living here? Did your boys serve in the army? What is your mother's maiden name? Who did you vote for in the last election? Where do you go for vacations?

You may raise your eyebrows and say, "How rude," or "How nosy." We look at it another way, because Israel is a unique "family of people" who have emigrated from 104 nations of the world. The push of persecution or the pull of the Spirit of God have put us all here. Everyone has a story and, in most cases, if listened to carefully, discloses their tragedy, heartaches, rejection, loss and much suffering. When one Israeli is killed we all feel it. When one soldier is kidnapped we are all involved. When a bomb goes off we all make phone calls to see if 'our' family members are safe. When war looms large on the horizon we all stick real close. When we are at war, we all stop bickering and stand together as one people!

You see dear reader, in Israel, 'we' are all that we have. There is no one else. Nearly no one wants us it seems. We are a people of "sorrows and acquainted with grief, no man cares for our soul". Isaiah 53:3 Altogether, we are now 8.3 million souls, with the oldest Christian community in the world. One in five of us are Arabs who enjoy their own representatives in the Knesset with full voting privileges and all basic human rights. While far from perfect, the Knesset or Parliament here is an anomaly in the Middle East. Consisting of Arabs and Jews, secular and orthodox, men and women. This makes Israel a unique liberal democracy - in fact the only one in the Middle East.

About ten per cent of us actively believe in the Almighty. The rest are open to everything... but at circumcisions, weddings and funerals, everyone shows up to recite the ancient Hebrew prayers.

We also love our Sabbaths, or the seventh day of rest, and of course the Feasts of the Lord. Ninety-seven percent of us keep Passover in some way... but hey, we are 90% secular. We try not to trouble God and we hope against hope that He would choose someone else for awhile!

So what am I saying? Family is what we are all about, all of us. We all love to gather together for the weekly Sabbath meal, from great grand-mother or great grandfather down to the tiniest babe. There is place for each one, place to flourish, room to differ and express that differ-ence openly. We would not be here if it were not for the endless sacri-fices of our ancestors. We do not forget them, we cannot forget them and we will never forget them! I ask you to keep this in mind as you work your way through the next chapters on 'family'.

Jay:

My rocky start on life's journey took place in Victoria, B.C. Canada. Because my father, Vic Rawlings, was serving overseas, in the Canadian Armed Forces, my mother, Sheila was alone for my arrival on planet earth which was rather eventful. Thank goodness for her eldest sister, Netta Chattel, an RN who was working as an operating room nurse on duty that day.

Meridel:

The following scenario was told to me by Jay's Mom, Sheila (Sheena). As the wife of her only son, I became the daughter she never had. She loved to recount to me stories of her past in her lilting Scots accent.

"February 22nd, 1944 arrived with a stiff south-westerly wind blowing from the Pacific Ocean, perfect on a wash day for drying the clothes. Everyone was away at work. Being very pregnant and unable to work, I was put in charge of family laundry. Wash day was a long and arduous process, which took many hours;

My father made sure the wood box was filled with plenty of dry, split wood. The old black Canada Pride kitchen stove with its gleaming nickel trim, was stoked with wood piece by piece. Before leaving for work the men hand carried in the necessary buckets of rainwater from a wooden barrel situated outside under the eaves of the house. They filled the large rectangular metal tub on the hot stove top. I dipped the hot wash water into the circular tub of the washing machine, supported on metal legs. Little wooden wheels enabled it to move. The handle of the 'clothes agitator' was cranked manually back and forth. Once the clothes were washed, they were put through the wringer made of wooden rollers. Most of the water dripped out of the wet clothes by turning the handle. The squeezed items then fell into another tub of fresh cold water. After soaking for a while and rinsing they were wrung out a final time by hand. Weather permitting, wicker baskets of wet garments and linens were carried outside to the clothes lines and hung up using wooden pegs. Warm sunshine and breezes took care of the drying. While cranking the washer handle I felt something deep within me 'give way.' About noon the first contractions took me by surprise. When the pains starting to get stronger and more rapid I said, "Ow! Ow! You precious wee thing! You got in there but you're no gettin oout the same way you got in!"

Jay:

That statement was soon to prove prophetic. Around 13:00 hours she ran to the wall mounted telephone as blood dripped down her legs and filled her shoes. Standing on tip-toe, she told the operator, "I have to get through to St. Joseph's Hospital. An accident has happened!" With rising panic she loudly asked the hospital switchboard for the operating room nurse on duty.
After what seemed like an eternity the familiar voice of her eldest sister said, "Operating Room..."
"Netta, Netta," choking back tears my Mom cried, "the wee bairn's comin but I'm standing in a pool of blood!"

Immediately sensing the danger of mother's condition, my aunt said, "Sheila, lie down right now and put a pillow between your legs. I'm coming in an ambulance to get you."
Blaring sirens and red lights flashing told everyone on the quiet street that there was an emergency. The ambulance attendants lifted Sheila, weak and pale onto the stretcher, along with the blood-soaked pillow. After examining her, the attending doctor radioed ahead, "We're coming in. *Placenta previa*." Sensing the extreme danger to both mother and child he ordered, "Prepare the operating room for an emergency C-section, with stand-by blood transfusions."

Minutes later, Sheila was wheeled into the OR. The surgeon on duty checked my mother's vital signs and started a blood transfusion. A wire mask was placed over her nose covered with gauze and ether dripped on it putting her to sleep. Her abdomen was swathed in iodine. The surgery began. A few minutes later I was literally lifted out of my mother's womb. Slowly her condition stabilized.

Years later Auntie Netta told me about my birth.
Blue and not responding, I simply failed to breathe. Aunt Netta had 'scrubbed in' and taken charge. She refused to give up and, put me into alternate tubs of warm and cold water, trying to initiate that first breath of life. Nothing seemed to work! She refused to give up and, finally after twenty minutes of this process, I sucked in my first breath and cried. After washing and wrapping me up they placed me at my mother's side. The following morning my mother sang at the top of her voice, "Oh what a beautiful morning. Oh what a beautiful day. I've got a wonderful feeling, everything is going my way."

Later we learned that very often in those days both the mother and the child would die during such a delivery, due to severe blood loss. To this day I continue to give thanks for the gift of my life.

This would be an appropriate moment to introduce you to my mother. She was born Jean (Sheena) Duncan Naismith Sneddon, on January 15, 1915 in a small village near Glasgow, Scotland, called Kirkintilloch or 'Church on the Hill.' The motto of this village in the ancient Gaelic language is, "caw canny but caw awa," which means "go easy but keep on going." That saying proved uniquely appropriate for the Sneddon clan as you will discover in the following chapters.

Meridel:

Kirkintilloch was an industrial village built on a hill with narrow winding grey cobblestone lanes. Gas-fed street lamps provided flickering light in the early dawn and dusk of winter. The clip-clop of horse's hoofs and creaking of steel-rimmed wagon wheels could be heard carrying heavy factory goods across town. Tidy shops and homes built of rough hewn grey and blackened granite gave the impression of permanence yet austerity. It was a 'dry' town meaning no alcoholic beverages were permitted. Fashionable tea and pastry shops were popular meeting places but only frequented by the few who did not work in the factories, mines or mills.

Local Scottish specialties included warm scones[7], whipping cream and strawberry jam, teas and coffee. In the streets, weary workers passed the bay windows. Hungry eyes glanced through the shinning beveled glass devouring the scenes of comfort and plenty. Small round tables with candles were strategically situated near a glowing hearth. Hard working men, women, teenage boys and girls, filed past exhausted after twelve hour shifts. Bundled up against chill gusty winds on foggy drizzly afternoons with empty stomachs they trudged on toward their poorly heated apartments.

For the working class, life was sober in those WW1 years. Shrill whistle blasts from local factories signaled the end of one shift and the beginning of another. Daily bread depended upon working the unending rounds of shift work provided by the foundry and garment factories. Large families, struggling to make ends meet, were relegated to the overcrowded east side of town.

---

[7] Biscuits cooked on a griddle bar in the oven.

[8] The Luggie Water is a river rather than a rivulet whose headwaters rise in the administrative council area of North Lanarkshire, north of Glasgow, Scotland.

Jay:

My mother was born in a cramped tenement building bordering the Luggie Water.[8] With labor-class families as neighbors their suffering was exacerbated with most men off fighting in WW1.

'Sheena', as my mother was called in Gaelic (for Jean), was the fourth living child of William Sneddon and Janet (Jen) Christie. A local midwife assisted with most of their home births. She took charge again this time. Netta, the eldest daughter was allowed "to help." During that austere era there was no hospital ward "enforced days of rest", or prepared meals for most postpartum mothers.

Meridel:

At seven days old, the nurse made her first, routine newborn visit. Sagging wooden steps, creaked under her weight, as she climbed to the second floor. Faded wallpaper in the hall was peeling. Sharp cries of small children in the adjoining apartment, followed by the impatient threats of a male voice, sounded through the adjacent door.

The veteran nurse, moved by the sounds of slapping, cuffing and finally gut wrenching whimpering, thought wearily to herself, *Another, man without work. Walls are thin in this place.*

Knocking on the Sneddon door she waited. Jay's grandmother 'Jen', known for her cordiality, welcomed her. "Come on in hen, I'm busy changing the wee lass." Her voice was deep and throaty.

The nurse stepped into a steamy room where diapers lined a wooden rack near the dead fireplace. Piles of sheet music lay stacked on top of the polished walnut Steinway that overflowed into nearby book shelves. Next to their fine piano stood a large black cello case and a music stand. This was obviously the humble home of gifted musicians.

"She's seven days old today, let's have a look." The nurse made a routine exam of mother and child. The newborn flailed her arms and legs when the cold air hit her bare chest. The nurse checked the baby's reflexes, and drying umbilical cord. "Now we need to weigh you... ah, you haven't gained your birth weight yet. There, there, all done!" she said, bundling her up into her tiny handmade woolen clothes.

Almost absentmindedly she offered, "It's chilly in here Jen, and she's a delicate wee thing." The nurse tightly wrapped up the newborn in knitted blankets and placed her securely back into her mother's arms. She cried, wanting to nurse.

"Our coal is rationed, so until afternoon we are without heat. I agree it's damp in here, just look at the condensation on the windows. Our landlord is a hard man, and does nothing to help fix up the place." It was the lament of a tired working mother.
"How is she nursing?"
"Fine, she doesn't take much, but I keep at it."
Looking closer at Jen the nurse said, "You are looking worn, very dark under your eyes and pale. Are you getting enough molasses? I know you are probably holding body and soul together with oatmeal porridge?"
"Yes, these are challenging times. I was up in the night with the boys, both have terrible coughs, but I got the eldest out the door to school today. I have taken two new jobs, but I just can't make enough on my own with the string quartet. The war you know! Now with my husband, the cellist, overseas, he has to be replaced. We still get gigs, but it's hard to be out at night having to leave the bairns (Gaelic for children) as you can well imagine."
"Uch, it's no easy," the nurse sympathized.
"I just got a part time job playing the piano for the silent movies, you know. It gives me two shillings an afternoon, which helps."
"Remember, you need to take good care of yourself. All of these kiddies are dependent upon you." The nurse's tone was serious.
"Oh, you make it sound so bad. Everything is fine, but thanks for coming." Jen Sneddon was a kindly, yet self-assured and independent professional woman.
Changing the subject the nurse went on, "What have you heard from the front lines? My son was shipped out last week but my husband is too sick with TB to be enlisted."
"I get little news; we keep our ear tuned to the radio. This war is Hades for the boys out there in France and for the rest of us left behind. I get some comfort from my music, which transports us all into another world, and the children seem to love it as much as I do. I play and sing them to sleep at night when I'm here."

"Well," the nurse asked, "When you are working, who cares for them?"

"I have John a blind neighbor who comes over. Dick is seven and Netta five, they help out too. Our little Jim there, sitting inside the toy box has a sweet nature, he's three. Wouldn't you now rest a while and have a wee cup a tea with me?"

"No. Thanks pet, I need to be on my way." The nurse pulled on her coat. "Say, your neighbor sounds ugly with the wee'uns."

"Yes, it's known in the building, but what can we do?" Their eyes met for a brief knowing moment, then they said goodbye. As the nurse started down the stairs, the foundry whistle sounded. It was noon.

Jay:

Meridel and I wrote this account based on my mother's conversations, but I am puzzled why my grandmother was living in such poor conditions. Some years ago, we were sent a sepia photograph of her family about that time. It shows my grandmother as the youngest child of the rather well-to-do Gartshore-Christie family. My great grandfather is wearing a *kippa* or Jewish skull cap on his head. My grandmother, a tiny girl cradled near her father, has bright dark brown eyes. She wears a silk dress with diminutive button-down shoes. Her hair a mass of natural chestnut curls.

We know that her older brother James Christie, my great uncle, an engineer, was head of the water works for the city of Glasgow, but that is about all that was ever told about these ancestors. More than a hundred years later, I can only imagine the difficulties of my grandparents as independent young musicians trying to make ends meet without taking 'hand-outs' from Jen's wealthy family.
Where were her parents and older siblings?, we wondered.
What caused the estrangement? Did Jen marry "beneath her station" in life or did she turn from her Jewish heritage?" It seems that she and her husband were considered 'common' entertainers.

Finally, November 11, 1918, the Armistice was signed and the bloody WW1 ground to a halt. Who wins in war? Thankfully, Grandfather William Sneddon returned to his little family.

Like the other bedraggled men, he was thin and weary, having led his platoon through the stark reality of gas warfare in the trenches. He suffered from asthma for the rest of his life. Everyone was grateful he survived when so many other lads worldwide never returned. The trauma sustained by the survivors of that generation has left an ongoing legacy of pain and dysfunction. The day after he left his beloved Scottish Argyle and Sutherland Highlanders Regiment as a Sergeant Major, he was out of work. He was a fine cellist who could play nearly all stringed instruments, but the day to day reality of making a living to support his growing family in Scotland after WW1 was grim. Beating the pavement to no avail, he tried to comfort himself with his music and a shot or two of Scotch whiskey in the chilly evenings.

Now just a short note about the Sneddon family: It is said they came to Scotland, as peddlers from Romania speaking Ladino, whose roots lay in Spanish Jewry. This is oral family history. When it comes to Jewish heritage, from generation to generation, the roots can be covered over for fear of even more persecution. They were dark-eyed and olive-skinned. Do not ever be fooled by the humble demeanor of a 'rag man'. Many in this family were gifted musicians.

Bill Sneddon's mother taught them all of the woodwind and stringed instruments. Their gainful employment was 'mean' in the eyes of the world, but they lived a life of hidden riches through their musical acumen. When my grandfather was a small boy, his family went to Arizona in south western USA to begin a new life. But the heat and harsh conditions, along with an accident that took the eye of one of his brothers, caused them to turn back to Scotland. But not before they visited friends who had immigrated to Vancouver Island on the west coast of Canada. Two of the sons vowed they would return to Victoria on the Island, "one day!"

At two and a half years of age, my mother Sheena met her father whom she had completely forgotten because he was off to war for most of her life. She was very shy and it took time for her to realize he was her 'Daddy.' Fondly she recounted watching him shave and trim his fine handle bar mustache. He loved to swing her up over his head and let her ride around on his shoulders.

Every Friday noon, he came home with a salted kipper-fish wrapped in newspaper to share with the family. He was fastidious in his dress and eating habits, a very slender and sensitive person. One of the fondest memories of her father was when he held her in his arms and tickled her until she was breathless with giggling, all the while rubbing his rough beard on her cheeks to say good night. She loved it. Finally, he found work playing with a string quartet. They worked in fashionable spots as well as at the local TB sanatorium. It was a stop gap measure, but did not pay enough to feed seven hungry mouths.

Finding no substantial work and with his wife's consent, in 1919, Grandfather Bill joined his brothers and left for Canada on a steamship from Glasgow to Montreal. His hope was to find work and thereby create a new life for his family. By this time, Sheena had a little brother John and her mother Jen was expecting yet again.

Not successful at first, Bill found that Canada wasn't the easiest place to make ends meet. He ventured west and as promised years earlier, found work in Victoria, B.C. on Vancouver Island as an iron molder. After several months, he put a down payment on a nearby two story brick home for his far away family. How thrilled he was to write Jen about their new home at 2944 Bridge Street. The purchase completely consumed his meager monthly earnings.

Soon it was clear that he could not earn enough to pay both the mortgage on the house and save enough money to pay the passage of his family from Scotland to Canada. It was a dilemma. Grandmother got a temporary job playing with the Glasgow Symphony as a second pianist but could barely provide for her growing family either as she was expecting her sixth child.

With the impossible financial strain, and with no end in sight, she gave her newborn baby girl, Peggy to her wealthy elder sister Margaret who had remained childless. Apparently this was common practice in those days. But by 1921 Janet had to make a heart-breaking decision. Forced by economics, she placed the five eldest children in a church run orphanage called the Quarryman's Home. It was embarrassing for the extended family and devastating for the children. The orphanage was operated by staunch Presbyterians, who rigidly enforced their inflexible religious rules and policies.

Meridel:

You can imagine the scene on the day of their separation. Jen Christie Sneddon, in the two year absence of her husband, signed papers giving the orphanage officials protection rights over her five children. Hugging and kissing each child goodbye, together they stood in a glum little cluster on the stone steps of the austere orphanage administration building. With immutable pain, the children watched as their only 'security' slowly walked away down the circular gravel drive. Sheena aged five and her younger brother John, aged three, screamed in agony and strained against the strong grip of their "dorm mothers." When the heavy ornate black iron gates slammed behind Jen with finality, her shoulders sagged. She sobbed with the weight of her loss. Pulling the black veil over the brim of her hat, she tried to hide her tears. Her pain was enormous. Years later when we took Jay's mother back to that very spot she fell into my arms sobbing with the deeply imbedded memories of those lost years.

Jay:

Each child was placed in a separate grey stone 'cottage' according to age. The cottages were scattered throughout the rambling well tended grounds. Sheena missed her own mother desperately and often cried herself to sleep at night; however, she always awoke cheery. The brothers and sisters saw very little of each other over the next seven long years. It was orphanage policy to keep siblings separated.

Many times throughout my life, with deep emotion, my mother told the following story:

When she entered the orphanage she was undernourished and tiny for her age. She knew that her beloved eight year old brother Jim, or 'Jimmock' as she called him in Gaelic, would deliver the morning milk rations at 7:00 a.m. for the children's breakfast porridge. In anticipation she would sneak out of her cottage to run and wait in the shadows behind a chain link fence.

When the milk cans were delivered she stretched her little fingers through the cold black grating attempting to reach 'her Jim'. For just a fleeting moment, he would hold and squeeze her delicate hand giving her a loving smile, as their eyes locked, "Uch, Sheena, my fine wee lassie," he'd whisper.

Seeing her brother, his red rosy cheeks and sandy hair sticking out from under his woolen "bunnet" or plaid peaked cap, became the hope and highlight of her day. She confessed that those longed for, momentary 'touches' kept her alive.

As a natural cleaner she was chosen by the Head Mistress to stay on to help with the kitchen clean-up. This included scraping the huge pots used to cook oatmeal porridge for the orphan children.

On kitchen duty she scrubbed the pots to her heart's content and was so tiny that sometimes she crawled right inside of the great iron pots to clean them. It was then she heard music faintly in the background. She discovered that it came from the open grating of the heating system in the wall.

Day by day in the kitchen she plotted how to be able to sit beside the warm air duct and listen to the music. The furnace grating was joined to the auditorium where older children sang hymns at their morning assembly, accompanied by a fine pianist on a grand piano. When the children were dismissed to go to their various classes, the pianist sometimes stayed behind to play classical music for her own enjoyment. The familiar music filled Sheena with a deep sense of longing for her own mother. She would curl up by the grating, soaking in the music, while lost in longing for mother love losing completely all track of time.

One of those days when she was absent from her school room, her angry teacher sent out a search party to find her. Once discovered, Sheena was made "an example of" in front of all the other orphans and labeled guilty of 'truancy' and separated from her class and punished. She suffered the consequences repeatedly. Her soul, so hungry to hear the comforting piano music, that she couldn't resist. Again and again she was caught at the grate and beaten.

The orphanage fed the Sneddon children enough to keep their bodies alive, but it miserably failed to touch their wounded souls.

No nourishment came from the harsh puritanical religion served up with injustice, unbending rules, isolation, ridicule and beatings. This so hurt my mother that, as a preteen, she promised herself that if she ever had children she would protect them from 'religion.' She vowed never to allow her children to be hurt by such practices. God to her, was authoritarian, mean and abusive, while her soul longed for a life that was glorious, full of hope, joy, music and family times.

About forty five years later, while I studied for exams at home, my mother loved to play her piano in the evenings. I fondly recall her playing Beethoven's Moonlight Sonata and selected pieces from Chopin, Bach, Mozart and other great classical composers. Sheena always felt she was a poor copy of her mother when it came to playing the Masters compositions. But history was repeating itself. To this day, I find listening to classical piano music a very riveting emotional experience. Mind you, when my mother was carrying me she lived in my grandmother Jen's home and I know that, in the womb I would have heard hundreds of hours of the finest music, both piano and cello played by my grandparents.

Now back to our unfolding Sneddon family story:

By 1926, grandfather sent all of the money that he had managed to save to my grandmother in Scotland. Thankfully, the church officials who ran the orphanage added the necessary remaining funds to send the poor Sneddon family to Canada to be reunited. Just imagine the children's joy when news finally came that they were leaving the orphanage confines of the last seven years. The little brood of Sneddons, now much older, packed up their few belongings and waited for their mother to arrive. They hadn't seen their father for nine years.

I leave the unfolding scene to your imagination:

Later at dockside on the Clyde River standing among the steamer trunks and cargo waiting to be loaded aboard the ship bound for Canada stood Jen's Steinway grand piano, a surprise gift from the Glasgow Philharmonic Orchestra for her years of dedicated service.
Traveling by steamer from Glasgow to Halifax was a huge adventure. Once at sea, they settled down and happily walked the deck with their Mom. Round and round they went, arm in arm, bundled up against the weather, talking incessantly. Hugs, kisses and tears, were frequent, making up for endless days and nights they had managed without the comfort of each other. Scenes from the many lost years of their lives were recalled. Tales of woe and victory along with peals of laughter over pranks played were recounted from their bunks. They were happy as the ship pitched and heaved steaming her way across the frigid and rough Atlantic waters towards a brand new life in Canada.

Late one afternoon the boys sighted the rock cliffs of Newfoundland glimmering gold in the setting sun. A plethora of sea birds followed, hoping the boys would toss them food scraps. Sea lions barked from the rocky eastern-most boundary of their new nation. Many hours later, they slowly disembarked at the Halifax harbor, each boy responsible for a small worn trunk. This was the experience of millions of European immigrants arriving in North America in that era.

Clouds of steam hissed from the mighty black train engine waiting nearby, filling the Nova Scotia train station platform. Big brother Dick leapt aboard and reaching down helped the little ones up the high metal stairs. All six souls boarded and found their assigned berths for a six day journey westward on the Canadian National Railway (CNR). Another adventure was underway. They scouted the train, and enjoyed sleeping in berths with starched white linen, grey blankets and small towels. The monotonous clickety-clack of iron wheels lulled then to sleep, while moving west across the largest country in the world at the time. Destination was the farthest point westward on their map of Canada; Victoria, British Columbia on Vancouver Island.

Mother told me, that as an impatient twelve year old, the long train journey seemed 'endless.' The vast prairies, golden with wheat, passed slowly. Suddenly, the Rocky Mountains were a thrill to behold and days later the city of Vancouver lay just ahead.

Grandfather Bill was waiting at the Vancouver Central Train Station. He was dressed in his best suit, with polished shoes, a peaked cap on his balding head, pacing back and forth smoking non-stop. Squinting down the tracks through his thick round tortoiseshell glasses he tried to catch a glimpse of the train whose whistle could be heard off in the distance. He held a bouquet of red roses in his hand, Jen's favorite. It had been nine long years.

Meridel:

The puffing engine shunted to a noisy stop with the screech of hot metal on metal, announced by a blast of the merciless whistle. Amidst the billowing clouds of steam and expectant crowds, the boys were the first to spy the silhouette of their wiry thin father. Jen, seeing her husband lowered her gaze. Upon meeting an awkward strangeness hung between them. Then, without words a tender embrace was followed by tears. The lanky teens now feeling shy, encircled their parents without words. Jen introduced their long lost father to each child according to age. The warm response was a unanimous flurry of hugs, which helped to break the invisible wall of silence that had separated them emotionally and geographically for too long.

They were assured by the Station Master that their cargo, including the piano would be delivered to Victoria within a week. Collecting his tired family, Bill Sneddon hired a horse and buggy, which filled up quickly. Misty rain fell softly, soaking them but had no effect on their indomitable spirits. They headed for the downtown Vancouver inner harbor. Bill had booked them on the Princess Margarethe, an overnight boat to Victoria, located on the southern tip of Vancouver Island. Arriving early the following morning Bill hailed a taxi. Quickly the windows were rolled down, the boys strained to see 'everything' en route.

Nearing their new home, he proudly announced, "Ours is the big red brick house, number 2944 down there."

"Stop the taxi...please!" Jim shouted in his thick Scots accent. "Come on kids, lets get out. We'll find it ourselves." The taxi pulled over to the curb, the boys piled out first, followed by the girls. They all dashed jubilantly down the sidewalk.

"Its number 2944," Netta reminded them while keeping up with the boys. When the taxi arrived with Bill and Jen, the young new immigrants were there already, sitting on the white front steps of their new home. Wide grins said it all: "Home at last!"

Jay:

The Sneddon house soon became a centre of attraction. In the process of settling in, the children's outgoing personalities blossomed. Their broad Scots brogue was quaint and entertaining. They soon became the talk of the neighborhood. Friends were easily made and brought home, one by one. Everyone was welcomed by grandmother, who always had the tea kettle boiling on the big wood stove in the kitchen. She baked her famous and delicious scones at the 'drop of a hat.' Mother attended nearby Burnside School and there the kids named her "Sheila" because they couldn't get their tongues around her Gaelic name "Sheena".

She was comical, enthusiastic and always ready to try something new. Being a popular daredevil she soon learned to swim and dive. Their spring-board was the rough hewn timber under girding of the nearby Point Ellis Bridge. She followed the boys as they climbed up the narrow wooden structure, which spanned a tidal inlet called "The Gorge".

There was no extra money for such frivolous things as swimsuits, so grandmother quickly created one by reworking an orange woolen jumper (sweater) into a 'bathing costume'. When wet, it stretched from her neck to her knees. This outfit caused the local kids to howl with laughter, but they were impressed by her courage in diving off the bridge. She told me about emerging from the chilly sea, unaware that a few tiny wiggling minnows stuck in the knit of her soggy swim-suit trying desperately to get away. There was never a dull moment when Sheila was around.

The Sneddon home was a house of music. Often, after supper, the family assembled around the piano in the living room with their instruments. Music was a necessity of life. Grandmother was at the piano, grandfather ensconced in his favorite chair, played his cello. Quickly they scrounged the neighborhood for different instruments, one for each child. Guitar, banjo, violin, flute and drums were all part of their ensemble. Sheila sat on the piano bench beside her mother. She wanted to be a pianist. The joyful sounds of Scottish music could not be contained, flowing out through the open windows and doors. Soon the neighbors came over to listen. In no time, they were drawn in to sing, clap and even dance the Highland Fling. The old brick house became a welcoming place with laughter and fun for all.

Grandmother always had an open hand and a warm heart especially to other new immigrants. The clip-clop of hooves, announced the arrival of a horse-drawn cart loaded with fresh fruit and vegetables, delivered to the neighborhood by an enterprising young Chinese man, Jack Leung. He couldn't speak much English and had difficulty understanding my grandmother's Scots accent. She called him Jack 'Louis.' He always came to the Sneddon house at the end of his delivery route, to give them the best bargains from his left-over produce.

He loved the openness of the home, the fun and laughter. Cultural differences melted when he gathered courage to put on his 'Cantonese magic tricks' at the kitchen table. Now, as the center of attraction he pulled marbles out of the children's ears with his sleight-of-hand tricks. His wide grin got wider when his audience squealed with delight, asking for more. He obliged. Every week he had a new trick to demonstrate and, when leaving to go home, he'd call back over his shoulder, "Don't worry, I come back, don't worry, I come back, new trick, next time!" Jack and his family stayed friends with our family all the years they remained on Bridge Street. He was an angel in disguise. His generosity helped feed the Sneddon kids and countless others during the Great Depression.

Sikh Raj Singh provided firewood for the great black kitchen stove and sawdust for the furnace. The sawdust was dumped via an outside chute into a huge bin under the house, to be burned for heat.

The hot air rose through the tentacles of duct work reaching the extremities of the house. Coming from Scotland where they were never warm, this was a 'modern wonder' for the entire family.

Raj Singh always came around to the back door of the house and knocked when it was delivery time. When welcomed in, he reluctantly hung back despite my grandmother's warm invitations.

Several years later, he entered the kitchen on a raw, wet winter day. Netta offered him a warm bowl of soup and some scones. Looking around he asked, "Where is the Mrs.?"

"She's gone to the hospital," Netta responded.

"Oh, oh! Is she sick? I didn't know. So sorry."

"Oh no, no," Netta laughed. "Mom has gone to have a baby."

"A baby!" His eyes widened with surprise.

"Yes, we now have a baby sister, Catherine," said Netta.

"Oh, tell your Mum to come home quick." He broadly smiled.

My mother told me later that grandmother always wore loose flowing dresses so hardly anyone knew that she was expecting. The diligent Singh family business grew to become one of Victoria's largest lumber companies, while the Leung family went on to establish one of Western Canada's most prosperous wholesale fresh fruit and vegetable businesses distributing to various chains of large supermarkets.

As the years passed, the new Scots immigrants settled down into Canadian life. Mom and Dad Sneddon enjoyed having young adults in the house and the jolly camaraderie that they brought to the daily routine. They all worked and helped pay some bills, which was a welcome relief. Dick became a men's clothing salesman, Netta was a registered nurse, while John launched a career in the Canadian Army, and James got a temporary job as a longshoreman at the dockyard of Victoria. Sheila worked at the Jubilee hospital laundry while Catherine, the youngest, now called "Kay" attended school.

James Christie or "our Jimmock" as he was affectionately called by all, was truly a fair-haired son. Full of fun and nonsense, he always kept the family and friends in stitches with his stories and practical jokes. Loved by everyone especially the ladies, both old and young alike, Jim had a very appealing jovial spirit.

One day he announced that he had finally found a high paying job. Everyone was excited for him. The only drawback was that it was dangerous. Up early for his first day, Mom Sneddon cautioned his enthusiasm with, "Be careful, son."

He bent down and planted a kiss on her brow. "Don't worry Mom, I'll be just fine! This is a really good paying job!"

Shaking her head, Jen smiled.

Grabbing his black lunch bucket off the kitchen table, he raced outside through the front door, leapt down the six stairs, screen door slamming behind him landing with both feet squarely on the sidewalk. He was ready to go!

Later the same day, the family received a visit from Jim's grim-faced foreman. He brought tragic news that left them speechless.

Their Jimmy, so full of life and hope, arrived at the busy dockyard ever willing to do anything the experienced longshoremen needed. However he was a greenhorn, without even a hard hat, or proper training for the dangerous work. A large hook attached to a crane cable caught his glove, picked him up and slammed him into the side of a ship, knocking him unconscious. He fell into the sea between the ship and the dock and drowned, lost in an instant.

He was only twenty-three.

The family never fully recovered from this shock. Their precious James Christie, the beloved little brother who knew just how to cheer everyone up in the hard times, was gone! Struck dumb at the news, each one was overcome with grief. The house was soon filled with mourners. Mom Sneddon, numb with pain, sat in silence, unable to lift a hand to serve anyone, the tea pot sat cold.

The light in her life somehow was dimmed and she became 'too quiet'. She'd just shake her head and mumble "Aye, there never was such a fine wee laddie as 'our Jim!'"

Dad too was very somber. The music ceased all together for a while and he took to his whiskey when night descended. Suffering and pain visits all families. Yet when tragedy strikes, somehow with time eventually life must go on.

Netta and Sheila grew to be beautiful optimistic young women, dreaming, as most girls do, of finding "Mr. Right." Whoever had a date got first choice of anything in their communal clothes closet. Nylon stockings were something only seen in the movies, and the trick was for one sister to take an eyebrow pencil and paint a line down the middle of the back of the legs of the other! From a distance it looked like the 'lady' was wearing the 'real thing'! The girls, cautioned by their parents, usually went out on double-dates.

Dancing was a favorite pastime. Tunes on the hit parade included: "Mares eat oats and does eat oats and little lambs eat ivy... I love you..." Then it was Christmas time and Bing Crosby crooned out, "I'll be home for Christmas..."

By now the whole world was in turmoil, listening to the threats of Hitler and his nascent Nazi war machine. Everyone felt uneasy. In a very short time, millions of families were again rendered fatherless, and parents were without their sons. It is estimated that up to eighty-five million people perished in WWII, among them, one third of world Jewry. Their only sin being... "a Jew".

But we are jumping ahead to a topic to be covered in the next chapter.

Timeless Secrets

"For I consider that the sufferings of this present time are not worthy to be compared with the glory which shall be revealed in us." Romans 8:18

One of the universal principles of life is "suffering." We all suffer one way or another. Everyone. The key is to see the suffering as a stepping stone, not a stumbling block. No matter what you are suffering in your life, take a moment and look back. Hopefully, in time, you will see a positive pattern emerge. Never stoop to play the 'blame game'.
Life comes out of death and we know joy follows the pain of childbirth. Learning to overcome may take longer than you realize but change and growth is always possible after we have suffered. A willing heart that sees with the eyes of faith will strengthen and embolden you to be willing to go on.

God loves you and has a wonderful plan for your life. Look for it and you will find it. *"Ask, and it will be given to you; seek and you will find; knock and it will be opened to you."* Matthew 7:7

You will be amazed at what is in store for you. Note this promise:
"Eye has not seen, nor ear heard, nor have entered into the heart of man, the things which God has prepared for those who love Him."
1 Corinthians 2:9

Post Script ~ Excerpt from a reader's quote:

"I'm glad Jay and Meridel, that you included several detailed chapters about Jay's family and more recent ancestors. It makes interesting reading, and provides a rich context to your life story. As you wrote, 'we do not, cannot and will never forget our ancestors'. Only now, at the age of 59, I can fully appreciate the truth of that statement— better late than never. The bitter-sweet part, or perhaps poignant would be a better word, is that the ones who were most involved in my life and who loved me so genuinely, consistently and unconditionally, all of them are no longer here. But love is stronger than death and their love for me has a powerful ongoing effect that does not die. Love is as eternal as God Himself, since it comes from Him." Joan, UK.

CHAPTER 4

The Ecstasy and the Agony

**"Grandfather Frank Rawlings booked passage to Canada for his
wife Miriam, pregnant with their second child. He ordered their
tickets on "The Titanic", the latest and greatest ship ever built to
that time. It was the spring of 1912…"**

The Rawlings, also new immigrants to Canada lived near the Sneddons
on Rock Bay Ave in Victoria on the southern tip of Vancouver Island.
Victoria is the capital city of the province of British Columbia,
surrounded on three sides by the Pacific Ocean. They were from
London, England and had six children as well.

My paternal grandfather, Frank Rawlings, had served with the British
Army in the Boer War in South Africa. He fudged on his age in order
to join up, and in 1899, found himself on a ship headed to Cape Town
at the tender age of seventeen.

When he returned to England in 1902, he met a tall dark-haired beauty, Miriam (Cohen) Cannon, one of ten children in a home so poor that
several of the children were raised in foster homes or with relatives.
Miriam was raised by two step-sisters who became her surrogate parents in London. She stood almost six feet tall, and carried herself in
a distinguished manner. Her pale skin and violet eyes were in stark
contrast to her raven black wavy hair. She was a shy, gracious lady
whom my grandfather nicknamed 'Pidge' for her soft comforting
nature. Miriam's Jewish grandparents had immigrated to England in
the mid 1800's from France. In order to avoid further anti-Semitic
prejudice, they changed their family name from Cohen to Cannon and
became "British".

After a whirlwind courtship twenty-six year old Frank and twenty three
year old Miriam, married in 1908.

The young lovers dreamed of moving to Canada and began making plans. Lois, their first daughter, arrived in 1910.
To help make their dreams come true, Frank immigrated to Canada in early 1912 to meet his half sister Kate who lived in Victoria BC.
It seemed a good place to settle. He was hired as a painter at the Bamberton Cement Plant, near Victoria and worked hard preparing the way for his young family to follow him.

Frank booked the passage to Canada for Miriam, pregnant with their second child. He ordered their tickets on The Titanic, the latest and greatest ship ever built to that time. It was the spring of 1912, but, their toddler Lois came down with scarlet fever, just a few weeks before sailing. Miriam had to cancel their tickets on that fateful ship. It sank on April 15th 1912, shocking the entire world and bringing the boastful words of her owners, "that it was unsinkable" to nothing. Their first son, Alexander, was born on October 8th 1913, in Essex England.

Finally, in late 1913, Miriam and her two children traveled for six days as 3rd class passengers, sailing from Southampton to Halifax, Nova Scotia. They lived on sandwiches, canned food and biscuits. Miriam found a kind-hearted second class passenger who offered to heat the baby bottles for her. After arriving in Canada and enduring the five day "express train" trip, cross country from Halifax to Vancouver, you can imagine the joy of Miriam and Frank's reunion. The final overnight boat trip to Victoria located on Canada's west coast ended this part of their saga.

Known to be 'more English than England' Victoria has a London-like climate that immediately suited the Rawlings. Frank Sydney Rawlings was a 'jack of all trades'. He worked as a chef in the elegant Canadian Pacific Hotel, The Empress. Meanwhile Miriam, a quiet homemaker, had time to consider her new life in Canada as an almost completely assimilated Jewess. Over the centuries it has been common practice for Jews to conceal their identity to avoid persecution.
Many intermarried with non Jews in the hope of avoiding further oppression.

Quickly, the Rawlings were absorbed into Canadian life, so much so, that in 1916 Frank patriotically enlisted in the Canadian Army. Miriam was pregnant with their third child Victor at the time. From England, he was mobilized to France in the heat of WW1. While on the front lines, he suffered from mustard-gas poisoning and was hospitalized in France. Upon his discharge in 1918, he was shipped back to Canada via England. Subsequently, weakened in body, he collected a lifelong disability pension. My father, Victor Rawlings, was born on November 25th 1916, while Frank was serving in the European theater of WW1. As you read on, you will see, how history has repeated itself in my family.

Evidently, my grandfather had a deep longing to understand the connection between history and, the prophetic passages of the Bible. He was a home-spun philosopher and gleaned insight and inspiration through his own diligent study each week. On weekends, he gathered his growing young family around the dining room table and expounded his latest thoughts from a specific Biblical text.

He wrote in 1933, Test Tube - Our World's Progress,[9]

"The first three principles of human existence are as follows: the spiritual, physical and material elements of life. Our interest is not for ourselves alone, but for our children in affording them a worthy inheritance. Life is no accident and the tragic conditions of today are the result of man's governing and the sequences of human error. Adjustment and change is possible by a complete realization and recognition of the universal laws of values, which are natural laws that demand a perfect balance in all things."

His life of scripture research suited my grandmother because of her Jewish heritage, which centers around the traditional study of the weekly Torah portion called in Hebrew the *Parashat Shavuah*. This yearly calendar of Biblical readings is consistent throughout the Jewish world. Today, weekly portions of the scriptures continue to be a source of inspiration, taught by Rabbis and laymen alike.

---

9   Rawlings, Frank S. **"Test Tube - Our World's Progress"**, Introduction page 1, unpublished manuscript 1933.

It was clear that my grandmother had a deep spiritual hunger and longing for her Jewish heritage. She was a quiet believer in the God of Israel and His Messiah. In many ways she was like the dove from Noah's Ark that flew over the water soaked earth trying to find a place to land. She quickly returned to the ark for safety. Miriam kept to herself, and poured out her life for her husband and children. Her youngest son, George remembers her sitting at the piano and singing to the Lord through her music. You could say she fell through the cracks, not belonging to any organized religious practice or community.

One interesting point to ponder about my grandfather was the way in which his Rawlings surname was preserved. Soon after he was born in England, his father died. His young mother married again and had five more children given the surname of her second husband, a Mr. Boulter. In order to keep the unity of the family, my grandfather Rawlings' surname was unofficially overwritten as Boulter. However, when he joined the British Army, the officials immediately saw on his birth certificate that his real name was Rawlings. From then on, he was Frank Sydney Rawlings. This part of my story is of significance when you read on to find out what happened to me more than sixty years later.

I believe that it was providential that the Rawlings and Sneddon families settled in Canada only a few blocks apart. The young lads played street hockey together, while the lassies skipped rope and tossed "jacks" in the mild Victoria climate.
Vic was popular in the neighborhood. The kids looked up to him. He built a Soap Box race car for George, his youngest brother. It was entered in the local Soap Box Derby. [10]

Our dear Uncle George began to write letters to our sons in Israel, telling them of the antics of his big brother Victor, their grandfather. During his latter years, whenever we visited Victoria, he made a point of filling in details of my Dad's life for me.

---

[10] Soap Box Derby: originally an American youth racing competition of homemade wooden "go carts" powered only by gravity.

I also think that George was longing to talk about Vic just as much as Meridel and I were eager to hear any news about him. He made a point of always taking us out for special dinners at the Oak Bay Marina restaurant.

These moments have become fixed in time for us. On one such occasion, laughingly, Uncle George quipped, "I knew Vic better than anybody. I should have, we slept in the same bed for ten years. In those days there were nearly always more kids than beds." George reminisced. There was Lois, my eldest sister, a kind-hearted soul who loved her three brothers, especially Vic. Alex, my older brother was jovial and played practical jokes on us. He was a very hard worker, and even as a boy found odd jobs to help the family out. Gladys, my next sister, was normally very quiet but giggled and smiled whenever Vic was around. Ruth, our baby sister, was a real "tomboy," eager to play with us. She called Vic and me her "heroes." Uncle George painted word pictures of what it was like growing up with his brother... my Dad.

He went on, "Vic always included me in his activities, even going so far as to take me out on his dates with your mother." He paused here and gave me a loving look. "When we built the Soap Box Derby race car we only used parts we could find or make ourselves. Vic was ingenious, and soon all the kids in the neighborhood were coming to our garage. We lived just down the street from where your mom lived. Every one was welcome to help out in the project. Vic was our leader. Later when he played football for the Victoria All Blacks, he made the team uniforms. Cutting them out individual sizes and patterns on newspaper. He then made them out of cloth and sewed them together using mother's sewing machine."

George paused, laid his fork down on his plate, threw his head back and chuckled, "Vic even created special pouches in the front of their shorts to hold folded magazines, which acted as light weight pads. At eighteen Vic earned his high school diploma, graduating from Victoria High School in 1935."

Meridel:

During the Depression years, my uncle John Sneddon became an ardent footballer with the Victoria All Blacks team. One of the star players on his squad was Vic Rawlings, a shy, handsome, young man. John often invited him to the Sneddon home but he declined. Finally, John convinced Vic to visit for a musical evening and join in the fun. Vic often turned red with embarrassment when the family pushed him to dance or sing along. Although hesitant at first, a friendship between Vic and Sheila sprang to life. During the late 30's and early 40's the courtship of Sheila Sneddon and Victor Alloway[11] Rawlings blossomed.

Jay:

While he took a break to finish his salmon dinner, I encouraged him, "Oh, Uncle George it's great to hear! No one, in all my fifty-five years ever spoke with me about my Dad like this. It's music to my ears." I knew that my four sons would be keen to hear more about their Grandpa. In my heart I held a picture of my Dad like an undeveloped negative. Yes, I could visualize my Dad, but as Uncle George dug deep into his childhood memories, that negative photograph slowly developed into a Technicolor movie, of a fun loving, bright, creative and kind individual. I needed this.

"Vic joined the Victoria Rowing Club," George continued. "This was a major commitment of time and energy and his team won many medals and cups for their skillful rowing. I remember when he was promoted by his team mates to 'coxswain.'"

"What's that?" Meridel asked.

"The coxswain is the captain of the team," George explained. "He calls out the rhythm of the rowers to insure that his boys all pull together to edge out the competition." Pausing for a moment, he went on, "Vic was successful I think, because he was not afraid to start new things. He also learned to play basketball, and even practiced with the famous Chapman brothers of Victoria, Art and Chuck, who were chosen to play on the Canadian Olympic Basketball Team which won a Silver medal in the 1936 Berlin games.

---

[11] Name derived from the Aloe plant known for its healing qualities. French Jews often name their children after flowers.

This victory stands to this day as the highest level ever reached by a Canadian men's basketball team in Olympic competition." He cleared his throat. "Vic also loved the outdoors. He and Alex and I often went on fishing trips for fresh-water trout and, of course, in quest of the famous West Coast Pacific Coho and its cousin, the larger Spring salmon."

I was so blessed to finally learn some details about my Dad. I had an insatiable thirst to know more about this man, whom I never had the joy of meeting or knowing.

Continuing over dessert and coffee, George explained, "For all his talents, Vic was painfully shy, just like our sedate and very lady like mother, Miriam. He loved to be at home by her side. As a boy he devoured her homemade bread, often holding one large buttered slice in each hand. I mention this as a family trait, because two generations later our three year old son Chris did the same thing when we lived in Ville Carros, southern France while sitting in his high chair watching his momma bake bread.

"Miriam and Vic had a special understanding. She depended on him to help out with the family. Being very frugal, as well as an excellent manager of his earnings, Vic always had a little "extra" to add to the pot. He was a stylish dresser with a keen sense of fashion."

He became a skilled draftsman by studying technical drawing at night school while he worked during the day with Alex, taking what ever jobs they could find. Finally, he became an apprenticed plumber. Alex went on to build Rawlings Plumbing and Heating, which for decades was the largest plumbing company in Victoria.

By 1940 Vic and Sheila became an item. She never really had any other steady boyfriend. Vic for all his shyness was creative in his romancing. In a unique way he proposed to her. They often dated on Saturdays going for drives around scenic Victoria in his Model A Ford.

One spring afternoon he took her to Mount Douglas Park, which at the time was a considerable drive. They strolled along under the great Douglas fir and Red cedar trees. Vic was the first to spot the swings. He raced Sheila to them.

Laughing and hugging, they sat together on one swing dreaming as lovers do. "Come on, I'll pump us up, hang on!" Vic jumping to his feet, took a standing position on the swing. Gradually he was able to get it going higher and higher. My mother squealed with delight at the feathery feeling in the pit of her stomach when they reached the highest level, and right then in mid-air he popped the question, "Will you marry me?"
The swing continued on its rapid arc downwards, breathlessly she shouted up to him, "Yes, yes I will!"

Sheila's father Bill Sneddon, the hard working Scot, could be crusty and unapproachable. He certainly knew how to discipline. In fact the one requirement he made for Sheila, his 'bonnie wee lassie' was that she be in early, especially on date nights. That evening she kept her secret, but joined the family in the living room to play music and card games as was their custom. At bedtime, she whispered, "Good night Poppa," bringing back one of her fondest childhood memories of him tickling her and rubbing his rough beard on her cheeks. But that night as she ran upstairs to bed, she knew that she had given her heart to another.

Vic went to see 'Pop' the following day to ask for her hand in marriage. Mustering up his courage, he asked, "I would like to ask for permission to have your daughter's hand in marriage."
The dour Scot broke into a big smile. "She is one of the very best, and we know that you are too Vic. Welcome to the family!"

At that time jobs were scarce and mother found work at the Royal Jubilee Hospital in the laundry department. There she met a team of workers led by Bill Haslam, the foreman. This fair haired, clean cut, young man had earned the respect of his co-workers, all but one, Sheila Sneddon.

One day the extremely shy Bill asked Sheila out on a date.
She immediately said, "Oh no! I am engaged to Vic Rawlings."
Bill was deeply hurt, because Sheila was the first girl he had ever fallen for and he didn't know anything about a Vic Rawlings.
"One day I am going to marry you!" he blurted out.

"Oh no you're not" she responded firmly. "I'm already spoken for."
"We'll see," said Bill.
Their working relationship cooled considerably, right up until 1940 when he signed up for the Canadian Armed Forces and was mobilized to England.

Prior to the WW2, Vic had joined the Princess Patricia Canadian Light Infantry Army Reserves. He became a drill instructor for the local recruits, to give them the basics before they left for overseas. Meanwhile, Sheila and Vic were married quietly on September 18, 1942, followed by an intimate but joyous reception of family and close friends at the Bridge Street home.

The regional commander of his regiment asked Vic to remain with him in Victoria to become the full time Drill Sergeant. But as WW2 was heating up Vic decided to join active service and refused this offer of safe employment. He plucked up his courage to tell his new wife of his plans. Trying to lighten up the very heavy reality, he mimicked her Scots accent, "I'm going abroad for kith and kin."
"Oh no Vic!" She was horrified and speechless. She cried and could not be consoled.
"I'll be home faster than you can wink an eye," he tried to comfort her but his words fell on deaf ears.
Sheila had this foreboding but couldn't put her finger on it. The trauma of those seven 'lost' years in the orphanage in Scotland had left her vulnerable to anxiety and deep loneliness. Taking her in his arms, Vic held her trembling body tightly in an effort to calm her.

He was preparing for mobilization, when after a visit to the family doctor, they learned that they were to be parents in February 1944. Sheila fought to be strong in the face of this news coupled with the looming separation. In her heart of hearts she wondered how she could manage with Vic overseas.

By the end of 1943, he went to Saskatchewan to join his new regiment, The Regina Rifles. There he started rigorous training as a signalman. These soldiers have the tough job of flanking the infantry and moving ahead to locate enemy positions and then signaling back to their comrades on how best to advance.

Sheila continued to be very anxious about his decision. She put on a brave front and, like tens of thousands of other Canadian women and their sisters worldwide, she busied herself 'on the home front' even during her pregnancy. Heavy laundry work was now out of the question because it was physically too strenuous. She could, however, drive a delivery truck.

In the absence of the men serving in the military this occupation was considered 'essential service'. She got a job with Dad's Cookies. Proudly she drove one of their Model A Ford delivery trucks on a route to various shipyards in greater Victoria. She delivered lunches as well as cakes and cookies to those who were working hard to build war ships for the Canadian Navy. Everywhere she went, she endeared herself to her customers. Her comical comments and genuine friendliness became the highlight of their day. The joke was always on her, and they loved to hear her Scots accent. She worked for a Jack Burridge, a real "*yekke.*" This Hebrew acronym describes someone who is fastidious and has to have everything in scrupulous order, neat, clean and tidy. Today we call it obsessive-compulsive. Jack was always polishing his latest car, this time a new black Packard sedan.

One day, Mom had just picked up a full load of food stuffs in the harbor area. She pulled up the steep incline beside the warehouse of Dad's Cookies. Behind her, at the bottom of the hill, was a wooden dock next to the Inner Harbor where Jack had parked his car well out of the way of the delivery trucks. When my Mom's truck crested the hill, she stalled it and it started to roll backwards. She put in the clutch and hit the brakes. The brake pedal went right to the floor with no resistance. Rolling backwards faster and faster, two choices flashed through her mind; either she could go off the dock into the icy waters of the ocean or broadside Jack's brand new Packard.

Swinging the steering wheel hard to the right she slammed into the side of his pristine Packard. Crash! Broken glass splintered along with the sound of crumpled metal, followed by.... silence!
Jack and the other workers ran out to see what had happened.
Wincing he said, "Well I'm very glad that it was my car that saved your life."
"I'm so sorry, she blurted out, "but.... I'm very glad that your lovely car was right where it should be!" Everyone laughed, except Jack.
By this time, they all knew that she was an expectant mother.

Meanwhile my father had been mobilized to Aldershot, England. One of my favorite photos of him at the time was taken while dressed in 'fatigues'. There he is, so handsome and strong, sitting on a log in the woods giving art lessons to his comrades. He wrote loving letters home to both of the mothers and of course to his wife. They were beautifully illustrated with his pen sketches and water colors. The only letter I have from him was penned at this time. It is a love letter of a father to his infant son he had never seen. It was filled with dreams and hopes for our future together.

Victor Alloway Rawlings (r) - Soldier - artist during WW2 near Aldershot, England

To minimize confusion, I , John Victor was coined 'JV' when just a few months old. Why? Dad's name is Victor Alloway and mom's brother is John. So, to keep us all straight in the many war time letters traversing the Atlantic, I became 'JV' and continue to be known as 'Jay" until today. With all of the letter writing back and forth from Canada to the war front in Europe you will see two of his letters on the following pages that I am always touched to read. Many others were illustrated with flowers that he had drawn and painted, using the small set of water color paints and brushes he kept in his breast pocket.

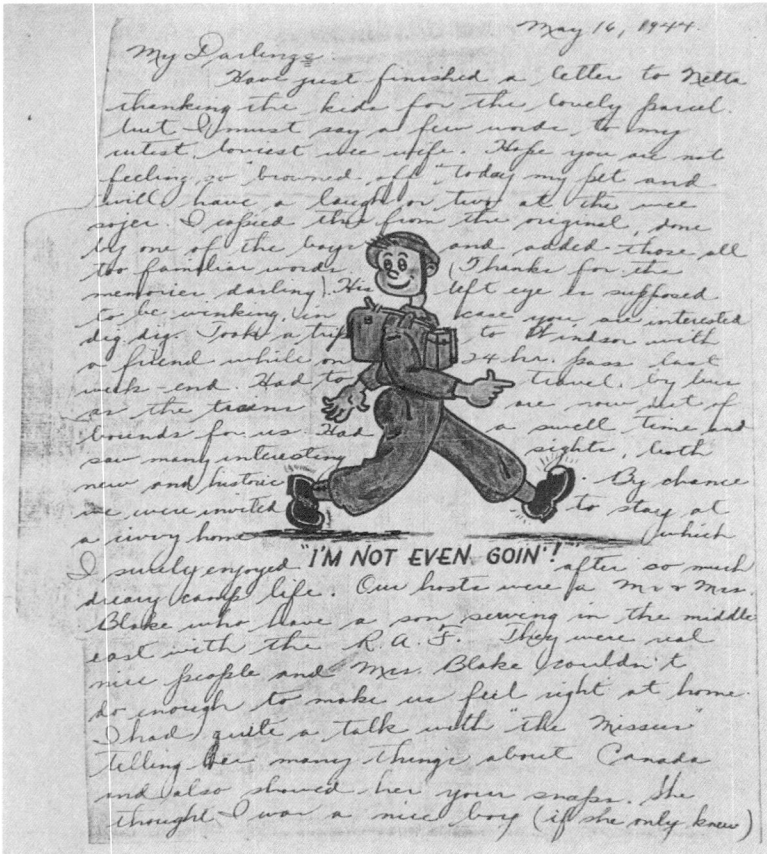

Victor Rawlings' illustrated letter from the WW2 war front, May 1, 1944

On June 6th,1944, known as D-Day, my father's regiment, the Regina Rifles got their first taste of combat. Landing on Normandy's Juno Beach, amidst a hail of Nazi fire, they were the first Canadian regiment to successfully secure a beach-head. Later, they forced the 12th S.S. Hitler Jugend Division back, clearing the way for their allied comrades. My father's May 16, 1944 letter was written just three weeks before this battle.

Victor Rawlings' illustrated letter from the WW2 war front May 16, 1944 (page 1 & 2)

On D-Day, 30,000 brave Canadian soldiers, sailors, and airmen assaulted the Nazis. They were part of 150,000 men carried by 2,154 vessels for the first phase of the operation. Ultimately, 6,483 ships and 2,000 aircraft were involved in the greatest invasion fleet of conventional armed forces in the history of the world. June 6th saw the invasion go as planned by the Supreme Commander of the entire operation, the American General, Dwight D. Eisenhower. Each of the Allied forces had different beaches to clear on the exposed northern coast of France.

The Regina Rifles First Battalion had waited for that moment for a long time. Former bank clerks, farmers, students, laborers, printers, plumbers, lawyers and many unemployed displaced by the Great Depression, had been transformed into a mentally and physically tough battalion. They steeled themselves for the most challenging moment of their lives when the ramps of their landing craft splashed down and they stood unprotected amid the oncoming hail of German artillery, machine gun and rifle fire.

It was as close to "Hades on earth" as could be. Canadian soldiers were among the first to land on those beaches. Slowly, over the next months, the allied troops, including the Regina Rifles, pushed the well equipped Nazi enemy back toward their border. In human terms it was a very, very costly ordeal. Canada lost more men per capita than any other country in WW2. One tenth of all Canadians at the time were in defense services.[12]

By September 1944, there was a major mobilization of Allied troops in an assault called Operation Market Garden. This time, British and American airborne troops confronted the Nazi war machine at a number of locations including a bridge over the Lower Rhine River in a Dutch town called Arnhem. It was the largest airborne offensive using conventional warfare of all time.

---

[12] see website: www. ca/regiment/50/the-Regina-rifles

Meanwhile, my father's regiment was given orders to push the German troops out of Belgium and Holland. It was a very tough winter. The Nazis were finally forced back across their border by April 1945 with the exception of pockets of German soldiers left in Holland, who had hunkered down. They were the old and very young Nazis that went unsupported and with each passing day they grew increasingly more hungry, cold and desperate in their isolation.

Canadian military historians have generally paid slight attention to the operations carried out by the 1st Canadian Army Division in April 1945. It is almost as if the great battles of February and March in the Rhineland exhausted the historians just as they wore down the men who fought there in 1945.

April that year is remembered as 'the sweetest of springs.' It was the month of the liberation of Holland, but April was also the cruelest month. Even though the war was all but won, the killing did not stop. The military cemeteries in Holland contain the graves of 1,355 Canadian soldiers killed in April and one hundred and fourteen who lost their lives during the last days of the war just prior to VE Day, on May 8th 1945. Their story and the record of the reunited 1st Canadian Army Division are well worth examining.

In my father's case, by April 8th the Regina Rifles Battalion had worked its way north to occupy positions on the south side of the Schipbeek Canal. Their task was to contain their sector in front of the nearby Dutch town of Deventer, while the Royal Winnipeg Rifles established a bridgehead. The records told me that my father's area was generally quiet, all but for two patrols sent across a small river that came under occasional sniper fire. That night, A Company passed through the Winnipeg Rifles position to clear the woods on the northern bank. German opposition was light, and thirty-five Nazi prisoners were taken. Many were just teenagers while others were old men. All were starving, cold and very desperate.
The next day, my father's battalion was ordered to bridge the Zijkanaal Deventer-Raalte in the vicinity of the village of Okkenbroek. The area was a little to the northeast barring the main approach to Deventer.

By noon, A Company secured a firm start line for C Company, my father's brigade and D Company who were to advance to their objective by 3 o'clock. The assault companies were given tank support as well as 'Crocodile' flame throwers. They advanced successfully to within two hundred yards of the canal.

Unfortunately, the centre span of the bridge they were to secure was blown up by the retreating Germans just as B Company reached it. During the attack, eighty more prisoners surrendered rather than face the formidable 'Crocodile' flame throwers. Also during the attack, D Company was able to get close in air support from a flight of allied Typhoon aircraft. The planes came in so low that one German machine gun post was destroyed, just a few yards in front of the leading platoon. It was this last major fire-fight, which cost my father his life on April 9th 1945. I was 14 months old then. A bridgehead had been established with my father's C Company dug in, at 22:00 hours, and twenty-five more prisoners were taken. It was the last major battle of his regiment for the remainder of the war.

A few days later, on April 16, 1945, just three weeks before the Armistice was declared, my mother received a curt telegram stating the following:

" Regret deeply K45415 Rifleman Victor Alloway Rawlings has been officially reported killed in action, ninth April 1945. Stop. You should receive further details by mail direct from the Unit in the Theatre of War. Stop. To prevent possible aid to our enemies do not divulge date of casualty or name of Unit. Director of Records, Canadian Armed Services."

Mother was devastated. She wept for weeks. We were living with her parents in the Bridge Street house. My Grandparents were able to take care of me during her worst periods of mourning.

My mother was breast feeding me during this time of trauma and every time she heard the air raid sirens sound in Victoria she broke into uncontrollable sobs. These sirens were sounded because of the potential threats of attacking Japanese aircraft over the Pacific at that time.

EXCLUSIVE CONNECTION WITH WESTERN UNION CABLE SERVICE

CANADIAN NATIONAL

W M ARMSTRONG GENERAL MANAGER
TORONTO

TELEGRAPHS

Answer by C.M.T
VA5 55 2 EX DL GB=OTTAWA ONT APR 16 1151P Telephone E.
MRS JEAN DUNCAN NAISMITH RAWLINGS, REPORT DELIVERY=
    2944 BRIDGE ST VICTORIA BC=

73159 REGRET DEEPLY K45415 RIFLEMAN VICTOR OLLOWAY RAWLINGS
HAS BEEN OFFICIALLY REPORTED KILLED IN ACTION NINTH APRIL
1945 STOP YOU SHOULD RECEIVE FURTHER DETAILS BY MAIL DIRECT
FROM THE UNIT IN THE THEATRE OF WAR STOP TO PREVENT POSSIBLE
AID TO OUR ENEMIES DO NOT DIVULGE DATE OF CASUALTY OR NAME
OF UNIT=
    DIRECTOR OF RECORDS.

Canadian National Telegram - KIA Victor Rawlings -
Killed in Action, April 16, 1945

My mother and I several months
before my father's tragic death

For years afterward I was always very frightened and confused when I heard a siren. The sound of an ambulance, police car or fire truck made me panic and I didn't know why. Later, I realized that fear, loss and a sense of abandonment entered my being with my mother's milk. The wailing of any siren was simply a subconscious pain trigger for me until I reached my teens.

A few days later Mom received a message of condolence from King George VI of England, dated May 21st, 1945.

BUCKINGHAM PALACE

The Queen and I offer you our heartfelt sympathy in your great sorrow.

We pray that your country's gratitude for a life so nobly given in its service may bring you some measure of consolation.

George R.I.

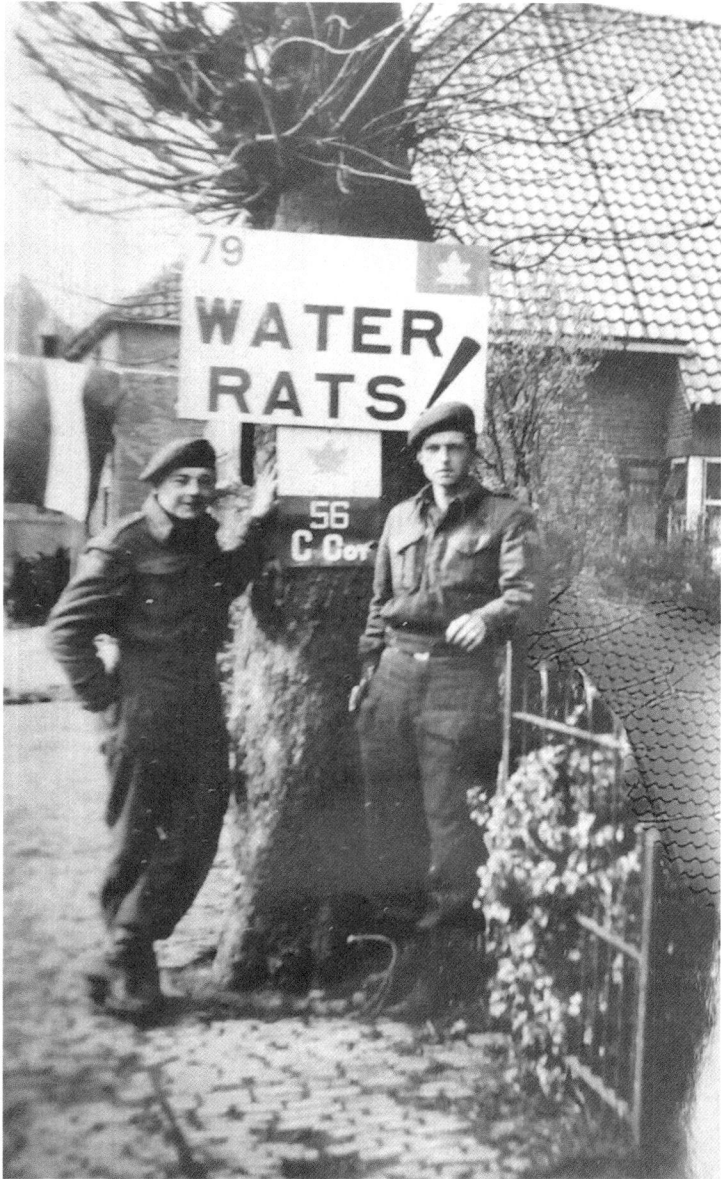

Signalman Vic Rawlings and comrade - Regina Rifles Regiment - Netherlands, 1945

Timeless Secrets

"He will swallow up death forever, and the Lord God will wipe away tears from all faces...For the Lord has spoken." Isaiah 25:8

Jay:

Coming to grips with the death of a loved one has to be one of the most complex experiences any of us will pass through. We all suffer keenly and differently. Only time and the love of family and friends along with the comfort of God's Spirit can help us at such moments. The hope of life after death eases the pain somewhat.

Meridel:

Faith in the resurrection of the dead is one of the foundational tenants of Judaism and Christianity. But grieving is a delicate on going process and takes time. The sense of loss can last a life-time, as in the case of Jay's mother and family, Vic's family and even Jay himself. I believe each one of our sons have grieved over the loss of their Grandfather. I know that I have.

No belief or doctrine can be dictated to one who is grieving. Listening and being 'present' is one of the kindest ways to 'help'. Grieving takes time and there is no 'right' amount of time.

Remembering is so vitally important. In Israel when someone dies their world stops. The home of that person goes into a seven day mourning period. Friends and family come to comfort the bereaved for that week, bringing food and their loving memories to share. For those seven days and nights the departed is the focus of attention. It is a healthy tradition. Custom allows the tearing of a garment while mourning, representing the tearing of one's heart. After thirty days the family gather at the grave site to lay the headstone. A year after the death, a further mourning event is then marked. This gives time for those closest to the deceased to slowly return to their normal flow of life.

Jews weekly recite specific Psalms during these mourning periods giving thanks to the Almighty reminding Him that He has promised 'not to leave our bones in the dust.' That prayer of faith expresses hope in the resurrection of the dead.

Modern burial practices have other customs like embalming which can be likened to ancient Egypt, but we will not go there.
Tears are a gift of release for all people when facing this kind of separation and deep sense of loss. Knowledge of the 'resurrection' is wonderful but only the comfort of one's own relationship with the Lord can ease a broken heart. This is where the consolation of the Spirit of God is vital.

"To everything there is a season. A time for every purpose under heaven: A time to be born, And a time to die, A time to weep, And a time to laugh; A time to mourn, And a time to dance, And a time to heal."
Ecclesiastes 3:1, 2a, 3a, 4

"Draw near to God and He will draw near to you." James 4:8

"He heals the broken hearted and binds up their wounds." Psalm 147:3

"...whoever believes in Him should not perish but have eternal life. "
John 3:15

Post Script:

This history is of particular interest to our four sons raised in Israel.
Each one has experienced many challenges with the Israel Defense
Forces. Two of them served in top combat units, but more about that
in later volumes. Three of their grandfathers and many great uncles
served in the in the Boer War, the Royal Canadian Armed Forces in
WW1 and WW2. My father is buried in the Holten Canadian War
Cemetery in the Netherlands, about twenty kilometers from Deventer,
where he fell. To this day it is a carefully groomed garden area with
immaculately trimmed lawns, banked with large beds of colorful
perennials.

Close attention is paid to each grave site and their white head stones.
The 1,355 Canadians laid to rest there, gave their lives liberating
Netherlands. The Dutch people have never forgotten the their
sacrifice. Every May 5th, Dutch Independence Day, the cemetery
comes alive with school children laying flowers at each grave site while
local dignitaries eulogize the Canadian soldiers. Every grave is routinely
remembered on Easter and again on Christmas Eve. Large Finnish
made candles are lit and placed at each head stones and burn for
twenty-four hours in any weather. "Lest we forget..."

We are profoundly comforted to know that Vic, our loved one, along
with his comrades, are not forgotten. We have visited his grave site on
three occasions and each time it has been a very moving experience
for Meridel, me and our sons. We were overcome with a feeling of
tragic loss and sadness. We walked the lanes of Holten and were
unable to speak for sometime, the grief was so intense.

We were deeply touched, remembering the ongoing respect given
them by the Dutch people. One of the local curators, seeing how
moved we were, took us home and served us coffee. He listened as
I spoke out my pain and grief. He told us, "The Canadian soldiers in
Holland were different from the other Allied troops. After the war,
many of them spent weeks, months and even a year billeted with us
and we became like family."

He was an expert in much of the military history of WW2 and, because we were doing research for a film, he pointed us to several military archives, which had just been opened in the year 2000.

The Dutch government bequeathed the land of the Holten War Graves to Canada. Thus the 1,335 Canadian boys who fell in battle nearby are laid to rest "in Canadian soil." My Dad's letters and photographs are in their museum. Now my dream is to take our four sons and eight grandchildren to the Netherlands to pay our respects to Grandpa Vic. One day!

The first time Jay visited his father's grave at the Holten War Cemetery in Holland, 1975

CHAPTER 5

The Best for My Little Boy

"... many people will do anything to ease their lonely emptiness like sports, work, drugs, alcohol, and sex, shopping or eating to quench this inner gnawing. They think buying a new house or a new car, new clothes, dieting, travel, self-help schemes, making money, even a new political system or religion will make them happy and secure. This is folly... "

Jay:

With the loss of her husband, mother busied herself with the task of being a single parent. Deciding to take a secretarial course in order to help find a higher paying job so she could support us. While living upstairs in her parents' home on Bridge Street she completed the course in eight months. My grandparents were very willing to look after me while mom studied. Some of my earliest memories of them are from this time. Grandma fed me oatmeal porridge for breakfast, and my grandpa blew on my hot tea in a saucer to cool it down for me to sip. Bridge Street was a child's dream house. Inside, the polished wooden floors were perfect for playing cars. Outside, I had a sand box and a large garden as well as a big woodshed where I could explore. It was a busy place with people coming and going. Music, of course, was part of our everyday lives.

I remember one morning I was playing in the back garden when I decided to go on an adventure with my little red wheelbarrow. I had to find my mom! Unknown to my grandparents, I embarked upon a rather daring journey. Somehow I knew she had a temporary job as a waitress in a nearby cafe owned by a long-time family friend. It was called Mac's Coffee Shop, a popular Victoria destination. To find her I had to go out onto Bridge Street, a truck route, cross the road, walk one hundred meters up to Gorge Road and then turn right and walk several blocks to find Mac's on the right hand side.

I remember upon arrival that the cafe door handle was too high for me and I had to wait until a customer came. Someone had pity and helped me inside with my wheelbarrow. Later my Mother recounted that I was dressed in an old sweater, overalls that were dirty at the knees from playing in my sand box, and scuffed boots.

"Oh my wee laddie..." Falling to her knees she embraced me, astonished that her two-and-a-half year old toddler managed to find her. My startled grandparents made sure I didn't try that stunt again.
Maybe this ability to find one's way runs in our DNA. I could never have imagined that fifty years later, our son David would be named in Hebrew 'hayal mitztayen' or 'most excellent soldier' in the Israeli Army for his orienteering skills!

Remember the head of the laundry at the Jubilee Hospital, Bill Haslam? He had survived the army and had returned to Victoria after the war. He made a point of offering his condolences to Sheila Rawlings. Then, some months later, when it was appropriate, he asked my mother to go out with him.
"Absolutely not!" she soundly rebuffed him. "What gave you the impression that I am even interested in dating?" she said indignantly. "I have no interest in anyone." With an unwavering look she assured him of her feelings in no uncertain terms. This second rejection devastated Bill, who slowly slipped into depression.

Sometime later, my mom was visiting a patient at the Royal Jubilee Hospital. When leaving the surgical ward she decided to pop down to the laundry department to say hello to some of her old friends. While chatting with the girls, she discovered that Bill had not been to work for six weeks. No one seemed to know what his problem was but my mother had her own private thoughts on the matter. On the way home, she changed her normal route and decided to visit Bill. She pulled her Model A Ford to a stop in front of his family home. Bill's mother, Mrs. Clarissa Haslam, a diminutive but jaunty lady from Yorkshire, England, opened the door and immediately invited her in. Speaking in hushed tones Clarissa informed her that because she rejected Bill he had become a despondent recluse.

Completely unaware of the depth of his feelings for her Sheila said, "Well, I only want the best for my little boy."
Clarissa immediately responded," Well, I only want the best for <u>my</u> little boy."
That did it! My mother agreed to at least talk with Billy. They began an eighteen-month courtship. With sound advice from family and friends, the passing of time, and my mother's desire to have a dad for her son, gradually allowed her to begin to see the sterling qualities of Bill Haslam.

They were married on October 12, 1947. The union was actually a cathartic for the entire Sneddon, Rawlings and Haslam clans who pitched in to make the ceremony and reception a success. It was time for Mom to start a new chapter in her life. Everyone worked overtime decorating the family home. I was nearly four years old and got a front row seat on the broad steps leading to the second floor watching the ceremony.

Wanting to live again, Billy, my new step-dad, mom and I moved into our own home. Life for me, however, as an only child was quite lonely after having been part of my Grandparents' busy home.
The wedding must have made a lasting impression on me.
A year later, as Mom was tucking me into bed one night, I said to her, "Mommy, I want someone to play with! I want to have a brother or, (after a pause) maybe a sister or, (after a longer pause) even a wife!"

Sadly though, few noticed at this time that my second Mom, my Grandma Sneddon's health was deteriorating rapidly.
She now developed difficulty walking and breathing. One day, her heart began to fail and she stayed in bed. This was very unusual as she had always been the busiest of homemakers. The doctor's diagnosis confirmed the family's worst fears. She had chronic heart failure due to blocked arteries. In an era prior to heart bypass surgery and vascular stents, her prognosis was not good. All she could do was rest and wait.

One morning she called her children together to tell them of an experience she had in the night. She smoothed out the bed covers, trying to be her old jaunty self and said, "Very early this morning my room was filled with Light. At first I was afraid." Her voice became almost inaudible, "and you know I am not a religious person, but," she paused, her deep throaty voice began to waver, "I want you all to know that I sensed a supernatural Presence... this has never happened to me before! I was overwhelmed but dared to ask this Living Light, 'Who are you?' The answer amazed me and melted away my uncertainty and loneliness.'" Lifting her trembling hand to her chest, she continued, "I heard the answer in my heart, "I AM that I AM!" Then, she went on "the light slowly started to fade, but a penetrating 'Peace' remained deep inside and calmed me. I felt completely accepted. It was the I AM that I AM[13] which brought it... I'll never be the same again." She started to cry. "Now, I am asking all of you not to worry about me. Just know that not one of us is alone here. Everything is going to be alright. Just trust in the "I AM". Don't worry; everything is in His hands, even our Jimmie!" (James Christie Sneddon, Mom's brother who died because of a dock accident.)

Silently they nodded and bowed heads signaling their agreement. My mom recounted this story years later. "According to age, with my Dad called "Pop" going last, we all took our turn tiptoeing up to the bedside and paid tribute to the woman who 'against all odds' had never given up. She had bravely fought and lost; and fought back again for us all. For one last moment we looked into her tired eyes, and kissed her pale damp cheek. Our tears, mingled with hers. The indomitable and gifted Jen, my wee Mom, slipped slowly away in her sleep. We were all left wanting. The old house on Bridge St would never the same again."
"Jen had no financial legacy to leave any of us, "Sheila recalled, "but that moment became an eternal treasure and has helped me define my heritage." She continued, "J.V., I want this story passed down

---

13 In Hebrew, the unpronounceable Name of God made up of four Hebrew letters: *yod, hay, vav, hey*. In English, the word 'Adonai' or LORD becomes YHWH (literally: "I will be Who I will be to bring about redemption). The root of the word is heh, vav, heh, as in *'ahava'* - love. Love for ALL of His creatures - for all mankind and His creation together.

from generation to generation. We all must come to know the reality of the 'I AM.' There will be an encounter for each one of us. We need 'The Rock" to hold onto day by day and especially in times of need."[14]

Jen's funeral came just months after Billy and Sheila's wedding at the Bridge Street house. This time the instruments were silent as the old home again became a gathering place for the many who had been warmed by her open hearted kindness, wise words, food and music. Grandma had never met a stranger. She was kind and accepting to those who found their way to her door. Hearts were warmed, no matter who she met. Her musical talents, heart of love and comforting words of wisdom over 'wee cups of tea and scones' made her unforgettable. Family and neighbors came to pay their last respects to Janet Christie Sneddon, "musician, wife, mother, grandmother and friend" young and old alike, everyone greatly missed 'Jen'. Then, folks came from many walks of life, languages and cultures to pay respect and to honor her memory.

Bill Haslam was a true gentleman and proved to be a wonderful husband and provider for Mom and a dedicated Dad to me. A man's man, he loved to play sports with me. One day he bought me a new baseball. After supper, we found old ball gloves, and went to the back yard, where he taught me how to throw and catch. Then I learned from him how to pick up grounders and to swing a baseball bat properly.

We moved into a new house that my parents built on Oak Crest Drive in a subdivision near Cedar Hill. It was an ideal place for kids because of the lovely garden and plenty of room for 'yard' baseball. Closest to the woods stood my two stories 'fort' that we had built using scraps of wood. My pals from the neighborhood, David Davies, Rick Gough, Ricky Gilman, and Bruce Morley helped me scrounge the wood and build it. On rainy days we moved our activities into the spacious basement for roller hockey and table tennis.

---

[14] "The God of our fathers…" 2 Chronicles 20:6; Acts 22: 14-16

Grandpa "Pop" Sneddon came to live with us. I don't remember him playing his cello anymore because he suffered from severe emphysema, the result of being gassed back in WWI. I never met any of his brothers who settled in the States. He grew weaker and weaker, and early one morning he slipped away in his sleep.
It was the end of an era.

We have a photo of him taken at Victoria's famous Empress Hotel, where he worked as a maintenance engineer. There he is, slight of body, fine boned, sitting with his beautiful cello cradled in his arms. Those crystal clear brown eyes still penetrate into me, in a 'knowing' way. His wrinkled and weathered face is stamped with suffering. I now understand he had an extremely sensitive and gifted soul; a man with multiple talents who could make any stringed instrument sing, yet he suffered for more than fifty years from being gassed in the trenches of WW1. In order to hold soul and body together, in Canada he spent years working in an iron mouldery. This job aggravated his lungs because he worked close to a blast furnace where iron ore was heated up to a molten liquid. He had to skim off the floating impurities. The iron was then poured into molds.
In spite of the pain, he took this job to redeem his wife and children out of dire poverty in Scotland. He worked hard to give them 'new beginnings' in Canada. It is important not to forget such sacrifice.

As an eight year old I soon learned how to do the chores I was assigned. First thing in the morning I had to feed my dog, Sporty, and my cat, Buttons. After school in the winter I had to chop the wood. Inside, I always had to clean my room and set the table, and often wash the dishes after supper. Both my mom and dad worked and, since I was an only child, I had to do my share around the house. The summer job I liked best was cutting the grass because after each time, Dad paid me fifty cents. It was just enough money to join my pals for the Saturday matinee western movie at the Capitol Theatre and still have some money left over to buy a Revel (chocolate covered ice-cream on a stick) and get the bus both ways. I enjoyed my freedom.

While playing one day I realized I was different from my friends. They all had two grandmas and two grandpas, but I had three of each! I ran to home. "Mom, I have a question!"

She looked up from her sewing machine. "What is it dear?"

"How come Ricky and David and Bruce have only four grandparents and I've got six?"

For a moment she was speechless, then took me to the living room. " Come here J.V., sit beside me, I have something to tell you."

I flopped down on the couch.

While straightening her apron, in a quiet voice and with tears running down her cheeks she said, "My dear wee boy, your real father is Vic Rawlings, not Billy."

Confused, I looked at her. "Why do you say that? I'm J.V. Haslam."

As if remembering, she looked down, and then away from me. "Your father was killed in the War, and I married Billy so you could have a dad. We both took his name."

"Okay, mom. Can I go now?"

Later that day, as we sat together Billy said to me, "Yes, J.V., your real name is J.V. Rawlings, but I don't care if your name is McGillicuddy. You will always be my son." I jumped up and gave him a big hug.

All through my growing-up years on into high school I kept the name 'J.V. Haslam'. When I enrolled at the age of twenty in the University of British Columbia (UBC) I needed a copy of my birth certificate.

The issue of my name came up again. A notarized piece of paper had been attached to my original birth certificate stating that I was 'also known as' J.V. Haslam, but my real name was J. V. Rawlings. I felt that it was now time for me as a man and for my future children to have our rightful name. It was a hard decision because I dearly loved Billy, my step-dad. I knew I had to have a 'man to man' talk with him.

"Dad this is a hard thing for me to bring up, but I want to ask your permission for me to use my real name from here on in."

He threw back his head and laughed while repeating his words from twelve years earlier, "J.V. I don't care if they call you McGillicuddy, you will always be my son!"

I was glad for his response because I didn't want to hurt him.

It was also a comfort learning that my own Rawlings grandpa had been faced with exactly the same dilemma as myself six decades earlier. I was told that my great-grandfather Rawlings died when my grandfather Frank was a baby. His mother remarried and gave him the name of her new husband. It wasn't until Frank went into the British Army in 1899 that he had his name Rawlings restored. I had come full circle. Again, the Rawlings name was preserved. In the ensuing years, God has blessed Meridel and me with four sons and four grandsons who now carry the name to their generations.

In 1954 my life got really interesting. Local sportsmen started Little League Baseball in my area. I remember reading the announcement in the Times Colonist newspaper. It said, "Try Outs to be held on Saturday from 9:00 – 12:00 for boys 10 – 12 years old at the Rotary Little League Park. Bring your birth certificate." I was so excited I could hardly sleep. I even took my old baseball glove to bed with me until the day "try outs" arrived.

That Saturday, I was up early and rode my bike to the park. I got there by 9:00 a.m. I was shocked! The ballpark was already filled with boys playing catch. I felt pretty intimidated with my old glove, sun-bleached ball cap and scruffy running shoes. I parked my bike, stood tall and tried not to look nervous.
Approaching a table with adults sitting at it, I began courteously, "Excuse me, I read your ad in the newspaper, what do I do?"

Someone pointed me to a nearby sign-up table where neighborhood ladies had volunteered to examine birth certificates and then issue each qualifying boy with a large identification number. I laid my papers on the table.
She read out my name, "John Victor Haslam,", and smiling warmly she studied my freckled face.
"Yes, that's me" I replied."
"Turn around son, I'm going to pin number 322 on your back. There! Now you are registered."

I did some quick math. All 321 other kids were trying out for 4 "major teams" of 15 players each. That meant that only 60 would be chosen. Most would not make it to the "majors." My heart started to pound. The coaches were all out on the field shouting orders. Some kids were pitching, others fielded grounders in the infield, six deep at each position, while others were in the outfield taking turns at catching long fly balls. When I went onto the diamond, one fatherly looking man asked me, "What position do you play son?

Unsure, I blurted out, "Second base."

"Good, go over there and field some grounders." He pointed to where I had to go. Grateful that my Dad had practiced with me, I didn't make too many mistakes. We had to do a rotation at all the positions and by twelve o'clock the try-outs were over. I was tired.

"Okay, listen up boys," the head coach shouted, "Next Wednesday, You will find out if you have been picked for one of four "Major" teams. It will be announced in the newspaper on the Sports page. That's all for today."

I couldn't wait. Awake early every morning, I listened from my bed, for the thud of the newspaper as the delivery boy hit our front door with it. Would I be chosen? My mind raced with anticipation. By Wednesday morning I was already up and waiting outside on the porch in my pajamas for the paperboy to arrive. I caught the newspaper in my arms, raced to my room, jumped on the bed, and threw it open to the Sports page, my hands trembling. 'Did I make it or not?'

The "Major Team" players were even issued uniforms and they were to play in the big new ballpark with grandstands. Or was I to be relegated to the "Farm Team" league? I checked each team roster. There were fifteen kids selected for each squad, five ten year olds, five eleven year olds, and five twelve year olds. There it was. My name 'J.V. Haslam' was one of the ten year olds on the list. I was now part of the "Major League" on a team sponsored by the Oak Bay Kiwanis Club. I was ecstatic. I woke up Billy with the news.

"Dad, I made it. I made it. I'm on the team," I shouted.

Sleepily he said, "Well, son that's great. We'll have to keep on practicing."

"Yes, yes! Let's go outside right now and practice!"

Billy looked at his watch, "It's 5:30 in the morning and I have to go to work soon, but when I come home we'll get right at it, OK?"

I bounded out of the room, repeatedly tossing a baseball in the air and catching it. I loved that familiar satisfying sound of 'thud' when the ball landed safely inside my trusty old glove. Dad volunteered to help coach our team and it turned out to be quite a commitment of time between official games, team practices and practicing with me at home. He did seem to enjoy it all. I'll never forget the ribbing he gave me after one Little League game that I was playing when I was eleven years old. I was up to bat and one of the local radio stations, CJVI, sent out a wellknown radio personality to announce the game in an attempt to bring out larger spectator crowds. As I got up to bat I could hear the announcer say, his deep voice edged with expectation, engaging a large listening audience, "And the next batter up is J.V. Haslam, playing shortstop today. His current batting average is 455; he's a very dangerous hitter."

Carried away with visions of grandeur, I didn't concentrate on the pitcher and struck out!

My mom and dad never did let me forget that one! I could now understand the meaning of the term, "grandstanding."

In all, I played fourteen years of 'organized' baseball. They were excellent learning years. I gained invaluable experience playing as a team member. When I was twelve our team won the local Little League Championship and I was selected to play on the All Star Team for the international competition. We were up against a very well-trained American team and lost. Yours truly tried to steal home with the 'tying run' in the bottom of the last inning. "You're out!" shouted the umpire as I slid over home plate. I was so disappointed for letting the whole team down. It took me a long time to get over that loss, but I learned the vital truth of 'team spirit' and something more of the principle of the 'unity of purpose'. It wasn't 'my' game, it was 'our' game. My single action affected the entire team and brought defeat. Two of my illustrious team members were Bob Cotton and Barry Hitchens. We used to say in jest that "Hitchen was pitchin and Cotton-batten!"

Just five years later, I was selected for an All Star Team from our Colt League in Victoria. That year, we won the Canadian championship with many of the same young men I had played with in Little League. The next year, at eighteen, I was asked to join a team in the Senior A Men's Baseball League that played in Victoria's old Royal Athletic Park with its professionally kept infield and wooden grandstands seating up to 5,000 spectators. We played teams representing various towns all up and down Vancouver Island. Occasionally we played exhibition games with ball clubs from Washington State USA, and once a team from as far away as Japan.

Often my uncle Alex Rawlings, my father's eldest brother, and his son James, my cousin just six months younger that I, came out to watch me play. They especially enjoyed the Men's League and that was a big encouragement to me. By sponsoring these teams, local businessmen used the advertising opportunities to promote their various business operations. Alex had built one of the largest plumbing and heating companies in Victoria and I was honored and delighted when he sponsored our team. Our coach, Herb Wetherall, was a man who had the ability to shape a group of guys ranging in age from eighteen to forty into a winning team. He used humor mixed kind insults that made everyone laugh and relax. It seemed to work. We won our share of games as Rawlings Plumbing and Heating.

One of the most promising young players in our league was George Hemming. As a tall, powerful left handed pitcher, he had a high strikeout rate. Scouts from Major League Baseball occasionally showed up at our games unannounced. They were looking for any talented young players. George was the one they kept their eye on from the time he was sixteen. Eventually, at nineteen he was drafted by the New York Yankees Class C farm team in Greensboro SC. It was a big honor for George and our league. Herb our 'tough guy' coach was delighted with George's success. "Coach" Herb later married Shirley, an especially gentle Christian lady. Over the last forty-five years we have maintained our friendship, mainly through letters and occasional visits in person.

It was during those teen years that I longed for something more.
My life was busy and filled with lots of friends, I had everything
I wanted... but something was missing... what? Yes, I missed my
grandmothers and remembered them both as amazing women of
faith in their very own ways. They both let me know that there had to
be more to life than just eating and sleeping. Secretly, in my private
moments, I wondered what it was that was tugging at my heart.
Mom, because of the hurts she had sustained as a child in the strict,
Calvinist Scottish orphanage, wanted to 'protect' me from religion.
In our house that topic was a 'no-go' zone. Strangely, this rule
actually had the opposite effect.

My spiritual hunger only increased. I was sorry that I was out of touch
with my living Jewish grandmother who quietly held some of the keys
to my spiritual heritage. Sometimes I visited her alone. She was very
shy and ill by this time. I realized she was failing. I couldn't help her
and so I felt awkward. She was as sweet as could be and happy that
I took time for a "drop in" visit, but I had to carry the conversation.
I realized she was too weak to turn back the pages of her life for me
to have a peek. Despite this reality the Creator was working...through
sports.

Allow me to explain: I also loved basketball and played on all of my
school teams. Firstly at Doncaster Elementary, next at Lansdowne
Junior High School, finally on the Mt. Douglas Senior High squad.
As in any sport, proper coaching is the key to success. At fourteen
I joined the First United Church Boys Basketball League. Their well
equipped gym was complimented by an excellent coaching staff.
I looked forward to playing there each week. This wholesome activity
brought together young men from all over Victoria to hone their skills
under the tutelage of various committed coaches. There was no cost
involved. The only requirement by the church for use of their gym
facilities was that we attend Sunday school each weekend.
Our coaches checked to see if our respective Sunday school teachers
had signed our attendance slips. If so, we could keep playing.

To comply, I went along to nearby St. Anselem's United Church. Groggily, I'd drag myself out of a warm bed at nine o'clock on Sunday mornings and rode my bike to church as fast as I could to get there on time by 9:30. We studied the Bible and were supposed to apply the spiritual principles that we learned to our everyday lives. It was a good idea but I just couldn't seem to understand all the details nor commit fully to them. Looking back, I realize now that I was like all the other kids on my basketball team. We only went to Sunday school to get that 'signature' so we could play together the next week at our church-sponsored indoor gym and basketball court.

But something must have rubbed off. When I entered High School I joined the Hi-Y Club. This high school service group was linked to the YMCA organization. We were a hand-full of guys who volunteered our time to provide important service and leadership functions at school. We ran the kiosk at lunch time where students could purchase milk, cookies, chocolate bars and chips to go with their homemade sandwiches. The profit we made helped buy sports equipment for the school.

Daily we rotated for traffic flag duty to help the very young children cross the road in front of a nearby elementary school. We also ran the outdoor hot-dog and cold drinks stand for the Mt Doug's annual "Spring Sports Day" track and field event, often attended by parents. Since I was an only kid I enjoyed the fun and contact with others. All of the profits from these Hi-Y activities were given back to help our school in various ways to upgrade sports equipment. We helped buy team uniforms and other supplementary items not covered by the local School Board budget.

In appreciation for all of our hard work and the money raised, the Principal of our High School, Mr. Muir, permitted our Hi-Y Club to play sports in the school gym once a month. It was a special privilege. In grade twelve I had been elected the president of the Club. One night while we played basketball, a young man in his twenties, who I didn't know, came up to me. As the leader of the group, I had to deal with inquiries and visitors. He introduced himself saying, "Hi Jay, I'm Doug."

"Glad to meet you." I offered my wet hand while sweat dripped off my chin from the game.

" I am impressed with how responsible you guys are," he said. "For your next meeting, do you think I could come to show some slides of a fantastic camp that we have established for young people just like you?"

I shrugged. "I suppose so. I'll ask the guys."

He showed me a brochure of a camp called Malibu and it looked amazing. Waving the open brochure, I gave a shrill whistle to stop the game and called the guys together. "I want you to check this out!" After snatching the brochure out of my hand they aired their opinions.

"Malibu? Never heard of it."

"Wow, where is it? Hey, check out these pretty girls."

"Cool..."

"What's the deal?"

"Guys," I said, "this is Doug, and he wants to tell us all about it at our next meeting. What do you say?"

Doug promised that his presentation of the camp would be brief. With hoots and hollers of enthusiasm, everyone agreed.

My life was very busy. I had a weekend job as a janitor at the Royal Jubilee Hospital. With my earnings I bought my own car. It was a 1960 VW Beetle. I had it painted sky blue with a special metallic paint, usually reserved for expensive Cadillac's, it

became my limo. It had shiny chrome hubcaps and tail pipes with black seat covers. Keeping it spotless, I felt a certain amount of pride when I drove into the student's parking lot. Only a few of us had cars. I also saved money to buy gas, clothes and shoes. I felt good, but, there was still something missing. That old sense of 'emptiness' still hounded me. What could I do about it? Perhaps I needed a girlfriend, or so I thought. I had many pals at school but no serious relationship with the opposite gender. There was, however this one girl Pam, that I regularly invited out to the movies and drive-in burger joints. We'd known each other since Junior High. She was a very special friend then and we have remained good friends to this day. I still couldn't shake the sense that I was missing something in life. But, the question was, what?

Our next Hi Y meeting was held in my home. Doug came with his slide-projector and more brochures. He explained that Camp Malibu was located on the pristine Princess Louisa Inlet, about five hours by boat north of Vancouver. Today cruise-ships bring tourists from all over the world to see the fantastic beauty of this part of the West coast of British Columbia, plying the waters north from Vancouver to Alaska.

At the meeting it was clear that Doug knew how to engage teens. First he turned on the projector and showed beautiful pictures of the camp and the kids who were obviously having a blast. The appeal was immediate. Camp Malibu was originally built as a private get-away lodge for the rich and famous of Hollywood. After many years of disuse due to its isolation, it was put up for sale and finally purchased by a California based Christian organization called Campus Crusade. They decided to use it to host their High School branch called Young Life.
Malibu was then totally renovated and opened as a first class youth facility. It catered mainly to high school students from western USA, including Washington, Idaho, Oregon, and California and now a few of us from Canada were invited.

Dough had gotten us thinking and, right then and there, several of us decided that after high school graduation and before our summer jobs started we wanted to visit Malibu. The pull, of course, was to meet all those beautiful young ladies from the USA. We were motivated!
We decided to hold several weekend car washes to earn the necessary funds to cover our travel expenses and the fees for a week's stay at this luxurious youth resort.

We made just enough money through our work projects for five of us to go. On departure day, we met a big group of kids from the States at the North Vancouver harbor. Boarding a chartered ferry for the long trip to Malibu, we were the only Canadians in the bunch. Finally arriving, enthusiastically we settled into our cabins.

Each day started off with an interesting presentation of Bible teachings. It was a fun time followed with great food, activities, games and evening camp fires. The leaders were experts at keeping all the kids laughing. The week sped by very quickly.

Among ourselves, we Canadians never broached the subject of those Bible teachings, which frankly made me nervous. I could never figure out what the 'pull' was to Jesus. I found the open discussions intimidating, but I liked the simplicity of the idea that one could have a loving relationship with Father God. I knew a big part of me missed my real Dad. But I couldn't relate to Jesus.

Coming from a family of assimilated Jewish grandmothers and a mother who had done everything she could to shield me from 'religion,' I was in a quandary. Nevertheless that 'ache' inside had grown during the week. As we were packing up and preparing to leave for home, our dorm leader asked me to take a walk with him to "Inspiration Point."

Sitting on a rugged rock formation overlooking the sea he asked me, "Jay, would you like to know God personally?"

"Yes!" I responded without hesitation.

"Have you ever prayed before?" He asked.

"I don't remember..."

"Prayer is just speaking out the thoughts of your heart to God. Would you like to do this? The Bible says that 'those who look for Him will find Him.'"

"Yes, I'd like that." I answered quietly.

"It's beautiful out here so keep your eyes open if you like," he spoke kindly to me. "God looks on our heart, and He understands what we are trying to express even before we say it."

My heart agreed and I thought, *This is the kind of God I've been longing for, a Higher Power that I could believe in as a loving Father.* At the same time another part of me found this whole thing unsettling, and I felt vulnerable and exposed. I was not used to this 'extra dimension.' But even stronger than my fears, I sensed that I was being embraced by a gentle 'Loving kindness', that my mind could not deny. I felt that I was "known", I was not a stranger, or orphan, it was a sense of being safe and well, yes, that gentle kindness that my mind could not explain away. I had to be honest about this 'reality'.

I knew deep down inside that my moment of truth had arrived.

The counselor led me in a familiar prayer and began with, "Our Father who art in Heaven…" I knew this prayer which I recited every morning at the school assembly. I mouthed the words, "Hallowed be thy Name, Thy Kingdom Come, Thy Will be done on earth as it is in heaven, give us this day our daily bread and forgive us our trespasses, as we forgive those who trespass against us. Deliver us from evil. For yours is the Kingdom and the power and the glory forever. Amen."

At least I knew something. Even if I don't understand what is happening to me, I thought.

"Jesus taught that prayer," the counselor explained, "He wanted everyone to know the Heavenly Father." Speaking slowly, he gave no hint of hurry or pressure. "Jesus gave His life for our sins. Did you know that?" his voice was relaxed and caring.

Nodding, I bowed my head.

"Shall we pray a simple prayer?"

Softened by the personal attention I swallowed the growing lump in my throat.

Let's be honest here, at first, I felt that I didn't know what I was getting into. I was wary like anyone would be. But, hearing the sound of the waves lapping below, accompanied by birdsong was soothing. A fresh breeze from the ocean rustled the circular leaves of a popular grove near us. It was pure and sweet and peaceful.

As fear faded into the background, I willingly repeated after the counselor, "Dear Lord Jesus come into my heart."

Instantly something happened. Swiftly, silently and invisibly that old sense of loss and emptiness began to melt away in this atmosphere of loving kindness.   My life was passing before my eyes. I saw it like in a film...my complicated birth, the death of my father, separation from his family, the recurring sadness of my mother, and my Grandma's last words to her family about the 'I AM that I AM.' Salty tears trickled down. It seemed that I was known and loved. I also thought about the main unanswered questions in my life. Was my stony heart turning soft? Was this the 'new life' that they told us about in the meetings? My heart said 'yes' but my head still held many questions.

On the way home I quietly leaned over the rail of the ferry. I didn't know exactly what had happened, but I knew that I was more alive than I had ever been. I felt loved and relieved of my many uncertainties and the constant pressure of the push to 'make it.'

How am I going to tell my family what happened to me? I wondered. They didn't want 'religion' and neither did I.

Walking through the front door at home I hesitated, took a deep breath and shouted out, "Hi?" We hugged happy to be together again.

"I'll make a cup o' tea and J.V. tell us all about your trip." Mom bustled around.

Munching on one of her shortbread cookies I said; "First, I want to be very up front and tell you both about an experience I had at Malibu." I tried to be gentle, "I gave my life to Jesus."

"Oh, no J.V.! Don't tell me that you got religion?" Mother was horrified!

Laughing, I said, "Oh no, mom, it's not about 'religion.' It's a relationship. I have been 'born from above', or I could say I have had a spiritual awakening, like a new birth."

Nervously she looked at me and shook her head. For her it was a 'worst case scenario' and I could feel the growing tension between us.

I decided that I would do my best to honor Mom and Dad, even in the midst of several heated discussions. I would not, however, go back on my new found faith in God. Finally I got them to agree with me that we would never, ever, under any circumstances, argue about the Bible, God, Jesus, or my future.

Timeless Secrets

"For You will light my lamp;
The LORD my God will enlighten my darkness."
Psalm 18:28

Strangely, it seems human beings will do anything trying to ease their loneliness and emptiness. I did the same using sports. Others turn to work, drugs, alcohol, sex, shopping or eating to quench their hunger. They think buying a new house or a new car, new clothes, dieting, travel, self-help schemes, making money, even a new political system or religion will make them happy and secure. This is folly. What everyone needs, and can freely receive, is an awakening from above. Put another way, we all need a spiritual new birth, which is given by the Spirit of the Living God. When we ask in complete honesty with an open heart it happens. There are many gods in this world, but only ONE that is Eternal and Living.

The experience I had is what people of every nation, tribe and tongue are searching for. There is a special place built into each of us that has been reserved alone for fellowship with our Creator. This is the good news. Being born by the Spirit of God is a universal principle available to all mankind. It is not a Christian 'idea'. The Spirit of God actually does visit us and as King David prayed, "light my lamp..."

Thus the origin and truth of "new birth" is actually a Jewish concept. This idea was introduced by the Hebrew prophets Jeremiah[15], Ezekiel [16] and Jesus [17]. They were the first to present this teaching with such simplicity, clarity and consistency. Most people are unaware of this truth because they haven't studied the Bible. This is Father God's heart for mankind; He waits for us to come to the understanding that we can open up to Him. If we seek, we will find.

---

[15] Jeremiah 31:31-34
[16] Ezekiel 36:26-28
[17] John 3:16

He desires to have fellowship with you, this is amazing.

"Behold the days are coming says the Lord when I will make a new covenant with the house of Israel and with the house of Judah... this is the covenant that I will make... I will put my law in their minds and write it on their hearts' and I will be their God and they will be my people... I will forgive their iniquity and their sin I will remember it no more."
Jeremiah 31: 31, 32, 33, 34 (excerpts)

"I will give you a new heart and put a new Spirit within you; I will take out the heart of stone out of your flesh and give you a heart of flesh."
Ezekiel 36:26

"One night, in Jerusalem, a man called Nicodemus, a ruler of the Jews, came to Jesus and said to him, "Rabbi, we know that you are a teacher from God; for no one can do these signs (miracles) that You do unless God is with him." Jesus answered and said to him," Most assuredly, I say to you unless one is born again, (born from above) he cannot see the kingdom of God." John 3:2,3

This is the most important Timeless Secret of all. If you would like to be born of the Spirit of God it is entirely up to you. It's your choice. When you were born naturally you had no choice in the matter. Now you can choose to be born of the Spirit and receive eternal life by saying the following simple prayer,

"O Father God, I open my inner most being to you. Please bring me to the truth of Your Salvation, Your Shalom, Your Life and Light. Thank you for Your power over darkness, and for Your gift of a new birth. I want to be born from above. I accept it now. Thank you Lord. I am willing to be taught. Please open Your Word to me and help me understand."

"For the mountains shall depart and the hills be removed, But My loving kindness shall not depart from you, nor shall My covenant of peace be removed, Says the LORD, who has mercy on you." Isaiah 54:10

Chapter 6

Steep Learning Curves

A new world was out there waiting to be discovered...

"For the lips of a strange woman drip honey..." Proverbs 5:3a

At the age eighteen I wasn't sure what my future held, but I knew that this new dimension of finding God's plan for my life took precedence over all my previous ideas. A new world was out there waiting to be discovered. The more I read, the more relevant the Bible became. I was keen to learn what it had to say. The eternal truths of the scriptures had my attention and I looked for somewhere I could get the same kind of teaching I heard at Camp Malibu. I went to several conservative churches before finally settling on one in downtown Victoria. I resonated with the excellent Bible teaching of its pastor, Bob Holmes.

Bob was a delightful person. Humble yet confident in his life. He took me under his wing and I started to grow in this 'new life'. Bob had been an athlete in his youth, until a bout of polio severely curtailed his mobility. It was not only his enthusiasm for sports, but his quest for 'Life' that drew me to him and his wife, Jean. They became like family.

That fall I started my first year university at University of Victoria. My life became very busy, between studies, weekend jobs, helping Doug at the local Young Life group, some sports activities and church attendance. Actually I was too busy. I quickly found out that university level academics were much more demanding than high school. I had cruised along with a minimal amount of home study. Not so at university. I found this out the hard way by failing three out of five subjects at the end of my first term in December. Shocked into reality, I knew I had to make changes. I prioritized my studies, cut way back on social activities and, with a lot of sweat, I was able to pass my tough first year finals in math, chemistry, physics, English, and Spanish. Greatly relieved, I made my first year.

I didn't have much time to socialize, but purposed to continue studying the Bible. Occasionally I went to the Young Life group on Wednesday evenings, and I tried to get out to church on Sunday mornings for Pastor Bob's inspirational sermons. One Wednesday evening at a Young Life gathering a gorgeous young woman came to play the piano. I had never met her before but secretly I was very impressed. She had long auburn hair, green eyes and curves. After the meeting I was too shy to speak to her but I found out her name was Gigi. [18]

I didn't see her again and, many times when I went to the gatherings wondering if she'd be there but it didn't happen. She had disappeared. About six months later I found out why.

When I was at the Royal Jubilee Hospital to pick up my pay cheque, there she was, walking down the hall towards me in her white, starched uniform and nurse's cap. She had begun nurses' training. Boldly I went right up to her. "Hi, Gigi! You were once the pianist at our Young Life meeting..."
Surprised by my forthrightness she remained aloof but when I asked her about her life as a nurse she seemed to relax. Mustering my courage just before parting, I asked, "Say, how would you like to go out on a date?"
"Oh, sorry, I'm very ... busy...." Her words slowed, as if she just had an idea. With her eyes fixed on mine, she leaned slightly toward me, her pink lips turned up sweetly and invitingly, "My parents have prepared a small birthday party for me this coming Friday. Could you come?"
"Sure, what's your address?" I wrote it down and eagerly looked forward to that event.

Arriving at her parent's old two-story home, I walked through the carefully kept garden up three stairs to the broad veranda. Gigi met me at the door and ushered me into the house. I could smell dinner cooking, and greeted her mom and dad. When I saw her father I recognized him as the man who sometimes played the organ and piano at church.

---

[18] Not her real name.

"Where are the other guests?" I thought there would be other young people invited as well.

"Oh no!" she laughed. "I like small, intimate gatherings and so it's just you, me and my parents." She smiled reassuringly.

"Ah, okay then." I didn't pay any attention to this strange set-up and also didn't pick up the little warning signs. Not knowing her parents, I felt uncomfortable and a little awkward. I somehow felt responsible to make light conversation around the table as best I could. Her enthusiastic mom chatted along, trying to help us all relax. As the evening progressed I got up my nerve to approach her father, "I'd like to take Gigi bowling next week. Would that be OK with you?" Reluctantly he agreed. "But don't you think a bowling alley is a rather rough place for my little girl?" His voice was stern. Lifting his head and straightening his shoulders he continued, "We have raised our daughter in a 'good Christian home.'"

Now I really began to feel intimidated. I liked the fun and competition at bowling alleys and didn't think there was anything wrong with them. Perhaps I just wasn't good enough for their precious daughter. I dropped the question immediately. He was 'religious' and my upbringing was completely different. Being new at this, I didn't know what was and what was not acceptable. Intentionally or unintentionally, he gave me the feeling that perhaps I was a little under par for his little girl. Uncomfortably I left the room, the hair on the back of my neck stood up and sweat dripped in my armpits.

But what really confused me was that when I said my good- byes, Gigi made sure to walk me to the front door, out of sight of her parents. Helping me into my overcoat she stood on tip-toe to throw my scarf around my neck. Then she planted a very passionate kiss on my lips and put her full figured body tightly against mine. Without a word I left, feeling dazed. *Wow, what was that all about?* I thought while driving home, *I like it!* I told myself, *but it was just a first date! Where is this relationship going?* It all seemed a bit overwhelming to me! Without sounding prudish, I did enjoy the affection that Gigi started to give me, but I knew that with hormones racing through our bodies it was a dangerous situation. This proved to be true.

Several months later, when I brought her back to the nurse's residence, from a night out, I recognized that I was slipping out of control as our good night kisses became increasingly intimate.

The faithful 'still small voice' kept gently reminding me, "Jay, be careful!" Yes, in my heart of hearts I sensed we were taking advantage of each other, but on the other hand I rationalized, "Gigi needs a lot of emotional support due to the tensions and stresses of nurse's training." I chose to believe this half-truth. She needed me and I could give her what she wanted, even if it simply physical comfort.
The lie began to grow.

I was also her sounding board. She poured out her frustrations, anger, and insecurities on me during our dates. On one occasion when she was taking Psychiatric nursing in a facility near Vancouver she called, pleading with me to pick her up. Crying uncontrollably, she seemed to break down completely. I decided on the spot to fetch her from the Essendale Mental Hospital. This took nearly a day of travel. First I had to cross by BC ferry to Vancouver, drive to New Westminster then back to the Vancouver ferry terminal, and finally catch a return BC Ferries boat to Victoria.

Once we were in the car she ignored me. At first crying hysterically she then became quiet and distant. I didn't know this person. It never occurred to me at the time to wonder where her parents were in all of this? Was she not their daughter?

Arriving at the family home, I found myself trying to comfort them. It was heavy. What had I gotten into?
Gigi's mother called the family physician who spoke privately with Gigi for some time before giving her sedatives. He arranged a week off from 'psych-training' in order for her to rest. Later, as I thought the whole day over again I wondered, *Why didn't she call her parents first? What is missing in this equation?*
In the process, I was becoming more isolated from my own parents. They had not warmed to Gigi and, since I was spending so much time with her, I was barely home except to eat and sleep.

By this time we had been seeing each other for six months. During that week of rest, she was at home alone. When she called I went over to console her while her parents were at work. And then it happened. As she served me 'tea' in the living room she clung to me in her silky pajamas. "I need you," she whispered. Her words beckoned me beyond what I could sustain. We ended up sleeping together.

Immediately I felt very ashamed. Here I was, a new believer, learning to love the Bible. My head knew the teaching to hold oneself in check from such intimacy, yet I enjoyed being needed and, of course, she gave me her beautiful body. I was on dangerous ground because of the mixing and the hypocrisy that was being set up in my mind and heart. I had no will power to make the changes I knew were necessary. Learning the hard way I discovered that it is one thing to accept God into one's heart and soul, and quite another to allow the truth of Scripture into one's mind and sexual choices.

Believing that I now loved her totally I tried to make everything right by rationalizing the event and bought Gigi a diamond engagement ring. *If we are engaged*, I thought, *then I won't feel guilty about our sexual activities.* All this time I foolishly allowed myself to get side tracked from my very demanding studies. Every mark I earned would make the difference in my future. My aims were very high but I had become double minded.

When Gigi was feeling better, we went for a drive.
"Gigi, close your eyes, I have something for you."
"Oh, I love surprises." She giggled like a little girl.
I parked the car. "Okay, open them now!"
While she carefully studied the diamond ring I asked, "Gigi, will you marry me?"
"Yes, Jay I accept your ring."
Her response was strange but I was so in love that it didn't matter. However, it did sound rather hollow to me. She didn't say anything about accepting or marrying me but focused all her attention on the ring!

Examining it in the light she mumbled to herself, "This really isn't what I would choose," and then pleaded, "Could we please go back and let me pick out the one I want so I can show it off to my classmates?"

"Yes, of course sweetheart." Vaguely I realized this was for her and not for us.

My mother had sensed that Gigi was very self-centered and demanding. "Son," she told me in a quiet moment, and I knew she was concerned, "Your girl is a spoiled princess. She has been over-indulged by her parents. She is not doing 'right' by you! I think she is using you!"

We rarely argued, and now Gigi had come between me and my family. Blinded by what I thought was love I defended her in every way. To me, no matter who said what, Gigi was the one and only girl for me!

However, this was about to change in the near future.
Continue reading to learn what happened.

Timeless Secrets

My son, pay attention to my wisdom; Lend your ear to my
understanding, That you may appreciate good judgment,
And your lips may keep knowledge, For the lips of a strange woman drip
honey, and her mouth is smoother than oil,
But in the end she is bitter as wormwood.
Proverbs 5: 1-4a

Beware! As soon as you decide to follow the Lord you will be tempted and thoroughly tried. I was no exception. The biggest enemy of my soul was me. That part of me which can be enticed away from the truth. Lust knew exactly how to play on my weakest place. I call it 'self' and more specifically 'the sexual urge'. All men are vulnerable in this area. I caution you to look out because the attack can come from the most unexpected source. Temptation will be tailor- made for you, using circumstances in which you feel relaxed and off guard.

Everyone is looking for love. The problem is that most of us end up looking for it in the wrong places. Human nature confuses sex with love. We are led away by our lusts, thinking that a physical experience will satisfy our longing for true love. Every person needs love. But how we get it and what kind of love we choose is the question. I was caught in this trap and I have tried to warn my sons about it.

The truth is, every one of us has been led away by our natural desires at one time or another. Some of us are never able to break free from the 'urge' to gratify self. The more we feed self, the more we die. It is the opposite to what scripture teaches... give it up and we gain life.

Jesus confirmed this when He said in John12:24, *"Unless a kernel of wheat falls into the ground and dies, it abides alone but if it dies it produces much grain."*
He was speaking from the Torah when he taught, that daily we are given the possibility to "choose life," by denying one self. This means giving up our old self-centered ways that crave to be satisfied.

If left unchecked they become self-destructive but it is always our choice, we humans are created in the image of God, with the amazing gift of choice for better or for worse. Remember, what you do with your body is your choice and there are consequences for our every action.

"Say to wisdom, "You are my sister," and call understanding your close friend." Proverbs 7:4

"Hear my son, hear the instruction of your father, and do not reject the teaching of your mother." Proverbs 1:8

"Keep your heart with all diligence for out of it springs the issues of life and death." Proverbs 4:23

Finding time to feed on the word of God will help you in many ways. If you can't understand it, begin with the Book of Psalms. David has masterfully penned his human reactions, responses and questions to the issues of life that touch each and every one. In spite of his mistakes, we read that he was a man after God's own heart. Why? Because he was childlike in his approach to the Almighty, and his focus was always toward his Heavenly Father.
That tells us something about the character of our Father doesn't it?

"Your Word, I have hidden in my heart, that I might not sin against You!" Psalms 119:11

Chapter 7

Duped

"Correct choices are the keys to a successful life!"

By the end of my second year at University of Victoria (UVIC), I decided to apply for medical school. I knew it would not be easy; every applicant faced strong competition. I had to graduate with a BSC and very high marks. This decision required that I complete my undergraduate degree at Vancouver's University of British Columbia in my chosen field of Biochemistry and Microbiology. This meant that Gigi and I had to endure long separations.

From childhood, my cousin James Rawlings and I enjoyed our mutual friendship at family gatherings. So now we decided to 'go it together' at UBC and rent an apartment off campus, which would be more economical than both of us living in dorms. We found a relatively cheap apartment in an old building in the Kitsilano area of Vancouver. We shared our sparsely furnished place with Terry Marlowe, a friend who was articling as a Chartered Accountant. We actually made out quite well 'batching' and split expenses three ways.

James loved to cook. His classes in Business Administration were over by two or three in the afternoon. My science labs went on until five or six o'clock in the evening. So each day, I got up thirty minutes early and prepared breakfast for us while James cooked dinner. Terry washed the dishes. We learned how to economize and didn't suffer much on our own cooking. To our parent's amusement and our chagrin we actually put on weight.

One day when I got home, four guys I didn't know were eating at our table. James explained that he had started cooking his mother's famous spaghetti sauce that afternoon. The aroma drifted along the halls and up the stairwells to the guys living above us.

They were all hungry UBC Forestry students, who descended and pounded on the door. One held up a bottle of red wine. "James, we are going to prosecute you for torture! We can no longer withstand the delicious smell of your spaghetti sauce! Please," they chorused in unison. Always the wonderful host, that he is to this day, James invited them in for dinner. This began our friendship and, whenever they had a special meal, they always invited us.

That fall Gigi graduated from Nursing School. I was in my third year at UBC, and motivated to get the best marks possible, so my visits home to Victoria were limited. I noticed that our relationship was cooling down from her side and I didn't know why or what to do.

In December, she told me that she had applied to be 'camp nurse' at Malibu over the holidays. I was surprised and a bit disappointed, but said nothing. I had been looking forward to spending time with her during my break at New Year's, but my ideas and hopes were not important to her.

Everything came to a head on a cool but sunny Saturday afternoon in February when I was back in Victoria for the weekend. We had gone out for a drive to 'catch up'; it had been a few weeks. I chose a lookout across the beautiful deep blue ocean up to the snowcapped mountains beyond. It was one of our favorite spots. Here, we had often kissed and dreamt of our future together.

I was caught off-guard for what was coming.
"Jay, I want you to know that while I was up at the camp over the holidays I met an American guy." Glancing up to see my reaction she rushed on, "He's a former Olympic athlete and we just connected!" She was far too happy for my liking. Now, it dawned on me that she was infatuated with him!
"Sorry," she said in a sing song voice, "I'm now in love with someone else." As if she were in a shoe store, choosing one pair of shoes over another, she gave me back our ring. Sounding so matter of fact and final I knew that she had made up her mind.

I had been duped and was being dumped! I didn't know whether to cry or blow up, and my startled emotions fluctuated between the two. My world ground to a halt. I was devastated.

"So, just like that; it's over?" I challenged her, steel in my voice but feeling as if I'd been dealt a blow under the belt. "Use it and abuse it, that's your style, isn't it Gigi? Where is commitment in all of this? How can you just toss my love away as you would a candy wrapper?" With my voice rising out of control, I pinned her to the seat with a furious stare. "You, young lady, have used me, and have done it all for yourself, your comfort, your sexual needs. When did you ever consider my feelings?... You know what? I'm so glad we have come to this."

Silence, cold and impersonal filled the gulf between us. This human being had become a complete stranger to me. I fought with the overwhelming sense of being completely betrayed and cheated. Nervously, the corners of her lips slightly turned upward, she tried to placate me, "But, Jay he is so...athletic."

"No, no!" I shouted. "Not one word about him! You have willfully used and abused me!"

I backed up the car and roared out of the parking lot. Fuming inwardly I drove her home and without a word dropped her off. In the privacy of my room I began to weep. At first, I accused myself that my angry outburst had caused the break-up. Then I apologized to the Lord for my divided loyalty. A few hours later the comfort of the Holy Spirit returned and slowly I began to sense the heavenly peace that I couldn't understand.

It was time to wake up, stop the pity party and seize the day! Now I was free to focus on my studies and other things in my life that mattered. I could rebuild my neglected relationship with my family and friends. I also took time to get back into the Word of God as never before. No longer, was I being pulled by my heartstrings for Gigi, often with little coming back in return. What lesson is to be learned in the character of a taker? But I had been only too happy to give.

My first plan of action was to devote all my negative anger and hurt feelings into something positive and creative. Setting my course, I studied with a new zeal and intensity. I was no longer divided. Putting my life and future back into the hands of God, I realized that I had compromised both for a while. Now, I sincerely wanted only what He wanted for my life. Avoiding contact with girls as much as possible now, I was not willing to squander any energy on a female relationship. As a kind of protection, I didn't date for nearly eighteen months. With relief and a sense of accomplishment, I graduated from UBC in 1966 with a BSC in Microbiology and Biochemistry.

That summer, I found out that I was not accepted into Medical School at UBC. I had failed a midterm exam right after my 'Dear John' experience that put my grade point average too low for med school. Yes, I paid a very high rice for the fling with Gigi. A few days later however, I received a letter of acceptance into graduate studies at the University of Toronto Medical School. They were offering me a two-year Hospital Administration course. I was gratefully amazed at how this new door opened to me.

Later, I discovered that it wasn't easy to get into this course at the University of Toronto. With about 40,000 students at the time, U of T was the largest and one of the most prestigious educational institutions in Canada. Now I set my sights on Toronto. From May to August, I lived at home in order to save money and set about earning extra funds for my new life and studies. I was fortunate to get a job as a lab technician at the Victoria Veterans Hospital, and glad to be included in some special research projects for the Pathologist who was the overseer of the laboratory.

I enjoyed my work and life returned to 'normal.' That summer I was still playing baseball and maintained my circle of friends. Occasionally I played tennis with Carol Dawe, a nurse, and good friend. My tennis coach was Jack Spratt[19], the retired Mayor of Port Alberni, the city touted to be 'the fishing capital of the world.' Even though he was in his early eighties he was extremely fit.

---

[19] His real name.

I loved to be with him on and off the court. He was a real mentor to me and regularly attended my ball games as a keen supporter.

My friends, Ian Young and George Ney had also graduated that year. We went sailing together, in and around the beautiful Gulf Islands between Victoria and the USA mainland. Getting back together that summer was like old times. With a sense of relief, I felt that I was 'on track' again.

Best of all, my relationship with my Mom and Dad was restored. I had been 'away' mentally and emotionally for too long. My mother was an open and honest person. She read me like a book and easily expressed her feelings. Her regular piece of advice to me sounded like this: "J.V. go out with lots of different women. It's important to be part of a group of friends. That way you can be safe and find the sterling qualities that you are looking for in a life's partner in a safe atmosphere." She also said, "There are many kinds of gemstones in the world. Some artificial ones and some genuine. Only under a magnifying glass you will find the authentic ones. You need to look very closely."

I had learned my lesson, held my peace, and let mom speak her mind regarding girlfriends. Honestly, looking back, I'm sorry that I didn't listen to her. Being inexperienced and impetuous, of course, I thought I knew better. I had learned the hard way, not build a love relationship founded on emotion and sex. A sexual relationship can be like the weather, hot one day and cold the next. Sheila had practiced what she preached. I am grateful that she brought Vic home to her family and spent time building a solid relationship with the family and each other. Together they nurtured a true love, which to this day remains an example to me. I also grew up living with the respect and loyalty shared between Mom and Billy, my step dad.

Timeless Secrets

But the fruit of the Spirit is love, joy, peace, long suffering, kindness, goodness, faithfulness, gentleness, self-control. Against such there is no law. Galatians 5:22

Jay:

Don't take anyone at face value: find out what's behind the physical attraction or the 'perfect' home. What is on the surface can be completely deceptive. People are not necessarily what they say they are. Character is determined by what we allow and what we stand up for, not just words or outward appearances. Listen to the Lord speaking to you via the 'still small voice.' Pay close attention to the relationships between family members. Watch and pray, but don't be religious, be real.

When you get a 'check' in your spirit listen to it! If you pray, don't do all the talking. Learn to listen. Trust your gut-level feelings, no matter who says or does what. The greatest commandment teaches us to: *"Love the Lord our God with all of our heart, mind soul and strength and our neighbor as our self."* Deuteronomy 6:4-5, Matt. 22:36-40

What's so hard about that?" you ask.
First of all, if I had given the Lord my undivided attention and loved Him enough to keep myself when tempted, I wouldn't have been led astray. It has been so aptly stated, "the greatest sex organ is the mind." The first place we lose the battle is in our minds. Unbridled sexual lust, buried offenses and unresolved conflicts produce negative thoughts. These negative attitudes can lead to anger, depression and even rage, leaving one with a weakened will, or inability to say 'no' when tempted.

From my experience, fear is the forerunner of angry outbursts that poison the atmosphere in any relationship. You will have to find the root of your fear. In this case, I was caught in the trap of lust, which made me feel guilty and fearful.

Secondly, if I had loved myself as I am loved by my Creator, I would have recognized I was stepping into a trap in Gigi's dysfunctional family. I would have seen that I was being used and cut it off. Also I would not have been hankering to have my ego stroked. I would have realized, or discerned that it was a 'set up' and I was being duped. I forgot my own chosen course, and was too willing to stoop down to whatever came my way. Wisdom is taught and learned, not caught. Call wisdom your sister and guys especially, keep her real close to your head and heart!

Meridel:

Have you ever wondered why in the Bible, the Creator set down a ruling that Jewish males enter into the eternal Covenant of circumcision on the 8th day? Yes, we know that scientists have proved that the clotting factor of the blood is at its highest level on the 8th day of life, but I believe there is much more. It is the keeping of this 4,000 year old Covenant, first given to Abraham that the Holy One of Israel insists on a very very personal relationship. The God of Israel is a covenant making and keeping God. The Jewish baby boy's blood is spilled by removal of the foreskin at circumcision. Thus this ancient covenant permanently marks all Jewish males as 'different' or 'separate' from all other non-circumcised males. It is a seal or sign of God's ownership or Covenant upon that life. I mean, how personal can God be? His mark of ownership is placed upon the organ that one's seed issues from? Talk about branding? A strong warning? Perhaps! But the eternal Covenant was to the Jewish nation and their ongoing generations. God wanted a "set apart nation" quite unlike the heathen nations.

If The Almighty teaches one to bring their thoughts into subjection, then does it not stand to reason that the sexual urge can also be subdued for His greater honor and glory? Consider this, a male holds his organ several times every day in the process of urination. Is this not a reminder of the life that issues through this vessel, whether circumcised or not? We are repeatedly exhorted in scripture to "choose life that you and your children may live."

It is also vitally important to understand the inestimable value of one's own body, which is our home while upon earth. It is the center from which you live and move and have your being! When it wears out the 'real' you is out of here. That is just how important your body is! The Bible also lays down a solemn warning about the consequences of illicit sexual conduct such as confusion, a broken heart disease, unwanted pregnancy ending in abortion.

"Therefore a man shall leave his father and mother and they shall be joined to his wife and they shall become one flesh." Genesis 2:24

"Do you not know that he who is joined to a harlot is one body with her? "For the two," He says, *"shall become one flesh."* 1 Corinthians 6:16

*"Flee sexual immorality. Every sin that a man does is outside the body, but he who commits sexual immorality sins against his own body. Or do you not know that our body is the temple of the Holy Spirit who is in you, whom you have from God, you are not your own? "*1 Corinthians 6:18, 19.

This sober warning spells out a mystery. During illicit sexual conduct, intermingling happens in one's person or character. Yes, one's sexual life is hopefully with the beloved wife of one's youth, which is the ideal. Whether under God's blessing or not, the Bible says 'they become one'. This refers in part to the physical and spiritual aspect of the sexual act. But never forget that it also means there is an actual spiritual transference. Without God's blessing, co-habitation leaves a stain (iniquity) in one's person. I can see the revulsion of many of our readers to these words. Choosing to live a clean life sexually is not an easy or popular concept to be sure.

One of the most interesting seminars I ever gave was to a group of professional men. They were approaching 35-40 years old and were accomplished and comfortable economically. However, a couple of them were divorced while most were unwed. We all discovered many amazing things that night as we began by studying our personal relationships with our parents. But they were, excuse the expression 'blown out of the water' when I opened these scriptures to them, for undoubtedly 99%

of them were very active sexually. They were incredulous, and had never before heard of any spiritual consequences from a 'fling'.

In Leviticus chapter 20 you will find a list of illicit and forbidden sexual activities. The Judeo-Christian faith, when lived sincerely, is one of morality. In Bible times pagans offered their first born to Moloch a fertility god, cruel, demanding and supposedly placated through child sacrifice by fire. In today's world, aborted babies are often burned up along with hospital refuse. Another point is that a high percentage of unwed mothers in the USA are young Christian girls who sadly were never taught the facts of life by their parents.[20]

In ancient times, involvement with this powerful spiritual force called Moloch included sexual deviations, especially homosexuality, bestiality and incest along with the consultation of mediums. These are everyday activities in our modern societies, which break the bond of holiness between God and His people. This is why the severe command in Leviticus 20:13 states that such a violator shall surely be put to death.
> Note: Fundamental preachers of Islam in many parts of the world support human sacrifice in the guise of suicide bombings or honor killings. Innocents are murdered without a voice. These cover the perverse practices of males in the family by transferring the blame to the abused girl. Note that in scripture God's heart is that the innocent were always saved. Today we see on our newscasts the wanton slaughter of innocent men and women by Muslim extremists on a global scale.

Moral decay in Moses' time was worthy of death for fear that this disease of the spirit would spread among the people of Israel. Being a specialist in the field of 'child sexual abuse,' I see the truth of this damage and disease. Yes, an illicit sexual union becomes a sin against one's entire person or being. The perpetrator is 'damaged' by entering or being entered by another sexually. Pay careful attention!

Do not open yourself up for this kind invisible damage. This is serious, and I am sure laughable to many in this day of wide-spread promiscuity, when multiple partners is erroneously considered 'normal.'

---

[20] "Focus on the Family," Dr. James Dobson's radio show.

When one messes up, and shame sits on the doorstep of your mind, learn to say sorry to your Creator and yourself and even your sexual partners if possible! Repentance is the key in learning to be honest with self and one's Maker. He is ready to forgive and forget, He is a God of Mercy.

Before we leave this subject, if you need help in this area get it. Sexual abuse affects more people on earth than Aids, cancer, heart disease and high blood pressure combined. It takes guts and lots of courage to break from any bondage, especially when you did not perpetuate it Shame and guilt are big silencers. Take yourself off of the hook, so to speak. So you fell. So you know what it is to be human. We all fail. This is where our Redeemer comes in, IF invited. He gives us a 'spiritual bath' and courage to get up and go on. Promiscuous young people often have a history of sexual interference when they were defenseless children.
Unfortunately, the pattern is repeated.

Jay:
So, to any young person reading this book, take heart and, don't be in a hurry to do anyone's wishes. Pay attention if you have reservations about someone or some situation. No matter what happens in life always try to see the big picture, try to keep a positive attitude, and never be afraid to walk away. There is no law against saying "NO". Don't allow any one else to define your worth. Faith is the antidote to fear. The Word of God, and obedience to it, is the key to vibrant faith.

"So then faith comes by hearing and hearing by the Word of God."
Romans 10:17

"Whoever listens to me will dwell safely, and will be secure, without fear of evil." Proverbs 1:33

Post Script

"Honor your father and mother that your days may be long on the land which the Lord your God is giving you." Exodus 20:12

Jay:
One other extremely important Timeless Secret, which is a universal principle, is to always 'honor your mother and father.' Notice I didn't say, "love your mother and father," because sometimes through difficult life circumstances love is nearly impossible. We have learned this reality through Meridel's counseling ministry to the abused. You can respect their position of parenthood. You make a choice to honor them. If you do you will be blessed with health and long life. How long do you honor your parents? If you are wise, you will honor them all the days of your life. It gets much easier as you have children of your own, then and only then, do you get a taste of just what your parents poured into your life, and the costliness of it.

Meridel:
Pay attention dear reader: if you are from a loving home, and there is trust between you and your parents, grandparents and siblings do not take this blessing for granted! You are favored, believe me. If you choose to become involved with a dysfunctional person, be forewarned. They can be a master controller, capable of bringing strain and distance, to break that bond of loving kindness, between you and your family. Jealous and needy for love, they can be serious manipulators. Beware! We know what people are by the fruit in their lives. Love tells the truth.

Jay:
Referring back to the experience with Gigi, it took time, but I was able one again to experience a fresh sweetness in my mind and heart. I was getting cleaned up on the inside. I sincerely apologized to my parents, for my blatant selfishness with Gigi. I tolerated her disrespect of my own loved ones. This was a gross error on my part. I also did all I could to be accepted by her family, which never happened.

Release from the heartache and shame came slowly as I renewed my commitment to My God. I committed to give Him first place and sought out my parents and friends whom I had blatantly ignored and not only did I ask their forgiveness, but my actions changed.
I put my money where my mouth was.

How happy I was when the day came that I walked through my parent's home whistling, with a light heart, and go on with life. With God's help I had cleaned up my act and could appreciate the value of my life with all of its potential once again!

Chapter 8

Still Small Voice

"Wondering how we were going to sustain such a long separation of nearly two years I had a deep sense of quiet peace that this was all somehow pre-planned.... There was however, a lot of water that still had 'to pass under the bridge..."

Jay:

One and a half years later, I'll never forget that warm and sunny Sunday evening in early May. Spring flowers were blooming and the air was filled with a heady fragrance. I was sitting in the back of the auditorium with my friend Ian, waiting for the worship service to begin. Rays from the setting sun shone in through the stained glass window filling the sanctuary with golden light.

With the seats filling up, in walked Carol Dawe my tennis partner. She passed me and continued on down to the front to find two seats. Accompanying her was a young lady I had never seen before. The sun glinted off her rich chestnut brown hair, pushed up into a very elegant French roll. The stranger was gorgeous in a pale pink dress with a short fur trimmed-cape. But more than that, there was just 'something' about her whole being that was special. Then I heard the still small voice say to me, "There is your wife and the mother of your sons." I was stunned. Shocked! I couldn't concentrate on the sermon or anything else that evening. All I knew was that, after the service, Carol said to my pal Ian that she and this stranger were going to attend the College and Careers get-together.

"Do you want to go?" I nonchalantly asked Ian.

"Sure, why not?"

So we drove together in my sports car arriving early, sitting around swapping news, sipping coffee and enjoying special desserts.

When Carol walked in I again sensed something special about this stranger.

Fueled by what I had so unexpectedly "heard" a few hours earlier, I went directly up to them. Greeting Carol I turned to her friend, looked full into her smiling eyes I said, "Hi. I'm Jay, what's your name?"

"I'm Meridel."

"How do you know our mutual friend Carol?" I queried,

"Well," she said, "Carol's dad, Rev. George Dawe, was my family's pastor in Kamloops."

We chatted for a while until Carol said apologetically, "We soon must leave because I have to get Meridel back to the Royal Jubilee Hospital. She's on night duty."

Watching them drive away in Carol's car I realized that I only knew her name and where she worked!

Meridel:

There I was, standing at the coffee table in a beautiful home in Victoria. The living room was full of young professionals swapping ideas and just enjoying the ambiance that happens when guys and gals get together. Meeting a very special person at this time of my life was not on my agenda, so it came as a total surprise. I had no idea when Jay and I met that he would indeed become the most significant person in my life! How did it happen? Well as you have read he was given a 'heads up' about me because he saw me before I saw him. I was pouring a cup of coffee when this very handsome fellow approached me. It was his gentle but direct manner that took me completely by surprise. His friendliness eclipsed any sense of strangeness. At that time everything was new to me: the location, the young people and the hosts.

Immediately he put me at ease by saying, "Hi, I'm Jay!" His warm green eyes, ready smile, wavy auburn hair and tall muscular physique got my attention as well. In that instant, time stood still for me. I had never loved a man. I didn't know true love. How could I be interested because I was on my way to India? But... when I met Jay, something inside of me recognized him as the missing half of my life. Yes, it was profound; and no, it didn't make any sense, but my knees turned to jelly and the delicate china tea cup in my hand slightly shook.

My hands were like ice. I was not prepared for such a nervous physical reaction.

Yet, I was very good at keeping 'cool,' having dodged several guys over the years. None had interested me. I had things to do with my life.

"Hi," I replied casually, returning his smile. "My name is Meridel."

We chatted for a few more moments. It was just that innocent.

As Carol drove me back to the nurses' residence, even though I knew that I had 'encountered' someone special, I wasn't sure what to do with it.

Jay:

Early one morning, several weeks later, I was driving dad to his office at the Royal Jubilee Hospital. It was exactly at 7:30 and the night duty shift was leaving. Dad was the Superintendent of Linen Services there and was nearing retirement after more than forty years of faithful service. I said good-bye and proceeded to my summer job at the near-by Veterans Hospital. Then I saw her! She didn't see me as she walked purposefully on the crosswalk directly in front my car. I understand now that she was going off night duty. Almost hidden in her nursing uniform she was covered by her scarlet lined navy blue cape.

All I could see was the profile of her face but yes, sure enough, it was Meridel. No mistaking that fact, I felt excited.

Later that day I was having coffee with Helen, one of my co-workers in the laboratory at the hospital. We had become friends in the process of work, even though she was married with teenage children, and twenty years my senior. I appreciated her balanced and pleasant personality. Suddenly she asked me, "Jay, do you have a girlfriend?"

"No, I said but I have friends who are girls."

"No... no?" she insisted. "I mean a regular, steady girlfriend."

"No." I looked at her quizzically.

She then asked, "Well isn't there anyone who you are even slightly interested in?"

"Well, actually, yes there is."

"So what are you waiting for?" She asked. "Go ahead and call her and ask her out."

"Well, yes, I'd like to but I don't know her phone number."

"No problem! I'll find it for you. Where does she live?"

"I don't know," I said.

"Well, where does she work?"

"At the Royal Jubilee Hospital," I replied, "but they won't give out her phone number because that's considered confidential information."

"Just you wait and see." Smiling, she picked up the telephone and dialed while I wrote Meridel's full name on a memo pad and slipped it in front of her. Then she asked for the Personnel Department. When told that they couldn't release Meridel's personal phone number she immediately responded in an authoritative tone, "This is the Victoria Veterans Hospital calling, we need it urgently." The secretary relented and Helen scribbled down the number. Tearing off the small note paper she threw it in front of me. "There, now you have no excuse."

After supper I took the number out of my wallet. Looking at it I tried to build up my nerve to call this person who was now constantly on my mind. Dialing the number, I thought, *Oh, she is probably out with someone already.*

"Hello?"

Swallowing hard I said, "Hi. This is Jay calling. Do you remember me? We met several weeks ago."

"Yes, yes. I remember." I could hear the smile in her voice. Immediately, we began to speak comfortably. It was like I had always known her. By the end of the conversation I had asked her to accompany me to a baseball game. "Oh I'd love that, with the popcorn, hot-dogs and the seventh inning stretch." she said.

"Great. I'll pick you up at six on Thursday." I chuckled.

As I mentioned earlier, I always took Jack Spratt with me to the games. So when I arrived with him at the nurse's residence in my two seated sports car, I have no idea what Meridel was thinking when I asked her to sit on the divider between the two bucket seats. I'm sure it was illegal to do this and rather immodest, but it was a short ride to the Royal Athletic Park. When we parked in front of the ball field and all climbed out, I pulled my equipment bag out of the trunk.

"Where are you going?" Meridel asked.

"Oh yes, didn't I mention that I will be playing in the game?" Seeing her face fall, I quickly added, "but Jack will keep you company in the grandstand."

Looking surprised, she said, "Well, OK!" and took Jack's arm as I went to the locker room to change into my baseball uniform.

Meridel and Jack found good seats, and just before the game began, who showed up unannounced but my Mom, Sheila. I had not told her about my date but she was unfazed. It was not unusual for mom to just show up at my games. She and Meridel 'hit it off' immediately. They talked non-stop during the entire time, eating popcorn, laughing and rooting loudly for our team.

That, to me, was amazing, because my mom had never ever warmed to Gigi like that. After we were married, Meridel told me that upon meeting Sheila that evening she decided to turn it into a night of learning about my mom's favorite subject: her son! To her satisfaction she learned that I had a BSC and was going on to graduate school. One of the vows Meridel had made to herself was that she would never marry a man who had not completed his education. Another stipulation, which I will not mention at this time, had to do with her Jewish roots.

After the game, Mom volunteered to drive Jack home while Meridel and I drove to the Oak Bay Marina for a meal in their upscale restaurant. The sea front location was perfect that balmy summer evening. Over dinner we had a lot of laughs about being accompanied by an eighty year old friend and my mother! She ribbed me and I loved it.

We were relaxed and natural with each other. After finishing our dinner, we strolled along the floating wharf among the variety of small boats and larger yachts. I took her arm when the wharf swayed slightly beneath us. There was no mistaking it, there was certainly a 'spark' between us. Twilight washed the quiet sea in soft pastel hues.

It was a magical moment for both of us.

The salty ocean air had cooled, crying sea gulls swooped in and out, while small waves gently lapped beneath the dock. What bliss.

I felt like I was walking on water.

123

Then Meridel revealed that until just recently, she had been 'engaged' to an Egyptian Pasha, or prince. He was a very special middle-aged aristocratic gentleman. That will be a story for her to write one day when she fills us in on her early years. She too had been hurt by misunderstanding. He gave her a ring on her 23rd birthday and proposed marriage. She explained to me that she had encouraged and helped him escape Nasser's Fascist Egypt in 1965. He greatly respected Meridel's quick thinking and her timely assistance in his dilemma. He was never her lover, only a true friend, who read her kindness as an indication of a deep commitment to him personally. He wanted to marry her but the feeling was not mutual. After hearing this, I opened up feeling safe enough to tell her about my failed 'love life'. There was no pretense between us. I also found out about her approaching plans to go to India. Meridel was amazing. Without being shy she let me in on one of her deepest, spiritual experiences. I began to realize what a deep and private person she also was.

Meridel:

When I was 13 and 14, I spent the summer holidays working at my extended family's summer resort located on beautiful Lake Joseph in the renowned Muskoka Lakes resort area of Ontario, Canada. It catered to generations of "well to do" families, including the rich and famous. The serene lakes, clean air, a pervading sense of peace and relaxation offered a special other world atmosphere that drew guests from Europe, the USA and Canada.

One day, Bill our hotel handy man announced an event for young people that evening. He even offered his Chevy convertible to transport us. So we all piled into his swanky car, happy for some down time. Most of us were students working for the summer. It was great to have some needed "R&R". The wind blowing our hair gave us a sense of freedom as we roared along the narrow winding country roads laughing and talking nonstop. Driving into the grounds of a prestigious resort called Windimere House, we passed hundreds of parked cars. Something was up! We found the auditorium packed to standing room only at the back. Once inside and oblivious to what was going on around me, I melted to the inspirational music, which filled me with a sense of reverence. The gentleman who spoke was direct, humorous and dynamic. He was very serious in the way he challenged the youthful audience, demanding that we think about the future. He queried, "How do you plan to spend your lives?" Will you step out and believe to do the unexpected? "Will you make a difference in this world?" Thus he challenged his youthful yet suddenly pensive listeners.

I listened with open mind and heart to the message and accepted his challenge to "live life to the full." I certainly wanted to live a life that would make a difference! Something absolutely amazing took place inside of me. God's love became tangible. I melted. My eyes became a fountain of tears but I wasn't sad. I had no resistance to the waves of invisible love washing over me. Instantly, beyond a shadow of a doubt I knew that one day, I was to go to India. Did I understand what had happened? No, of course not, but it was absolutely life changing.

I said nothing upon return to Glen Home the hotel where we teens were employed for the summer months. But I couldn't join in the joking and fun. My mind was still involved with the spiritual experience I had just had, and so I slipped into my cottage and closed the door. Kneeling down at my bed, I wept. I had no idea why I was crying. I couldn't stop the tears that fell. The Lord God was allowing me to come so close. His love overwhelmed my heart. It reminded me a little of the time when I was four years old... but this was different.

Word got out, and my Auntie came to my bedside inquiring about my emotions. I tried to explain what had happened, but I knew she didn't 'get it'. The following day I sat down and wrote to my parents and grandparents, attempting to put into words this life changing experience. Never once was I concerned about how I would go to India. I had already decided that I would never be a missionary because I had been negatively influenced as a young child. So perhaps it is amazing that I was able to accept this direction as fact.
I kept 'hope' hidden in my heart, while completing high school and nurses training. How very special it was to share this part of my life with Jay, and to feel so safe with one whom I had just met. It was like we had always known each other; there was no sense of strangeness.

Jay:

Ten years later, upon her arrival in Victoria she was introduced to CUSO or Canadian University Service Overseas, a humanitarian organization patterned after the American Peace Corps. A CUSO poster hung on the wall just opposite the door of her room in the nurses' residence. "You are needed in India" it read, and there stood a mother holding her starving child. The message pierced her heart bringing back 'the call' to India. This program immediately appealed to Meridel.

It offered university graduates and RN's the opportunity to serve for two years in various places around the world assisting people in developing countries to become self-sufficient. As we continued to walk and talk, I told her that I too had applied, a year previously, to join CUSO. We both sensed this was an unusual coincidence. Privately I realized that there was more to this 'drawing' to each other than we knew. Meridel was certainly assured in where she was going in life. I told her that I was about to embark on a challenging two year course in Hospital Administration at the University of Toronto. It seemed that our lives were headed in opposite directions. As we drove back to her residence I thought, *Does this relationship have a chance of survival?*

"I have really enjoyed getting to know you a little and I respect your plans for India," I told her. "However, I guess we are, as that old saying goes, 'like two ships passing in the night.'" Immediately I felt a deep sadness for I didn't want to get involved again with someone and then get hurt and I knew she felt the same way. But there was something happening between us!

After we parted, I prayed for her and it felt good. Now I had a friend where romance was second to our zeal to try to make a difference in this life. In spite of what I had heard from the 'still small voice.'

Our parting that night was rather final.

Meridel:

That night I wrote in my diary, "*I don't understand this but I think I am going to marry that man.*" I didn't even know his last name. But from that moment on, I prayed fervently that somehow he would find me again.

Jay:

The next few weeks were difficult. I was torn in different directions. I knew I wanted to go on with my relationship with Meridel but I really didn't know how it could ever work. Time passed. I was busy and I didn't call her but, back at the lab, Helen was curious.

"How's your friendship going with Meridel?

"Well ..." I paused. "It just didn't seem to work out." When I spoke those words, it was like a knife went into my heart. I realized now that I was not being true to myself. What was I going to do? I really did not want a relationship like the last one, but I missed Meridel terribly. I was confused. I breathed a silent prayer, *Oh Lord please show me what to do, and let me meet her again.*

A few days passed. While driving to work I saw her, this time at a bus stop. Pulling over to the curb I leaned over to open the passenger window. "Hi." My heart was thumping and I found I was a little shy.

"Hi Jay!" Her bright smile was instant.

"Tell me, how was your interview at the University of Victoria? What about your application for Canadian University Service Overseas?"

Bending down by the window of my sports car, she surprised me with, "I've been accepted to go to India in September. It's for sure now."

"Congratulations," I said enthusiastically.

Beaming, she said, "I'm on my way to the University right now to learn all the details. Then next week I must go to UBC for six weeks of orientation and language study on campus."

"How do you plan to get to Vancouver, I asked?

"I don't know, to tell you the truth, I haven't even thought of it."

"Well, I volunteer to drive you over to the mainland. We can go on the ferry with your suitcases."

"You mean with my steamer trunk. I'm not kidding."

"Absolutely! No problem!," I responded, even though I had yet to see the size of it. I was quietly surprised at the rapid turn of events.

Yes, I felt very grateful for the quick answer to prayer and relieved to know I would be able to spend a little more time with her.

Meridel:

On the day of my departure, we agreed to meet at my nurse's station at 0800 am. I worked nights up to the very last minute. As a surprise, my head nurse ordered in coffee and muffins for a little farewell.

Jay arrived in the middle of a down pour. I enjoyed the ease with which he met people, he was friendly yet comfortable to be with and oh so handsome in his trench coat.

Jay:

I noticed then and ever since that Meridel makes lasting friends wherever she goes and this was no exception. After coffee and a brief chat, we said good-bye to her nursing colleagues. She quickly changed and threw on a bright red rain coat, belted at the waist. *What an eye catcher*, I thought. I complimented her on how chic she looked with her hair turned up in an elegantly even after working all night! Together we bumped her heavy trunk down the stairs and into my sports car. It looked ancient and closed with leather straps. Thankfully it fit. Well... almost!

The cloudy day gave way to a light drizzle soaking everything. Her trunk was so big I had to leave the boot of my car open tying it down with rope. Fortunately, the rain stopped while on the way to the ferry terminal. On board we enjoyed a Canadian breakfast as the ferry navigated its passage through the scenic Gulf Islands. The whole time Meridel chattered away comfortably. It felt so good to be together. We were relaxed and at ease, just like it was always meant to be.

All in all, the travel time to Vancouver was three hours. As a student, I had traversed this exact route so many times in the previous two years, I felt I could do it in my sleep. Upon arrival, I took her straight to her dorm at UBC. My cousin James was taking a summer course that year and lived in the men's dorms close by. I introduced them. James looked at me quizzically, offering me his dorm room, which I gladly accepted. Meridel was to begin her orientation program for India later that afternoon. I suggested we meet the next day, Sunday morning, for breakfast and later some sightseeing. Her schedule was free until Sunday evening, so we arranged to rendezvous.

Sunday, bright and early we met and I guided her through the almost deserted downtown Vancouver, including China Town. I made a point of taking her to several beautiful places like Stanley Park, which she loved. We walked among the magnificent fir and ancient cedar trees, flowering shrubs and Japanese gardens. The splashing fountains created an 'other world' atmosphere. Together we stood, gazing toward the western horizon where dozens of ships from around the world lay at anchor. After lunch the sunshine was brilliant and we drove with the top down up to Burnaby Mountain, which overlooks greater Vancouver, the Coastal Mountains were off to our right and Vancouver Island lay mysteriously on the distant horizon surrounded by shining sea. Meridel told me of her application to study a Master's Degree at Simon Fraser that fall. She was accepted, but, instead, chose to serve in India with CUSO.

We were just about to leave that scenic spot, and, without thinking, almost magnetically I leaned toward her. She responded. We kissed. It was an instant attraction, fireworks, electricity, passion, and love all rolled into one.

"Wow!" I said. "Is that how you feel?"

Blushing, she only grinned, her hazel eyes sparkling. Now, when you read Meridel's story you will realize why she had never responded to any man like that before. You must know that I was one amazed guy after just one kiss! Something inexplicable happened!

That afternoon, when I dropped her back at UBC to begin her India initiation courses and Tamil language studies, I already planned how to see her again. We only had six weeks before she was to leave, and in seven I was off to Toronto. We decided that we both wanted to spend as much time as possible together before our "D" day – Departure Day. I returned to Victoria feeling exhilarated on one hand and very thoughtful on the other. I knew that this woman was going to be an instrument of 'change' in my life. And change for me has never been easy. Back at the lab, now the time dragged by. Helen was 'tickled pink' to hear of our progress.

I invited Meridel to come over to the Island the following weekend. She arrived as a foot-passenger on the BC ferry, this time to the hub city of Nanaimo, 100 kilometers north of Victoria. I picked her up and we continued north on Vancouver Island to Oyster Bay, where Mom and Dad had rented a lovely little summer cottage right on the beach.

We were delighted to be together. Meridel slept with Mom, while Dad and I shared a bed. In the morning Mom made us all laugh by saying, "We slept as snug as two spoons in a drawer!"

These were days of good old fashioned fun. We kept busy swimming in Englishman's River, fishing and barbecuing the salmon that we caught. Later, Meridel and I strolled along the beach in the moonlight. Being so completely comfortable with each other was a sweet and precious experience. It was a gift.

Meridel just loved "Billy and Sheila", as she called them.

On Sunday evening it was hard to say good-bye, but again I planned for Meridel to come back to the Island each weekend so we could be together to make all kinds of meaningful memories before India. She even watched another of my ball games, a doubleheader, this time in Courtenay. It was a steamy hot day and, after the game I was exhausted having been 'catcher for 18 innings. As we drove south I started to feel refreshed. I was, however taken by surprise when she brought up the subject of the number of children she hoped to have. It was an unusual chat yet so completely natural. In fact it was the first time either of us had ever verbalized thoughts about a future family!

Another weekend, we stayed with Mom and Dad in their own quaint little cottage with a 180 degree view of the Gulf Islands across the Strait of Georgia (now called the Salish Sea). The stunning snow-capped peaks of the mainland Coastal Mountains are clearly visible in the distance. To maximize our time together, Meridel and I stayed over on the Sunday night, and rose very early Monday morning in order to make the two hour drive south to Victoria to my folk's home on Locarno Lane. Meridel made breakfast while I got ready for work. We ate out on the patio in the warm early morning sunshine. I was so grateful to the Lord for giving me this lovely friendship, with someone whom I could share my hopes and dreams. We enjoyed a fun relationship, clean and dedicated to God. I remember taking Meridel's hand in mine as we gave thanks. She was the only girl I had ever prayed with. It was great. It was foundational. It was long term! We raced to get her to the departing Vancouver ferry on time for her classes.

The next weekend, she had to stay in Vancouver for more CUSO tests. It was very hard to be apart. I guess you might say we were 'falling in love' in spite of the fact that a potential two year separation was looming closer and closer.

On the final weekend before Meridel left for India, I decided to go to Vancouver because I had something planned as part of our farewell. On the Saturday morning, while she was in a final orientation lecture about their departure details, I hurried downtown before the stores closed.

At Berk's Jewelers main Vancouver store I picked out a simple gold band. I wanted to give Meridel a ring but knew it wasn't appropriate to send her off to India with a sparkling diamond. This ring would fit in perfectly as she went about her village work with the poorest of the poor. I saw it as our 'betrothal' ring. A sign of our promise to each other concerning our future married life.

That last day we lingered over a private lunch, knowing that the following day was our "D" day. We couldn't bring ourselves to discuss our parting, not with so little time left. It was an emotionally charged moment. After coffee I drove her along Point Grey, the peninsula that is the geographic home of the UBC campus. I stopped and parked at the little university inter- faith chapel just off the main tree lined boulevard. It held fond memories for me as a student where I attended regularly. Rev. Bernice Gerard, a Vancouver City Councilor often addressed students there. She was like our "chaplain". For decades she hosted a popular radio and TV talk show. She was also a pastor, and tried and true friend of Israel. Selected 'Woman of the Year' by the Vancouver Jewish community, she inspired me with her world view. Her audiences loved her positive yet disarmingly honest approach to issues in the media and to life itself.

Luckily, at that time, the chapel was empty. Hand in hand we walked down to the front and knelt together. While continuing to hold her hand I quoted the scripture containing the word, *"Mizpeh"* in Hebrew meaning, *"May the Lord watch between thee and me while we are absent from one another."* Genesis 31:49

Taking the ring out of my pocket, I opened my hand for Meridel to see and explained the inscription of the word *"Mizpeh"* engraved inside. Opening my little book of Psalms, together we read: *"Oh magnify the Lord with me, and let us exalt the Lord together."* Psalm 34:3

I asked Meridel to accept the ring as a symbol of our commitment to each other until we would finally be united as man and wife. Smiling, she nodding her approval. Then, I slipped the ring on the fourth finger of her right hand.

As we knelt there in the soft afternoon sunlight, our hearts melted in the tingling presence of the Living God.
"Father in heaven," I prayed, "please preserve our relationship for your purposes and our fullness.
"Amen," Meridel whispered. "And please watch between us while we are absent one from the other."

That night, Meridel's dorm was full of activity. Parents and friends were coming and going, saying good-bye to those who were on their way the next morning to Malawi, Thailand and India. It was a party with champagne and revelry. Preferring each other's company, we decided to walk over to James' empty dorm room where I was staying. We sat and talked throughout the night instead of the ribald atmosphere in the nearby CUSO dorm.

Being impossible dreamers and idealists, we believed that if God was for us nothing could be against us. We also believed that if we agreed together on anything it could happen. I sensed that with the Lord 'watching' between us, our love could grow even if we were apart. This would be the foundation needed to withstand tough days ahead.

Finally, talked out and exhausted, we curled up, fully clothed on my cousin's single bed. I'll never ever forget that night. We fell asleep comforting each other. Of course we both longed for each other's bodies, but I had previously determined to abstain from sexual relations. I loved Meridel in a different way than I had ever loved anyone before.

The uniqueness of this love gave me the strength to refrain from insisting upon a physical relationship. We cuddled and it would have been very easy to go all the way, but I made the decision instead to respect myself, and my sweetheart. I have no regrets and neither does Meridel to this very day.

After a final packing and a quick breakfast, we were off to the Vancouver International Airport to say our good-byes. These special young Canadian ambassadors were given the use of Prime Minister Lester B Pearson's private jet to transport them to their various destinations.
Travel plans involved four days in Hawaii for R&R followed by an 'orientation stay' on the island of Guam. The 'sensitivity sessions' in the jungle, gave them a taste of the primitive conditions they would face in, Malaysia, Northern Thailand and India.

I stood with her for a brief moment at the foot of the stairwell to her plane. Holding hands I said, "I'm not saying good-bye. Just, see you later."
Her eyes brimming with tears she didn't say a word, just squeezed my hands.
I watched her disappear into the private jet and then she was gone. Waiting to see her plane lift off, I wasn't sad. Immediately I missed her, but now I felt that each passing moment only served to bring us back together. Of course I wondered how we were going to sustain such a long separation. Yet I had a deep sense of quiet peace that this was all somehow pre-planned, and it was something much bigger than we could ever understand or imagine. There was however, a lot of water that still had 'to pass under the bridge.'

Timeless Secrets

Oh, give thanks to the Lord, for He is good! For His mercy endures forever...
To give thanks to Your Holy name, to triumph in Your name. Blessed be the
Lord God of Israel From everlasting to everlasting. 1 Chronicles 16: 34, 35b, 36

Meridel:

In looking back, I am grateful and blessed to have been given this kind of relationship. And I am just as glad that we kept ourselves from a sexual relationship, especially with my history of abuse. The memories we had of each other over the next twenty months of separation were built on honour and trust. Some intrepid young people today, are bravely choosing to wait until marriage to begin their exciting and intimate part of life. Premarital sexual relations do not necessarily lead to emotional intimacy or stability in marriage. Physical intimacy is one of many avenues of communication given for natural comfort and enjoyment. Sanctity in any relationship must be treasured and safeguarded if it is to last. The ongoing responsibility of bringing new life into the world is a very important part of the intimate relationship. My mother used to say, "When Father God sees a couple, he sees the next generation."

Jay:

Through our forty four years of marriage I've discovered that respect for one's partner is of paramount importance for keeping the relationship fresh and exciting in every way. Experts in psychology and counseling have found that transitional events in life are our primary causes of stress. Taking a new job, a death in the family, divorce, separation, and moving to a new location are some of the main ones.

Meridel and I were now dealing with three. We were separated, moving to new locations, and confronted with a whole new set of responsibilities. Transition is a continuing process in life, I'm sure you'll agree on that. Pause and reflect upon nature all around you.
It is continually in a state of change. People today are much more mobile than in previous generations. So, separation from loved ones happens all around us, all the time. The question is, how do we deal with it? How were

we going to survive? It is essential to understand the importance of deferred gratification, learning to wait and to anticipate.
Here is what helped me the most:

THANKSGIVING
I always say, when in doubt... Give thanks to our Creator. Thankfulness shows that you are looking beyond yourself and your limitations to a greater source for what you need.

"Be thankful to Him, and bless His Name. For the Lord is good; His mercy is everlasting. And His truth endures to all generations." Psalm 100; 4b, 5

PRAYER
Try to see the big picture; prayer will open your eyes and your mind. Worry and anxiety plagues most of humanity but, if you can place your list of needs and hopes and desires before your Heavenly Father who loves and cares for you, you can then rest in His peace. It works!

"Be diligent to be found by Him in peace without spot and blameless." 2 Peter 3:14

> **Strong's #4704** definition of "diligent or eager" is: 'to exert oneself, make every effort, give diligence, make haste, be zealous, strain every nerve, further the cause assiduously. Combine thinking, acting, planning and producing. It sees a need and promptly does something about it. The word describes inception, action and follow through.

CONFIDENCE
Believe that Abba Father will give you the final victory. His still small voice is your instant connection to His perfect and timely instructions. They will bring you through life's bumps and challenges. His promises never fail!

This little sister from the Missionaries of Charity and Meridel
made medical visits to the 'busties' or shanty towns up and down the
hills near Darjeeling, N W Bengal, India.

Chapter 9

The Paniya Tribe and Progress

"My media career began by showing slides of Meridel's public health work in India. Dramatic pictures, linked with a compelling narration has a powerful impact and effect...."

Meridel and forty-five other CUSO colleagues were winging their way west over the Pacific, while I flew east to Toronto. I decided to go a few days early to get settled before the academic year began. Mrs. Eva Holmes, a gracious widow, the mother of Bob Holmes, my pastor friend in Victoria, rented me a room in her home. Immediately she made me feel welcome, which was comforting now that I was 4,500 kilometers away from family and friends, and about half way around the world from Meridel. I didn't know a single soul in Toronto, a city of two million at that time.

The first thing I did was build myself a study desk. From my years at UBC, James and I had learned how to furnish a student apartment on a 'shoestring' budget. Plywood cut to measure about two centimeters thick was first sanded and then varnished. Next I fixed legs to it. Placed in front of the only window in my tiny room I barely had space enough to open the door. It was small but comfortable and homey. My monthly rent included breakfast but I had to take all other meals out. Eating by myself was an ongoing exercise in loneliness!

Moore Park, directly across the street, was enjoyed by the community. Families relaxed on its expanse of lawns and playgrounds. Young mothers made good use of the space for their small children, while teens used the basketball courts in their free time. It was early fall in Ontario and the leaves were just beginning to change color. That area of the city is called Mount Pleasant and it was truly a 'pleasant' neighborhood.
Each brick home, built around the turn of the century, had a veranda looking onto the park. Sitting on the porch in their rocking chairs the kind neighbors greeted the people walking their dogs.

This world has all but disappeared. Pioneers built Toronto from scratch on an ancient First Nations tribal village called, in their dialect, 'tor-on-to' meaning "gathering place." Later, the conservative, hard working, law abiding people of early Toronto gave the city its name "Toronto the Good."

There was always lots of activity going on outside at all times of the year. I was grateful for my window on this interesting world. I have always enjoyed Canada's four distinct seasons. Here they were played out in full color.

Everything was new to me. I caught the tram in the mornings to St. Claire subway station. The famous red and cream colored street cars were novel to me. They looked like those in San Francisco. Their miles of tracks slicing through the streets made driving a nightmare. Connected to electric wires overhead, they shot out sparks that sizzled and fuzzed with blue smoke. Bells signaled the arrival at each stop. This gentle sound seemed out of place in the modern hustle and bustle of Canada's economic capital.

After a short subway ride, I jumped out on College Street and walked west toward the University. The wide streets and huge glass buildings were quite daunting for someone who had grown up in the more subdued 'quaint Victoria.' On that first day of Grad School I felt quite insignificant. The sheer size of U of T's city centre campus was impressive. Ivy-covered granite buildings standing alongside modern award winning architecture exuded the feeling of 'establishment.' This was contrasted by the carefully tended gardens and squares on campus. What a refreshing change from the madness of the city. The air even felt somewhat cleaner.
Today, more than 70,000 students attend U of T annually.
Among those enrolled are 7,000 international students mentored by 4,500 faculty members of which ten are Nobel laureates.
My academic home for the next two years was the three stories Sherman Building. Walking up the worn stone steps, I entered a narrow door into a distinct world of academia. There I found shining halls and book-lined offices.

Learning was serious business. I found the room where I was to enroll and meet my other classmates. We were a small group of twenty two students from all across Canada. Several were pharmacists in their forties, along with other obviously mature students. Some had already held various management positions in hospitals and government. Two Catholic sisters, one from the Grey Nun's Hospital in Winnipeg, and another from St. Joseph's Hospital in Hamilton provided a startling contrast in their austere black and white habits. There were also a few young grads like myself.

We met our professors and, later that day, attended a welcome reception party with wine and cheese. Everyone was very friendly and talkative, yet I felt the underlying weight of the academic tradition. In fact, forty five years before, a Nobel laureate, Sir Fredrick Banting, a Canadian medical doctor, along with his assistant Dr. Charles Best, had discovered insulin in the very building where we were standing.

The days and weeks passed quickly. Each evening when I arrived 'home' I checked the carpeted steps leading upstairs to my room. Was there a letter or aerogramme from Meridel waiting for me? She was a very faithful correspondent and usually once or twice a week her letter was there, which made my day. Indian air- letters are unmistakable. They are a pale greenish-blue color, of very poor quality paper, so thin and fragile they sometimes almost fell apart in my hands. There was Hindi writing on the edges but always I could recognize Meridel's unique handwriting.

Her world became mine through her vibrant descriptions. Eagerly, I read of her public health nursing in the Nilgiri Hills of N. W. Madras State in Southern India. I quote from her letter:

"My three-roomed thatched mud house with no facilities is located on the side of the only dirt road snaking its way upward in the rolling Nilgiri Hills. Across the road, an industrious family has their tea shop, constructed of bamboo and mud. Truck drivers and locals stop for their sweet 'chai' served in disposable clay cups without handles. It is very busy here; the tea stand also serves as the post office."

"This entire area of jungle had been subdued by British colonist's generations before, and developed into thriving tea and coffee plantations along with holiday resorts. It's a bit like visiting a lost world here. The air is much cooler in the hills than down on the steaming plains. This is where tourists and locals alike come to 'get away.' One hears the English accents of upper-crust ladies carrying white parasols in the streets along with the constant beep of annoying horns and the local Tamil language interspersed with several European languages."

"You mustn't worry about me, I have a constant companion, who is my cook, housekeeper, chaperone and guide. She is called an 'Amah.' Wizened and bent, this toothless Hindu grandma, speaks no English, only her native Tamil, a Sanskrit language which forces me to speak her language."

Meridel had wrestled with its pronunciation at UBC for eight hours a day. But now, her working vocabulary enabled her to run two jungle hospitals and make weekly 'rounds' to local villages, often assisting mothers delivering babies in their huts.

Meridel working alongside Dr. Narasinham with jungle tribes people. Nilgiri Hills, N W Madras State, South India.

She worked with Dr. Narasinham, a famous Indian public health specialist, decorated by Prime Minister Nehru for his outstanding work among the Paniya people and eight other indigenous tribes. He introduced Meridel to the tribal people in their protected remote settlements. They had been driven up into the Nilgiri Hills over generations, as civilization encroached upon their dwindling lands. The Paniya's are an aboriginal people group, descended from some of the earliest known inhabitants of Madagascar. Anthropologists suggest they floated on reed rafts and sailed to the south western coast of India from their African origins.

Meridel operated two jungle hospitals in South India

Meridel was the first white woman they had ever seen when she visited their remote settlements. The Paniya adults and their children would run away screaming as she approached. Her letters were very descriptive, but it wasn't until I had developed the film she sent that her daily activities took on a new dimension for me.
Carefully, she had listed the subject of each slide in her descriptive letters so I could later understand what I was seeing. It was true, once I saw the slides, I was touched and deeply moved.

The people were poverty-stricken and yet how happy they seemed with very few earthly goods.

Meridel was the first white woman that the Aboriginal Paniya people of India ever saw. They fled screaming when she first approached them.

While Meridel worked in the area of public health, her CUSO volunteer colleague was an agronomist, whose task was to assist the Paniya people in becoming an agrarian society. His outstanding work is published in his book concerning the three years he spent in the Nilgiri Hills based on his letters to his mother and fiancée.[21]

---

[21] Mundel, Hans-Hennirg, *My Life Among the Paniyas of the Nilgiri Hills*. Carpe Diem Mundel Publishing, 2007

Meridel was often in my conversations. My classmates were also keenly interested to see her slides. I attended a local congregation and there the youth group regularly invited me to present slide shows of her work. Pictures are worth a thousand words. Showing Meridel's India slides is actually how I began my media work. I saw the powerful impact and immediate effect of dramatic pictures plus compelling narration when linked together to tell a story.

My studies in Hospital Administration were sponsored by the Department of Public Health Administration of the Faculty of Medicine at U of T. It was very demanding and included Health Care Statistics, Economics, Accounting, Medical Law and Jurisprudence, Communication, Administration, and Anatomy. We had to study physiology of the human body, taught by a professor of the Medical School. We learned all the terminology of the medical profession so that in the future we, as Hospital Administrators, could speak with the doctors on any subject concerning health issues. In addition, we had various visiting professors teaching us about their specialties. It was rich in content but I had to work hard to keep up. Field trips to various kinds of hospitals included everything from the large teaching facilities associated with university medical and nursing schools, to the medium-sized community hospitals in outlying towns' right down to tiny rural clinics with just one or two beds. In all, it was a tremendous learning experience. We wrote many papers and sat rigorous examinations. I did not have much spare time, but enjoyed long talks with Mrs. Holmes. This elderly widow was a fount of compassion, wisdom and knowledge; we became fast friends.

Wanting to see something of Ontario, I signed up for a Canadian Thanksgiving weekend 'student get away' at a place called Campus in the Woods. There I met Grant Bartlett in the cafeteria at the camp and we have remained good friends over the last nearly fifty years. Together we headed to this beautiful recreation centre on the Lake of Bays in Muskoka. This area of Ontario is known as 'cottage country' north of Toronto in the Lake District. It is thickly forested by spruce, birch and poplar. The fall colors were spectacular. We rode our bikes along leave strewn trails and took boat rides on the surrounding lakes. Talk about inspirational! But only one of the speakers had the ability to bring Biblical truth to life for me.

He had a refreshing, confident enthusiasm. Curious, I approached him and asked, "What's your secret? How is it that you are able to communicate so clearly?"

"It's the Spirit of the Lord," he said in a quiet voice. "Just go and ask God to fill you to overflowing with His Spirit."

Obviously, at this gathering it was not appropriate for him to speak openly about the infilling of the Holy Spirit as mentioned clearly in Isaiah 28:11. Subsequently, this experience bursts onto the scene in Jerusalem as described in Acts 2:4.

It was all new to me but, whatever he had, I wanted! I was hungry to grow in God and desired to be used by Him. I knew one thing. I didn't want 'religion' but I was eager to learn every aspect about God's character. I was fascinated by the many different ways God's spirit was able to reach people. Jesus said it all as follows,

"But the hour is coming, and now is when the true worshippers will worship the Father in spirit and in truth: for the Father is seeking such to worship Him. God is Spirit and those who worship Him must worship in spirit and truth." John 4:23,24

Making the effort to be there for the weekend was well worth it. Now I was open to learn how to 'worship in Spirit'. After the weekend we returned to our busy academic lives in Toronto but I could not forget the words of that inspired speaker.

After the first hard freeze of winter, the basketball court in the park across the street was flooded by local firemen. Overnight it froze into a sheet of glass, providing a lit hockey and skating rink for the neighborhood. Hockey is Canada's national sport. For about five months of the year, ice rinks are the focus of most local sports activities. Canada brought hockey to the world. A weekly Canadian ritual is Hockey Night in Canada, broadcast nationwide every Saturday evening. Grant and I treated ourselves to a few NHL games when the Toronto Maple Leafs played their famous rival team, the Montreal Canadians.

We also worked with under-privileged youths, arranged outings and sports activities and had great fun. However, when it came to presenting deep spiritual truths and eternal concepts, I was at a loss to know how to connect with them.

I remembered how easy it was for the guy whose teaching I ate up at that weekend getaway. What was it he had? How could I be filled with God's Spirit?

To get some exercise, one afternoon Grant and I put on skates and played hockey at the rink across the road from my room. At the time, we were the only ones on the ice. Shooting the puck at the net, I shouted to Grant, "Do you remember what that guy at the retreat said about being filled with the Spirit?"

"Yeah, I remember." He sent the puck whizzing back across the ice, hitting my stick with a loud smack.

"Well, what do you think about that?" My words seemed frozen like the air.

"I just don't know," he shrugged, catching my pass. "I haven't thought about it that much."

"Well I know this," I skated closer, "I read the first few chapters in the Book of Acts and those Jews had an amazing life changing experience that gave them the courage and heart to turn the world upside down. I can't even imagine it."

"But Jay, let's not get carried away here." Skating backwards, he shouted, "Anyone I've talked to says it's not possible for today."

"Yeah but I think it is! Isn't God supposed to be the same yesterday, today and forever?"

He fired a slap-shot that hit the boards. It went flying off at a crazy angle. "So, what do you say?

"Let's ask the Lord to fill us. I need some support here." I caught up with the puck.

Grant stopped skating and leaned on his hockey stick. "Okay, Rawlings, where and how?" he challenged. His words hit the freezing air like steam from a hot engine.

Now, I started to feel a bit uneasy. Was I getting into something over my head? But I was running on empty. Actually I was tired of the routine we know as nominal living. Boldly I suggested, "Let's go to my room and pray right now. We can ask God to fill us today with His Spirit."

Cautiously, Grant agreed. I understood his reserve.

Bending down to take off his skates he said, "It feels a bit daunting to ask God in such a direct manner."

We both wondered what was going to happen next.

Dropping our skates and sticks at the door we tip-toed up the stairs. I knelt down at my chair and Grant by the dresser. We prayed in turn, "Oh Lord, please come and fill us right now!!"

We waited in silence. Nothing happened. After a while we got up, feeling a little self-conscious not knowing what to do so, we decided to go out for a burger and fries. In the restaurant, I said "About our experience, or should I say lack of experience, the only way I can explain it is that we must already be filled with the Holy Spirit."

"Yeah." He dipped his chips in ketchup. End of discussion.

Much later, I would remember this frustrating time and chuckle, but only after I had a real, deep and life changing experience in the Holy Spirit.

At Christmas break, I decided to stay put in Toronto and get caught up on my required reading. Besides, I didn't have the return airfare to Victoria. Some of my married classmates said, "Don't worry; we'll have a class party. So they set up an evening and we all chipped in for the food and refreshments. The guys in our class with pharmaceutical backgrounds offered, "We're experts at mixing up potions so we'll bring the punch." I now know that this was dangerous! Ken, a classmate from the Vancouver area brought his young wife Gina. They picked me up.

We met all the family members of the married classmates. Chattering ladies and men's light hearted banter was well underway, fueled by a large amount of punch. Unknown to most of us, the pharmacists had spiked it with pure, 100% alcohol. Being clear and tasteless, it packed a powerful wallop!

After a couple of hours, the sound level hit the roof as most of us were tipsy. This was my first experience being inebriated. Fortunately, because Gina was expecting, she sipped ginger ale and was in great form to drive Ken and me home as he was also looped. The moral of the story: beware of pharmacists who offer to bring their punch to any party!

Terribly ashamed I sneaked back to the home of teetotaler Mrs. Holmes. Navigating the icy front steps was a challenge with my double vision. I got to the front door and very quietly slipped my key into the lock, it turned but the door opened only two inches and went 'clunk.' Thinking I was already in for the night, Mrs. Holmes had secured the door! The safety chain was in place. What was I going to do? My friends had driven away. It was freezing outside in the ice and snow. Focusing, I carefully examined the lock and this time I pulled the door to me ever so gently. Sliding my fingers in through the crack, I undid the safety clip. Thankfully, the door opened. I slipped in without waking anyone. Gratefully, I fell into bed, asleep in an instant.

The next day, I slept very late and never mentioned my near calamity to the gracious lady of the house. Late the next morning I finally dragged myself down the stairs to brunch. Groggily I focused on a post card thoughtfully propped up at my breakfast plate. It was Meridel's specially crafted Christmas card poignantly showing a collage of her photos of Indian, Nepali and Tibetan faces, old and young. In her delicate handwriting she wrote,

"Beloved Jay , this quote is from a poem, written by Dr Tom Dooley,[22] during his years in Cambodia. 'Listen to the agony of Asia, I who am fed, who never yet went hungry for want of bread... I see and try to pray.' "

Immediately I felt convicted of my overly comfortable life style. Spring term flew by. We had many essays and papers to write and exams to prepare for. The weeks just disappeared. Meridel kept up her correspondence and told me of her challenges and successes. The Indian doctor that she worked for was expanding his medical services to other tribal groups and brought in three nurses from Germany.
Meridel was to mentor them so they could take over the work that she had started. For her second year, CUSO headquarters in New Delhi challenged her to go ahead and travel around India to find the next position she wanted to fill. We were both in a state of transition.

---

[22] Dr. Tom Dooley wrote these words while serving as a humanitarian medical doctor in Cambodia.

A Tibetan young man

As I was wrapping up my first year of graduate studies my classmates and I waited eagerly for our second year residency assignments. Now we were to spend one year alongside an experienced hospital administrator. This year of mentoring proved to be extremely valuable grounding for us as future health care administrators.

The School of Hospital Administration had several hospitals in the southern Ontario area to choose from. Our professors selected the location for each student. I was sent to the Hamilton General Hospital which was a part of the Hamilton Civic Hospitals Group.

This multi-hospital unit with 1800 beds was the largest of its kind in Canada at that time. The sister hospital, The Henderson General, located on Hamilton Mountain had other medical specialty departments. This network arrangement was considered the way of the future. As I look back now I realize this 'choice' location would play an important role in our future.

On the world stage not only Israel and the Middle East but the brutal Chinese takeover of Tibet were grabbing headlines. Meridel wanted to get as close to the conflict as possible.

The CUSO volunteers often used their free time to travel by 3rd class train to visit their colleagues working all over India, swapping stories, sharing the latest news and encouraging one another. A fiery red-headed Sandy visited Meridel and said she had just come from Darjeeling where she saw the work that the Missionaries of Charity were doing among the poverty stricken Tibetan refugees. She put 'a bee in Meridel's bonnet.' Meridel received permission from CUSO headquarters in New Delhi to pursue her dream. She caught a train to Calcutta for an interview with Mother Theresa, Founder - Director of her outstanding Missionaries of Charity work. Mother Theresa had only a few minutes to meet with Meridel but agreed to accept her. Her orientation in Calcutta, began immediately.

Mother Theresa had a special understanding with the Military Governor of NW Bengal State where Darjeeling is situated. At that time it was closed to the general public as this area had been secured militarily due to the Chinese invasion and takeover of the isolated and proud nation of Tibet. She recommended that Meridel's nursing skills could be well used in northern India. She would help with the massive influx of Tibetan refugees pouring into Darjeeling District from Tibet. Thousands were fleeing on foot over the treacherous mountainous snow filled Natula Pass.

**Mother Theresa's Missionaries of Charity, medical clinic
in the back of their Land Rover. Serving the Tibetan refugees,
1967 - Darjeeling, India.**

The Missionaries of Charity desperately needed medical help with
their many outreaches, especially now with the destitute and sickly
refugees.
She became one with the Sisters helping wherever needed in their
daily routines: Feeding the poor in the slums, washing dying bodies at
the Home of the Dying, and giving out medicines in a leper colony as
well as delivering babies. Her work was never finished.

Meridel's slides displayed the spectacular beauty of this Himalayan
region. The human plight she caught on film was heart wrenching.
Darjeeling, located 7,000 feet above sea level is perched on foot hills
overlooking the magnificent Kanchenjunga mountain range just south
east of Mt. Everest. She lived in a convent with the Irish Sisters of
Cluny who created a homey residence for college students. Meridel
also was in house counselor to female students from across Asia.
Miles from home, they attended the local prestigious schools for,
which Darjeeling is famous. Dinar, a diminutive beauty from Iran
shared her room. Her father, a proud Zoroastrian, a religion founded
in Persia, was the Iranian Ambassador to India.

Meridel spent her mornings going out in a large Land Rover with a
team of Sisters to the Tibetan monasteries. They handed out cooking
oil and milk powder along with medical care. Afternoons were spent
with one little sister who knew the language. The women climbed up
and down the steep sides of the 'busties, or shanty towns precariously
perched on the impermanent hilly slopes. Again she did medical work
in one shack after another.
Getting back into Darjeeling in the early evening she often went into
the market for supper in a Tibetan food stall, which was a shack
constructed of old scrap pieces of corrugated metal on the roof with
canvas sides. A large old fashioned cooking stove located at the back
gave off a blast of heat that warmed all within the cloth walls. Several
giant pots of food bubbled noisily on the stove. Meridel enjoyed
helping herself to soup, noodles, and local steamed vegetables with a
hint of meat thrown in. She wrote me about her joy of just being with
the locals even though she didn't speak the local dialect. It reminded
me that after her rigorous psychological testing at UBC, before being

allowed to proceed on to India, the Professor told her, "You are a born communicator and will never have a problem that way."

Caring for abandoned newborns was a daily routine. These preemie babies were found on railway tracks, in the garbage bins and in fields. Others were left on the doorstep of the Sisters of Charity Orphanage. Meridel had charge of them during the night and carried them to her room in the Convent for feeding every two hours with eye droppers. She placed them in the drawers of her dresser, because there were no bassinets. The mortality rate was almost 100 %. She told me later that it was at this time in her life that she began to search out what it meant to be filled with God's Spirit. Living with so much death was breaking her down emotionally and she needed added strength and comfort that could only come from above.

Now we go back to Canada...

With my year long residency assignment in place I packed my bags and said good-bye to Mrs. Holmes, promising to bring Meridel 'home' to meet her one day. I drove to Hamilton, Ontario in my Triumph TR3. Feeling lonely when I arrived in "Steel town," I settled quickly into my own room in the medical interns' residence on that hot sticky day.

The Hamilton General on Barton Street is located in one of the oldest areas of the city. Surrounded by heavy industry, the huge Stelco plant nearby provides Canada with much of its steel, so the air quality around the hospital is poor.

The next morning the staff and medical professionals of the hospital greeted me warmly. I felt welcome. I was shown to my new office near the main entrance. This was my very first office. Opposite my desk, glass panels facing the reception area, allowed me to easily observe the nonstop traffic of humanity moving in and out. I took a survey of the office. Fortunately, I had an air conditioner. Taking a moment I re-arranged the furniture to my liking with a new sense of anticipation and possibility. I even had my own Dictaphone and secretarial service. Now it was getting exciting.

Very soon, I noticed that sitting behind a desk day in and day out left me out of shape. To remedy this I tried jogging in the area, but the air quality was so bad I soon gave it up. I tried out for the local class "A" baseball team, the Hamilton Red Wings, and was selected as a back-up catcher. I usually worked each game in the "bull pen" warming up pitchers who were called in to relieve the starter. It was good exercise in a league that was much more professional than my teams back in Victoria. I even played in a few games, but it required a major commitment of time for practices and games as well as travel. My priority was keeping up with my studies and hospital administration work.

Quickly, June 1967 arrived. I'll never forget going out each morning to buy the daily newspaper. I made a point of keeping abreast of world events and that morning, thick black headlines glared out, "War in Israel." [23] Up until then, that little desert country in the Middle East always seemed so far away to me, but the events of this conflict brought the land and people of Israel right into my world. The world stood amazed at how quickly the conflict ended. Who had ever heard of a 6 - day war? What a miracle: Jerusalem was now back in Jewish hands. Somehow I remembered reading in the Bible that Jerusalem would come back into the hands of the Jews so I looked it up and discovered that for the first time in 2,000 years the Holy City was united under Jewish sovereignty. That fact made a deep impression on me.

Did Jesus refer to this development when He said in Luke 21:23, *"Jerusalem will be trodden down by the Gentiles until the time of the Gentiles is fulfilled."* (NKJ)
Vociferously I read everything: from Scripture to historical books to the daily newspapers. I had to know about the significance of modern Israel. I read, trying to understand. I was fascinated by the prophetic significance of this unique land. My heart was moved by the love of Father God for His People. What a love story! I ate up the passages telling how He longed for, cajoled, rebuked and even wept over His people Israel. He promised to once again return them to their land,

---

[23] The Six Day War as described in the *Hamilton Spectator*, June 2, 1967

which He did in 1948. I saw it as 'history in action!'

It is really "His story" I thought to myself. Little did I know that one day my life would be completely involved in Jerusalem and Israel, and that my sons and grandsons would be planted in that land. Also, I could never have foreseen myself writing film scripts or making documentaries to be used worldwide by the Israeli Foreign Ministry. I was still asleep to the call 'to broadcast' news events from Israel and link them to the eternal words of the Hebrew prophets spoken from Jerusalem. My audience would be the world.

The Bible exhorts, *"do not to despise the day of small beginnings."* During those first few months in Hamilton, it came clear to me that I was on my way.

"Yes," I told myself while leaning back in my desk chair, in my new office, "this is **my** good day of small beginnings."

Timeless Secrets

"For I know the thoughts that I think toward you, says the Lord, thoughts of peace and not of evil, to give you a future and a hope."
Jeremiah 29:11

Man only limits God! But one can choose to look for Him at every turn of our lives or not. If we do "look up" then when we "look back" it's not so hard to discern that He has been with us all along.

This last chapter has taken us into many situations, some heart breaking, others requiring endurance. Both Meridel and I were being tested so that our 'faith' would be as natural as our next breath. This means wanting to listen and to learn. God looks at our hearts, and gives us the desires of our hearts when they are for Him. You will be amazed at how He will open to you His treasuries in the Holy Spirit. Little did I know that, by showing Meridel's slides of India the Lord was beginning a career for me in media? It began with my love for Him, and then Meridel and my desire to share her medical work with others. An invisible seed in my mind eventually grew into my life's work.

When you are in a study program or some line of work, do not worry if, at the moment, you do not know your exact career goals. Let the Lord lead you into His perfect will for your life. Be sure to make time to meditate on the Word of God as diligently as you study your courses.

Here is the Lord's success plan:

"This Book of the Law [teaching and statutes] shall not depart from your mouth, but you shall meditate in it day and night that you may observe to do according to all that is written in it. For then you will make your way prosperous, and then you will have good success." Joshua 1:8

Chapter 10

In All Your Learning Get Wisdom!

"These Scriptures, hand painted in your Tibetan tradition, describe the King of all mankind and will teach you about the King of Love… ." Meridel speaking to the King of Mustang

My residency year in Hospital Administration went by very quickly. That was actually a blessing in disguise as I was missing Meridel more and more. She was faithful to keep sending me her letters, which by now were arriving about every ten days, even though she was also very busy. Her slides of India continued to show her sensitivity and were deeply moving because of the needs of the people all around her.

Hospitals are very active places. At 08:30 each morning I met with the senior management team for the daily briefing. The group consisted of Ray Walker, and John Haselhurst, the Administrators, Dr. George Woodward, the Associate Director, Miss Margaret Charters, the Director of Nursing and me. It was a brand new learning experience but I managed to keep up by taking notes. I was intrigued to learn how decisions were made. Quickly I realized that vitally important issues were always carefully discussed. The opinions of each of the management team were considered. Sometimes the relevant department head was called in for further consultation and fact finding. I discovered that searching out as many details as possible on any given topic was essential for making good decisions.

I also realized the value of clear communication skills. An effective leader has to be able to quickly analyze information and then effortlessly think and speak on his or her feet. Confidence building and the fostering of a team spirit within an organization started from the top and worked its way down.

Management's purpose was to create a positive and inspirational atmosphere in the hospital that ultimately benefited the patients who were, after all, the ones we wanted to serve and hopefully help. We also had a weekly meeting with both management teams from the Hamilton and Henderson Generals.

That meeting was always presided over by Dr Bill Noonan, Executive Director of the entire operation. He was a no nonsense man, a brilliant communicator, and a tough leader who demanded excellence from his staff. The Chief Financial Officer, Bob Krebs was an acerbic, cynical Englishman, Bill's alter ego. He swore like a trooper but his financial reports were spot on, providing the necessary information required by management to steer the ship, as it were, through rough fiscal waters. As I look back, I realize that I was given a plum residency location. Professor Eugenia Stuart, my U of T residency mentor, had placed me in Hamilton. I'm sure she did it to toughen me up. Looking back, I fondly recall those days, because I internalized many basic principles of management that have benefited my life these last four and a half decades. I learned how to make decisions under pressure, and graduated with the basic tools of how to run any size of corporation.

As my confidence grew I began to spend more off hours in the residence where I lived. There I met many interesting young doctors from Canada and around the world. Some were finishing their internship training and had gained 'hands on experience' in surgery, internal medicine, obstetrics, pediatrics, psychiatry, intensive care, emergency, geriatrics and oncology. As their year came to a close, these young doctors took their final written and oral exams at the Medical School of their enrollment. Once successful, after their seven years of rigorous study, they were awarded an MD degree and could then go into a local medical profession as a General Practitioner or Family Physician. You will soon discover how I became directly involved in a Family Practice Unit. Another option for the interns was to become a specialist which would require four more years of study and residency in their chosen field. The Hamilton General was a teaching hospital so we enjoyed the presence of numerous residents in various specialties.

Guy Favelle, a Swiss intern and I became good friends. He loved outdoor activities, especially mountain climbing. Then because he didn't mind getting his hands dirty, he taught me how to tune up my Triumph TR3. "It's just like doing surgery, messy but necessary," he'd tell me.

"Let's take your car for a test run," he suggested, raising his head out from under the hood. We drove around Hamilton on the ring road, and he pushed the speed up over 100 mph or 160 kilometers per hour. That was fast in 1968. Fortunately, there were few cars on the road that day and the Ontario Highway Police Patrol radar system missed us.

By September I had to go back to the U of T for Friday classes on how to create my Masters Degree thesis. It had to include original research and discovery concerning some aspect of health care. Dr Faulkner, my advisor, suffered from severe spinal arthritis. Bending over to give me instructions, he grimaced with pain. His skin was almost transparent but his mind was clear, calm and creative. I shared several ideas, and we finally settled on my making a study in two different General Practitioner's clinics. Each clinic had four doctors, their nurses and a central receptionist. One was a traditional GP clinic in the community while the other was a Family Practice Unit located in the Henderson General Hospital's out patient health care services clinic. It operated under the auspices of the McMaster University Medical School, Graduate Program in Family Medicine.

The thesis objective was simple yet original: I was to examine and monitor each nurse's activities in both clinics. I had to measure exactly how much responsibility the doctors were delegating to the nurses for direct patient care. This required me to go to the clinics, establish a range of activities that the nurses carried out and codify them.

How much time they spent per day on each activity was the question. The forward thinking of the day was that the Family Practice Unit doctors were delegating more direct patient care to their nurses than in traditional GP Clinics. To my knowledge, never before had anyone measured the actual time spent by a nurse with each patient in such a comparative study.

When I wrote to Meridel about the time consuming project she teased me, *"After six long years of university you have finally figured out a way to legally watch pretty young nurses all day long..."*

Writing my thesis was exacting and technically demanding, requiring analysis, tables and graphs. I measured each nurses' activities and projected them unto graphs. This enabled me to make clear comparisons, and keep the footnotes and quotes in proper reference order by numbers. Remember, this was before the era of computers and the internet. Makes me sound ancient, doesn't it? We did have electric typewriters though!

Finally, my results showed that the Family Physicians did indeed delegate more direct patient care to their nurses when compared to the traditional GP's. In my mind I couldn't help but contrast their eight hour shift with the hours and hours my sweetheart spent every day out there with the Sisters, doing their very best for the poorest of the poor on the hills of North West Bengal.

With little time for socializing, I appreciated the occasional dinner with Jean and Norm Smith, Mom's cousins, in Hamilton, who treated me like family. Jean even made scones and served them with steaming cups of tea, homemade raspberry jam and, of course, whipping cream. Their down to earth goodness reminded me of home.
These visits were a perfect antidote to the many trips back and forth to Dr. Faulkner's office in Toronto. He gave me endless recommendations and always, it seemed, yet more changes. I was under stress to get my thesis finished on time.

By February 1968, I had completed my research. A literature search at the time showed there were no similar studies done on this topic. After extensive proofreading my secretary, Joanne, typed out the final draft, which was bound into two separate volumes. One was given to my Faculty Advisor at the U of T and one I still have in my library. The date given me 'to defend' my thesis was April 26, 1968 at 09:00. Without this oral examination I could not graduate.

By this time I noticed that my weekly letters from Meridel had trailed off. With only one letter in February and one in March, I became concerned. I had also cut down on my letter writing to her due to my thesis deadline and final exams looming on the horizon. But, I sensed that she was doing a lot of soul searching because she mentioned going to Nepal with her very special friends Roy and Alma Hagen.

Meridel:

Roy and Alma Hagen, Americans, spent years preparing to live and work in Nepal. However, their application for entrance was rejected in 1948. In those days, Nepal, a Hindu kingdom was ruled by a god-King, and remained firmly closed to the West. Some of the only foreigners permitted entrances were medical doctors and tourists.
The literacy rate was only 2% and the Hagen's goal was eventually to establish a publishing facility. It was obvious to these dedicated Christians, that a modern version of the biblical narrative was needed in every day Nepalese. Undaunted, they moved to Darjeeling, located at India's eastern border with Nepal.

They studied the language and later began a Bible School for Nepalese, training them to work with their own people and created a corre-spondence course for those wanting to study Scriptures in Nepali or Hindi. Through the publishing program modern versions of the Bible found their way into Nepal for the first time in history. Nepal has a fierce record of persecution of the early Christian believers.

Spunky and vivacious, Alma was the mother of four very bright and active sons by the time I met her at a social function in Darjeeling. With an exemplary heart to serve others, she invited me for a home cooked meal and became like a big sister. One of the most positive women I have ever met, her joyful laughter was her way of showing love. She connected with the many local ethnic groups and always wore an Indian sari.

I best remember her navigational skills in monsoon season.
Alma, clad in a delicate sari, drove their mud splattered jeep along the slippery precipices on winding muddy roads.

Often skidding around rutted trails she was on her King's business. She took me along on trips to visit local towns people up and down the business districts located on the steep hills of Darjeeling. Here I saw another side of life very distinct from the utter and abject poverty that I worked with daily assisting outstanding Missionaries of Charity servants. I met many internationals, Anglo Nepalese, Indian Nepalese, students from Assam, mountain climbers, bankers, clothiers, photographers and artists. I watched how Alma reached out, encouraging and kind to everyone. Back in her humble home, I also noticed how she made do with very little. For example, to create her weekly children's radio broadcast without a proper sound booth, she made her own by sitting under a blanket in a clothes closet.

Her children's radio program was carried by short wave over the Far East Broadcasting Company reaching English speaking children all over Asia. Kids everywhere wrote back saying they loved Alma's stories. The other thing I noticed about Alma was her basket of letters, which seemed to accompany her like a woman's favorite hand bag! I couldn't get over her dedication in answering those who took time to write her with a personal note. Little did I realize then that I too would spend my life away from my native land and I would be sending letters out to encourage and help our partners to understand and support our work in the media. To this day I try to answer them all.

One day on a sunny morning I met Alma, while on my rounds to the various drop off spots for the oil and powdered milk that the sisters and I distributed. Quickly, she stopped her jeep, drew up along side of our Land Rover and after greeting the sisters, told me about two very unusual American women, Ruth and Susan. Over the years they visited the publishing center in Darjeeling. Then, Alma invited me to travel overland with her family from Darjeeling to Katmandu Nepal in their jeep. We would be guests of a large family; the American father was the Administrator of the large mission hospital there. She also mentioned that in the course of this visit she wanted me to meet Ruth and Susan, who had contacts with the Nepali Royal family. I lost no time asking Sister Damien for permission to take leave.

Smiling, she said in her slow and barely audible English, "Go, Meridel, you've been working very hard and need a break."

It was during this time that my letters to Jay slowed considerably. I had been released to enjoy a brand new adventure and there was no time to write. Especially not from the back of a crowded jeep making its way across bumpy Indian fields and on up into the dry hot jungle lands of Southern Nepal.

In Katmandu, Alma and I were invited out for dinner by her friends Ruth and Susan. They chose a restaurant in the prestigious Royal Hotel frequented by mountain climbers, tiger hunters and local and international businessmen. After dinner we relaxed in the hotel's overstuffed leather chairs close to the fire in the famous Yak and Yeti Lounge. Tiger skins covered the floor and walls. Completing the ambience was a circular fireplace, which warmed the chilly room. The nearby bar was empty. We sipped our coffee in this warm and congenial atmosphere. Cheerily the fire crackled heating the chilly night air in this high altitude 'roof top of the world.' We were com-fortable enough with each to tell snippets of our many and varied experiences.

Jay:

When Meridel wrote me about her experience in this posh Katmandu hotel I became alarmed when I read the following:

"Alma and I were prayed for to receive the infilling of the Holy Spirit." Meridel went on to explain, "With great difficulty, I spoke in other tongues. At that time I was given a prophecy that I would soon go to visit the people whose tonal language I had spoken!" She also wrote; "Several hotel guests pulled their chairs up around us and watched as we prayed and praised God. One gentleman, a local guest, told Ruth that I had spoken dialect of Tibetan."

My first response was "Wow"! Suddenly concerned, I couldn't even imagine what was happening to Meridel. Being afraid, my response was curt and hasty. "Grant and I asked for this blessing over a year and a half ago and nothing happened!"

After I cautioned her against religious fanatics, tension began to build up in our relationship.

Meridel:

Following my experience with the Holy Spirit, and having spoken a 'known' language' of the area, I was given the opportunity to trek up into the mountainous region of my new language. I shared this unique adventure a few days later with Susan. We flew from Katmandu to the village of Pokhara. In fact it was a hair raising experience. Descending rapidly in a four seated Cessna, I was shocked to see how swiftly the pilot landed in a virtual cow pasture. First, though, he had to sound a fog horn out of the window of the cockpit. It worked, scaring cows that ran off of the runway just in time. This was a low tech way to clear space for our bumpy landing.

We headed straight for the local market to find an interpreter. Carefully we explained in very simple English, that we wanted to trek up into the rugged Annapurna Range in north western Nepal. Pointing at the bundles lying at our feet, we explained, "We need porters to carry these little Nepalese books telling of the wonder and love of the greatest King of all. Could you find us reliable porters to carry our cargo and lead us high up into the secluded villages there?"

The interpreter grinned, nodding as the plan unfolded. He easily found us porters for our extended trek. Sir Edmund Hilary, the first man to conquer Mt. Everest, had taken a similar route. In no time at all four bronzed and muscled men gathered around. Each wore a wool toque on his head, even though their wide calloused feet were bare. Chewing 'beetle nut' leaves laced with lime they looked us and our cargo over with interest giving us friendly, albeit quite toothless grins.

Releasing their large woven baskets from their backs, held in place by strong head bands, four of them squatted, right there as the interpreter explained what the job entailed. As if in agreement, they took turns forcefully spitting the red beetle nut juice into the powdery dust at their feet. It was mid-afternoon when they heaved our 'treasures' onto their backs. Among the Gospels of John, I carefully hid a different package, entrusted to me. I knew there would be a special soul who was to receive it. More on this subject coming up.

Having befriended Sherpa watchmen in South India, I felt strangely at home, ready for the adventure. Our porters were local villagers. Sherpa's, renowned for their fierce loyalty and bravery, are hired worldwide as body guards and watchmen. But in this area they are hired as guides and porters to lead the mountain climbers on their expeditions up into the highest peaks on earth.

The porters turned out to be diamonds in the rough. Born with huge lung capacities, they are able to bear heavy burdens in rarefied mountain air. The price of the sojourn was set in Nepali rupees. They agreed, that with the emptying of each basket, it's carrier would descend back to Pokhara. All arrangements were finalized. With their burdens in place we began. Susan was conspicuous in western dress, I wore local garb and we followed meekly on through the market, out of the village and up into the cool foothills by sunset. Many booklets were distributed that first evening. A road side inn, reminiscent of the ancient khans of Asia used by travelers over the centuries, provided us shelter and a flat wooden surface as a bed.

The next full day began in the cool of dawn. We continued on the ascending trail. It snaked its way up and up. By mid-morning we stopped to catch our breath among narrow stone terraces. The vistas out over the deep bottomless valleys that had disappeared out of sight, were breathtaking. Ancient hand crafted terraces stood preserving what little top soil there was in this harsh region. A hard won reclamation project of precious land up and down the steep mountain sides, reflected the hardy tenacious nature of these village farmers.

It was harvest time. Golden stocky grain, bowed full mature heads, waved gently in the cool mountain breezes. Stopping to rest, we watched the ancient process of cutting and tying the grain into bundles for drying. It was being done the same way it had always been done down through the centuries. Little had changed. The entire village turned out, from the eldest to the youngest child who was carried around on the hip of his mother or big sister. Suckling babies were bundled on their working mother's backs.

The wheat farmers Meridel met on her mountain trek in Nepal

Seeing us round the narrow trail with four burdened porters, the sunburned villagers stopped harvesting. They dropped their scythes and came running and smiling. Here in the heart of their world, happily we could fill their eager hands with the little books of life. No one refused the gift. Twenty years had passed since 1948 when the literacy rate was only 2%. Now educated most of the young Nepalese were hungry to read anything they could get their hands on.

After only one day full day of hiking higher and higher, the rarefied air proved to be too strenuous for Susan. Panting, she stopped and asked me if I wanted to return down the mountain with her. I breathed a prayer for direction and felt strongly to continue on up the trail. We said goodbye and she began her decent toward the plains. I was placed in a protected position between the three remaining porters.

I followed them slowly and carefully as we crossed a crevice by means of a hand-woven suspension bridge strung above the abyss. It was the only way forward. And in dozens of other villages the inhabitants ran out of their mud and stone houses after me begging for a book. The supply was going down. Only two porters were left. We continued to climb higher and higher until nightfall.

You may wonder why I was on this journey in the first place. Even Westerners living and working in Nepal at the time, never even considered such an undertaking. Perhaps it was a case of 'fools rush in where angels fear to tread'? Perhaps?. But when this door of opportunity opened, I did not hesitate to go through it. I love adventure. I had not been fearful in other cultures and am comfortable being alone. The truth is, I seldom feel alone. In this case I had those capable porters with me as well. The whole thing came by inspiration and opportunity. I believe that the 'tonal' language that I choked back and stumbled over the night of my encounter with the Holy Spirit was part of this miraculous connection with these very special people.

I remembered how my jaw ached, because it was so difficult for me to trust and relax to allow the foreign sounds to issue forth. Those utterances, so strange to my own ears seemed like gibberish. I remembered that in the hotel bar not one negative word was spoken. Recalling this strange encounter gave me physical courage to keep putting one sore foot in front of the other.

Ruth had told me that I would go to the people whose language I was speaking. So, I knew that I was here on a divine 'assignment' and never experienced a moment of fear. I was filled with expectation, even though I became completely exhausted in the rarefied air and was only able to drink water. Taking my worn running shoes off at night and dropping them wearily to the floor, I felt as though my poor feet had expanded two shoe sizes. I lay down in my dusty, sweaty clothes. Sleep was an instant mercy.

Two days later, while trekking along a high snow covered pass some-where in the Annapurna Mountain Range, I was met by the forerun-ners of a descending Royal yak train.

A Yak train in the Himalayan Mountains

One of them delivered the following message to me personally and my porter gasped at the special news:
"The King of Mustang has heard about you and desires to meet you. You are invited to have lunch with him today in the next village, higher up on the trail."
What? Who is this King of Mustang? I wondered. I never heard of him or his kingdom of Mustang!
Sweaty and tired after four days of strenuous hiking, I stopped at the next roadside inn to wash my hands and face. Struggling in the rarefied air I had been too tired to eat, but now I knew I had to prepare myself to encounter a monarch and to eat his royal fare.

Later, I learned that this king ruled over the Kingdom of Mustang. This royal protectorate of his lay in a remote, isolated Tibetan speaking part of the world squeezed between Nepal and Tibet. This was a feudal society, with no telephones or other connection to civilization.

They had no automobiles, electricity or running water. Until recently, the local inhabitants believed that the world was flat! You can imagine it was with a keen sense of anticipation that I approached the next village and waited for the king's arrival on his annual trek down the mountains for supplies. First, I watched as his servants laid down a raised platform or dais, which allowed him to sit above the common-ers. As the king approached I stood back among the gawking villagers. His throne was a simple wooden chair, probably borrowed from a lo-cal. A rich silk tapestry was thrown over it, all was in readiness for his royal highness. He came quietly and sat down on the makeshift throne.

I was invited to move forward. Bowing, I greeted him according to protocol and honor and was instructed to present him with three white gossamer scarves or "katas" which had been spread over my wrists. Keeping my head bowed I approached this mountain king on his throne. According to Tibetan custom I put the katas on his outstretched arms. The nod of his royal head told me that he had received my peace offering.

Then I presented him with the most valuable gift of all - a unique hand written Bible. It was the special package I had carried up into the mountains by faith.

Instinctively, I knew this magnificent Bible was reserved for him. It was a work of art, hand written in black ink using a calligraphy brush on parchment leaves of rice paper. It looked identical to Tibetan Buddhist scriptures found in ancient mountain monasteries. Their custom is to read each unbound page and then lift it up from the pile and place it carefully face down on the outspread silk directly behind. The entire Bible was ten inches or twenty-five cm thick and held together by saffron silk wrapping cloths.

Bowing, the king showed his appreciation for my gift. I was then led to a hand woven Tibetan carpet laid down on the ground. This was my seat. The Tibetan kata or offering scarf symbolizes purity and compassion. It is usually made of white silk symbolizing the pure heart of the giver. This ceremonial scarf is common in Tibetan and Mongolian cultures and may be presented at any festive occasion to the host. The guest must remain two and a half meters in front of and below the king. I sat on this guest carpet in front of a wooden stand. Servants brought a large silver tray of food placing it on the stand in front of me. The royal banquet consisted of curd, stew, rice and Nan bread.

While we ate in silence I discreetly observed the royal monarch. He was tall and rugged looking with a dry and weathered skin. Rows of wrinkles ran across his high brow, accentuating his almond shaped eyes. Bright scarlet ribbons woven into his long braided hair circled his head as a crown. His dark Tibetan robe made of silk crossed over his chest and hung to his knees. A rich fur lined chestnut colored jacket of silk brocade hung over one bare shoulder leaving one arm free. Dark baggy trousers tucked into high leather hand sewn boots turned up at the toe, completed his royal garb.

Through an interpreter the king inquired, "Have you heard my language before?"
"Yes, it has been my privilege to work with Tibetan refugees in Darjeeling," I answered. "As you know sir, they have fled Tibet. I help them with their medical and social needs and consider it a great honor to do so." I was touched by his inquiring respectful manner, especially about his language.

"Where are you from?" he asked.

"I was born in Canada and have come to India to serve as a nurse,"
I responded. "I work along side the local people and teach them the
skills I learned in Canada. In return I receive the same wage they do."
Obviously surprised, he asked "Are you frightened to be alone here?"
"Actually not at all," I replied. "I believe that I came on a special
assignment to give you the Book of Books. May I now tell you about a
king named David? You will find his wise words in the Scriptures I gave
you".

"Why would you bother to bring such a gift to me?" He was curious.
"These Scriptures are hand painted in the Tibetan way. They describe
the King of all mankind. They will teach you about the King of Love.
He is a Servant King who called himself the Son of Man. He came to
show us the love of Father God. One day all men everywhere on earth
will see him as the King of Kings... for all tribes, tongues and nations."
"I will look in these very special Scriptures. Thank you" was the careful
reply through his interpreter. The royal head nodded ever so slightly in
my direction.

Then, as quickly as the encounter unfolded, it was over. His yak train
drew near. The King mounted his beautifully decorated yak and once
settled on the embroidered saddle, he nodded farewell.
Standing on the side of the narrow trail, I watched the king depart with
regal authority. His considerable entourage moved slowly, amidst
shouts from the yak herders. The living train of sure footed beasts
lumbered past me. The yaks were tied together by thick ropes strung
through their nose rings and their tinkling bells added a very special
sound that followed them on down the steep and narrow rocky slope.

Now, I knew that my trekking assignment was completed. Paying and
releasing the remaining porter I began my own descent back to
Pokhara. The two and a half days descent, although quicker than the
climb up, was often more difficult because your knees take an awful
beating. As you read on you will discover the vitally important
significance of the timing of my departure.

Timeless Secrets

"But seek first the kingdom of God and His righteousness, and all these things shall be added to you." Matthew 6:33

Putting into perspective one's priorities is always a good exercise in life. Otherwise how can you be sure that you are on the course that God intended for you? Every one of us living in the privileged West has the possibility to search out what we are gifted at and can find ways to pursue it. The majority of human beings on earth never have this option. At that time in my life, I was very busy learning all I could about running a hospital, and I felt that I was preparing for the future. My goal was to be a good provider for my family, and to do a job that would make a difference in society. Meridel, on the other hand, was 'out there on the edge' saving life in all of its rawness. The extremity she lived with created a hunger in her mind and heart to know more of the reality of the Kingdom of God. There in a nutshell is the great tension between the natural and spiritual worlds. Amazingly, Meridel found it very easy to speak to the King of Mustang about the Kingdom of Heaven with God as King. As head of a kingdom he immediately 'got it'.

On the other hand, there I was in comfortable North America, also seeking the Kingdom of God but in a much less dramatic fashion. It's clear that someone has to go and someone has to stay. Thank God that King David taught his troops the principle that "those who stay home and faithfully watch the 'stuff' get the same reward as those who go out to the front lines in battle." The key is that everyone has to be faithful where ever they are!

"For who will heed you in this matter? But as his part is who goes down to the battle, so shall his part be who stays by the supplies; they shall share alike." 1 Samuel 30:24

Chapter 11

Witnesses

"I stood up behind my desk and firmly spoke into the telephone, "Meridel, now look, we got engaged in person so I think we should get disengaged in person, face to face. Please come back to Canada so we will really know what to do!" After a long pause she said quietly, "I'll come..."

Meridel:

As I stood alone waving goodbye to the King of Mustang somewhere in the Annapurna Range of the Himalayas in Nepal, my heart was thumping with joy. What a very special privilege I had just been granted. Gratefulness overflowed my heart as did the tears in my eyes. Watching the royal yak train slowly and rhythmically move down the mountain out of sight I sensed two things; my assignment in the Himalayas was completed and secondly I must immediately begin to descend the same torturous route down to the plains and return to Katmandu as quickly as possible.

On the way back through the villages where I had spread the "good seed" of the Scriptures, I noticed that many of the booklets had been gathered up by Chinese communist infiltrators. They were thrown into piles and burned publicly. I prayed that the majority had been hidden. I made the descent back to Pokhara in record time.
The sense of urgency was providential.

Returning to Kathmandu on the last flight from Pokhara, several days later, I discovered that the Nepali god-King had recently experienced a massive heart attack and lay in a coma. While the country mourned news spread that the borders of Nepal were being sealed.
This requiring the fast exit of all tourists. Ruth, Susan and I were on the very last flight to New Delhi the next morning.

When the borders were sealed indefinitely, persecution of local believers began because Hindu leaders considered them to be a threat.[25]

Tired but happy I made my way by train from New Delhi back to Darjeeling. Sister Damien, head of the Missionaries of Charity, was waiting for me with open arms. World wide Catholic believers were receiving the infilling of the Holy Spirit and I very openly shared my recent experiences. This kind and wise leader asked me to explain in more detail. Sister Damien listened intently, silently nodding her approval. I also found the courage to say that I felt my work with them was completed. Sister Damien promised to share this inspiring news in Hindi with all of her sisters who would be praying for my future. I was excited to be moving on, but also filled with a deep sense of loss. I had made so many friends and knew that I would never see them again. It was a bitter sweet experience.

CUSO head office approved, and arranged for my return to New Delhi for the necessary medical exams and debriefing before returning to Canada. I packed my bags and said good-bye to my cadre of friends in Darjeeling, including the Tibetan monks, who were deeply appreciative of my work with the Missionaries of Charity concerning their own poverty stricken refugees. They knew we helped to save many of their lives. Other special friends who came to say farewell were many of the Sisters of Cluny from Ireland.

I was deeply moved by the trekking experience, but nothing could compare to the in-filling of the Holy Spirit. New horizons were beckoning. Ruth and Susan asked me to join them in their life of adventure for the Lord. I sensed, in fact that they were trying to talk me out of my engagement to Jay. They even told me to take the gold ring off, if you please. About this time Jay's letter arrived in which he asked ,

"Why have you stopped writing to me as often as before?
Are you confused? Are you still in love with me?"

---

[25] Hagen, Alma. *Then Nepal's Door Opened*

He could imagine that the prospect of married life for me back in Canada would seem pretty dull and dreary compared to my exciting encounters in India and Nepal. After all, I was out here on the cutting edge, living a life most people only dream of.

I struggled, because of the fact that since childhood I knew that I had a 'call' on my life. Ruth and Susan told me that the 'perfect will of God' meant celibacy. They intimated that 'if' I married Jay, the 'call' would be thwarted or null and void. Susan even suggested that I just go back to Canada, see Jay and even sleep with him!
I quote: "Get it out of your system, because there is no such thing as love, it is just lust."
Revolted by this suggestion I didn't tell a soul about these cruel insinuations. Consequently I was pained and torn because they didn't even consider Jay and me as engaged. This may sound unimportant to our readers, but I was a committed and determined person and would do what I believed to be 'God's will'! But now I was unsure, even though Jay and I had prayed and pledged ourselves to each other.

Jay:

Meridel shared one of my last letters with Alma, her trusted friend, who was also a married woman with a lifetime of experience.
"Do you think that a phone call to Jay would be in order?" she asked her.
After reading my letter Alma handed Meridel the phone. "Marry him! He will be a wonderful provider for you. There is blessing in his hands. Here, call him now!"

When Meridel's call came through I was amazed at the clarity of the connection. It was to be our one and only phone call. Closing my office door I said, "Hello, Meridel! It is so good to hear your voice." Sensing the strained silence I asked, "What's going on? Is there some-thing wrong?" Our circumstances had become radically different and frankly, at that point, it was hard to know what our emotions and feelings really were about each other. It had been a long separation. All I knew was that I still deeply loved and respected her.

"I will soon be released from CUSO and have the opportunity to travel the world with my American friends," she said.

"Are you saying you want to break off our engagement?"

"May be..."

After what had happened in her life it didn't come as a total surprise to me, but I was still shocked. Standing behind my desk I firmly told her, "Now look, we got engaged in person and I think we should get disengaged in person, in fact face to face. Please come back to Canada so we will really know what to do!"

After a long pause she said, "I'll come." And then in a lighter tone, "I'll let you know my arrival time in Toronto by telegram."

After we hug up I felt relieved because there would be a resolution of the situation in person. Busying myself with work I knew I had to trust God that I had indeed heard the 'still small voice' when almost two years previously He said: "There is your wife, the mother of your sons."

Meridel in Darjeeling, March 1969, with Kipu. Sadly, both puppies died in quarantine on their way to the USA.

Excerpt of of Meridel's last letters to Jay before leaving India:

"During my stay in Darjeeling, I fell in love with the Lhasa Apsos known as 'lion' dogs, used to guard the Buddhist temples in antiquity. Apsos are fiercely loyal creatures and will attack anything if threatened, no matter its size. When I was packing, a Sister called me to the visitor's room in the Convent. There stood a shy monk from one of the Tibetan temples. We had distributed food and medicines together. He bowed; his broad grin was toothless."

"He then took two adorable Lhasa Apso puppies out from inside his wide sleeves and placed them in my arms. I was speechless and thanked him with a bow. What a meaningful going away gift. Delighted, I gave them Tibetan names. The very small blond female I called Kipu, or 'princess' in Tibetan, and the male I named Kusho, or 'brave one.' We will have to figure out a way to get them into Canada..."

"Dinar, my roommate gave me her mother's engagement sari, it is a deep ruby red heavily bordered with hand embroidered silver threads. Over the months we have talked heart to heart over many issues. Her religion centers on belief in 'earth, wind, fire and water'. Trying to bridge our cultural gap, I shared my faith in the love of our Heavenly Father. This sari, her priceless gift, said it all."

Meridel:

I left part of my heart in those high foothills of Darjeeling. As I boarded the narrow gage cog-wheel railway, a band of souls, whose lives I shared for that brief time waved and smiled from the platform. The Catholic contingent consisted of Sister Mary Joseph, my house mother from the Sisters of Cluny, Sister Damien, head of the Missionaries of Charity and Father Bob, a Jesuit priest, head of food distribution to the poor. The Protestant contingent consisted of Alma and her young son Kenny. Beside my roommate Dinar were students from Assam that I had counseled. Also Hindus, Anglo-Indians and Anglo-Nepalese, shop owners, and a Tibetan monk represented the many friends I was leaving. What a vibrant bouquet of life they made each with a unique color, shape and perfume!

The shrill train whistle sounded and black billows rose from the smoke stack of the little green engine. I leaned out of the narrow window, waving, laughing and crying. As the train rounded the first extreme switchback descending toward Calcutta, I lost sight of my precious friends. Two little puppies poked their noses out of their wicker basket and looked into my face with tails wagging. Leaping into my arms, they licked the tears streaming down my face.

In Calcutta I immediately went to say good-bye to Mother Theresa and to thank her for the privilege of working for her and with her outstanding sisters in Darjeeling.
I walked quietly into her office and when she acknowledged me I said respectfully, "Mother Theresa, it has been life changing to serve with your selfless sisters. Thank you for opening this door for me. I have been greatly enriched, thank you."
She looked tired and diminutive behind a large wooden desk in a darkened room with closed shutters to keep out the afternoon sun and heat. The fan whirled slowly over-head, laboring to move the stifling air. It was a short meeting, and as I was about to turn and leave, Mother Theresa fixed her eyes on me with a penetrating gaze. Clearing her throat, in a simple matter of fact, motherly tone, she asked, "There is a young man in your life, yes?"
"Yes," I responded meekly.
"Well," she said with firmness, "you need to go home and marry him!"
"Thank you for this insight, Mother Theresa. It is very timely for my life." I left quietly.

Jay:

Because she still was not sure what to do about her future, the words of Mother Theresa's kept ringing over and over in her mind. Once in New Delhi, she went through medical testing which qualified her for ongoing intensive medical treatment in Canada for a serious infestation of amoeba and other parasites in her intestinal tract and an enlarged liver. Having lived in a closed military zone in West Bengal, she also had to be debriefed by CUSO. Her flight was prepared for the 15th of April. She received her last pay check of nine dollars.

Here is another excerpt from Meridel's letter to me:
"During my last week in Delhi, I was invited by Ruth and Susan to experience an Indian Christian tent meeting. The visiting evangelist was a big, burly Texan who had lost one arm in a farm accident. What a striking contrast this blond Texas cowboy with a heavy drawl was to the fine-boned dark skinned locals. He walked over to me and asked to have a word with me. "Yes," I nodded.
"Young lady," his manner was honest and straight forward, lowering his voice to a whisper he said, "I saw you at the meeting here yesterday. I don't know who you are; I don't know anything about you, but last night the Lord woke me up to pray for you and gave me this message. "There is a young man in your life. You need to go home and marry him! Then he bent over and whispered, "Do not listen to the two women who brought you here!" "

Meridel:

I was at war with myself over Jay. Ruth and Susan had almost convinced me that I was being selfish. How could God allow me to be so happy and have a love like this in my life? Did I not have to suffer? But, now I dared to believe for the best and highest. Receiving this clear encouragement from an unknowing stranger definitely helped me to believe in our relationship.

Jay:

From the perspective of time, I see that Meridel was amazed because she had spoken to no one about these things. She had two women telling her not to marry, but three other deeply spiritual people were saying the opposite. They were Alma Hagen, Mother Theresa and now the Texan evangelist. The Bible says that 'out of the mouth of two or three witnesses every, word will be established.'[26] I say, 'Praise God! Thank you Alma, Mother Theresa and the faithful Texan!'

With her plane tickets in hand, and following her debriefing by CUSO, she sent me a telegram about her travel details:

---

[26] Deuteronomy 19:15b; Matthew 18:16; 2 Corinthians 13:1

To Mr. Jay Rawlings. Stop. Arriving, CP#106 on Apr. 15th at 13:10 via London. Stop. See you. Stop. Love, Meridel Stop.

I had only two days to get ready for her arrival. I arranged for her to stay in the Medical Library dorm across the road from the hospital. Putting my nervous energy to good use I washed and waxed the Triumph TR3.
On April 15th, I left the hospital in plenty of time to get to the Toronto International Airport to meet her plane. It was a lovely sunny but cool spring day in southern Ontario and I waited outside the "Arrivals" gate at Terminal 1 with great expectation. Lots of excited people came through the sliding doors to meet their loved ones. As the automatic doors opened and closed, I strained to see inside and finally caught a glimpse of her waiting for her luggage.

She was beautiful, wearing a beige raw silk sleeveless coast over a cedar green silk dress. A soft scarf lay around her neck, brown wedge shoes and small matching leather purse completed her ensemble. Impatiently I paced back and forth until she finally appeared, carrying her big heavy black suitcase. I was nervous; she was nervous. She was shy; I was shy. When she approached I quickly went over to help her, threw my arms around her and just held her close. We both melted. "I missed you so very much," I confessed. "But now it's like we've never been apart."
"I know, I missed you too," she whispered.

As I lifted her suitcase on to the luggage cart the handle came off. Wanting to be suave I felt so foolish but it broke the ice and we both started to laugh. Instantly our endless lonely days and months had vanished.

Driving into Toronto on the crowded six-lane 401 Highway we made light conversation. En route she dug in her purse for our gold band I had given her in Vancouver. It seemed a thousand years away. Holding it up she said, "I'm not sure what to do with this."
"Here give it to me." While keeping my eyes on the road, I asked, "Please give me your left ring finger."

The ring slipped on easily and then, at the speed of ninety kilometers per hour I said, surprised at my boldness, "Now, please marry me and don't ever take it off again!"
Looking at me, Meridel responded, "Yes! Yes to both!"
The brief moment our eyes met was eternal.

By this time it was mid-afternoon and, before returning to Hamilton, I decided to play a prank on my friend Grant Bartlett. He had never met Meridel but had seen lots of her photos and had prayed for her. He was unaware of her quick return to Canada. Months before, he had given me the keys to his apartment just in case I ever needed it when in Toronto.

We took the Avenue Road exit and I pulled up in front of his apartment block. *Good,* I thought, *his car isn't here.* We made ourselves a cup of coffee and, shortly after, I heard him unlock the door.
At my prompting, Meridel hid in the pantry off the kitchen and closed the door. Grant was surprised to find me there but took it all in stride as we were good friends.
"Well, I'm sure glad to see you, Grant. I was really missing Meridel, but I thought I'd drop by while in the city."
"Yeah, good," he said, "it would be great to see her! Any news yet?"
"Well turn around and you will get the news directly!"
Grant was flabbergasted when Meridel stepped out of the closet.
He hugged her shyly. "Welcome home!"
"Thanks!" She smiled.

Together, we made a lovely Italian dinner and cracked open a bottle of champagne to celebrate Meridel's homecoming. We decided to get married as soon as possible for we had waited long enough.
Grant would be our best man. Looking at the calendar we chose Thursday, April 25th - just ten days away.

Timeless Secrets

*"He who finds a wife, finds a good thing,
and obtains favor from the LORD."* Proverbs 18:22

Marriage is the key building-block of society and it is under attack. Major attack! Marriages worldwide are breaking up at the rate of one every eight to ten seconds. More than 51% of marriages end in divorce in the USA and Canada. We are including Jews, Christians and non-believers alike in these figures.[27]

Marriage is God's idea. Creation was not complete until He formed Adam and created a wife, Eve, for him. She was handcrafted out of Adam's body from right next to his heart.

"Therefore a man shall leave his father and mother and be joined to his wife, and they shall become one flesh." Genesis 2:24

Eve was not called a wife but a "helpmeet," which means in Hebrew that she was like a mirror for Adam, so he could see himself as he really is and not as he thought he was!

"And the LORD God said, It is not good that man should be alone; I will make him a helper comparable to him." Genesis 2:18

The first husband and wife, father and mother of us all, were created to be a model of love and commitment to each other and their Creator They failed, and in that failure continue to be an example of blame, shame, disobedience and disappointment. This is not the end of the story however, only the beginning.

---

[27] http://www.cdc.gov/nchs/data/nvsr/ncvsr58/nvsr58 25 pff

I believe the most important decision a person ever makes is when he commits himself to his Creator. The second most important is when he commits himself to his spouse for the rest of his life. This principle applies equally to women. The first time is easy, the secret is to keep making the same commitment to the Lord and to wife/husband on a daily basis. Even though we fail, our God is a Father of mercy and helps to pick us up and show us the way of Life.

Like all couples, Meridel and I have had times of tension in our marriage, but I must say we have never considered divorce; murder perhaps, but divorce never! (Just kidding)

"Live joyfully with the wife whom you love all the days of your life... for that is your portion in life." Ecclesiastes 9:9

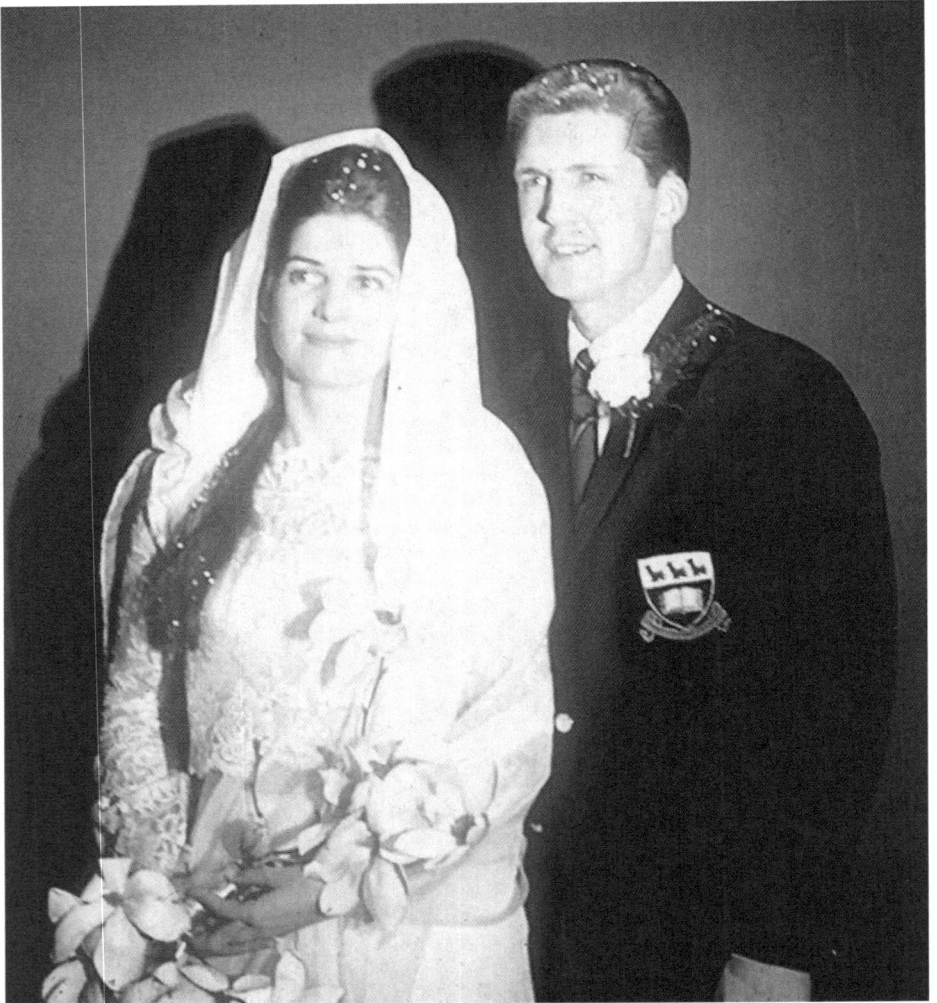

**Jay and Meridel married in Hamilton Ontario, Canada
April 25th 1968.**

Chapter 12

Magnolias

"Mrs. Rawlings," I chuckled over the clinic phone, "according to the test results... you are going to have a baby...no, we are going to have a baby."
"Oh... Mr. Rawlings," she responded very quietly.

Jay:

Our love story quickly unfolded and our relationship was thrown into high gear. The very next day, even with Meridel in jet lag, we decided to ask her friend, Rev. Paul McCarroll to marry us. Paul was Vicar of the Presbyterian Church in the frontier fishing town of Prince Rupert, BC, when he and his wife Kathy met and befriended Meridel years before while she was nursing at the hospital there. Subsequently, they had been assigned to Hamilton and were the obvious choice to perform our marriage ceremony.

I called Meridel's parents and formally asked them for her hand in marriage. Together they happily agreed and wished us every blessing. They made me promise that I would bring Meridel 'home' in the summer for a formal reception in Red Deer, Alberta. Her three little sisters insisted upon it. Also in the midst of my busy resident activities just before graduation, I was called into the office of my boss, Ray Walker. He sat me down, and to my surprise, offered me a job as Administrative Assistant in the Hamilton General Hospital. It was a position they had created for me. The timing was perfect.
I was beginning to see the responsibility of our marriage looming on the horizon and needed the job. I accepted immediately. He told me the salary would be $1,500 per month before taxes. I was ecstatic, having lived for a year on a stipend of $175 a month from the hospital. This was a clear answer to prayer for our future. I was amazed at the timing of the Lord. He used my professional mentors to further us on our way.

Rev. Paul McCarroll readily agreed to perform our wedding in his traditional grey stone Presbyterian Church, St. Cuthbert's on King Street West in Hamilton. Paul's lovely wife Kathy immediately accepted Meridel's invitation to be her matron of honor. Paul required that we meet in his office located near the McMaster University campus, for a session of pre-marriage instructions. He told us that because of his long term friendship with Meridel, and our nearly two year separation, he would waive the usual six weeks of pre-marital counseling. We were glad of that! Together we set the date of our wedding according to the first available evening at Paul's church. He was very popular with the students at the nearby McMaster University and their activities often filled the church, keeping it a busy place. The sanctuary was free on the evening of April 25, 1968 exactly the same date we had privately planned. It was very short notice, but everything fell into place!

I called my parents in Victoria to inform them of our wedding date. Mom made me promise that we would come to them for a "West coast" reception in the summer. They were thrilled. We invited Mrs. Holmes from Toronto to Hamilton to stand in for our folks. Our official witnesses for the church registry were my hospital intern friend Dr. Don Stemp and his wife Heather as well as my classmate Ken and Gina Reynolds from Vancouver. By Canadian law, we were required to register our proposed marriage at the Civic Registrar's Office in Hamilton and have blood tests done. I proceeded to invite the guests we selected as our wedding party, including the McCarroll's and ourselves. We were twelve in all. It was to be a quiet, private affair.

Meridel busied herself preparing her gorgeous, yet simple, wedding dress, an Indian sari. It reflected her eastern experience and fit our budget. She had the foresight to bring six meters of white silk organza from India in her suitcase. Seamlessly she pieced the French lace bodice together which could have been a Vogue creation, for it looked like a million. As for flowers, she had spotted a huge magnolia tree in full blossom, just down the street from the hospital.

Explaining to the homeowner she was going to get married Meridel asked if she could have a few flowers for the wedding bouquet. The lady was so excited that we could take all the flowers that we needed, even to decorate the sanctuary if necessary! I made several trips to the church with my small convertible sports car over-stuffed with fragrant white and ice-pink magnolia blossoms. To create a magnificent bridal bouquet Meridel placed branches with their unopened buds into a warm bath. In time the blossoms opened to be six to eight inches in width. She then arranged them to reach all the way to the floor and tied the branches together. It was the most exotic bouquet I had ever laid eyes on. It matched her dress perfectly.

Meanwhile, I reserved a private dining room for our reception dinner in a nearby well-known hotel. I calculated that I had just enough in my savings account to pay for this expense, with something left over for a short honeymoon.

In true orthodox Jewish fashion we decided not to see each other on our wedding day until she came down the aisle. We were also committed to staying apart physically until the wedding night. That was hard, because we were so in love.

Peter Johnson, the young up and upcoming Assistant Administrator at the Henderson General, heard about our wedding plans. He and his wife, Judy, had a brand new home in Burlington near Hamilton. They planned to be away on a short vacation weekend, which coincided with our soon coming wedding day of Thursday, April 25th. Without hesitation they offered it to us. When Judy showed Meridel around their lovely suburban home and came to the master bedroom, she whispered, "You'll enjoy our king-size bed, but look out... It makes babies!" Only several weeks later Meridel told me about this conversation.

The day before the wedding, I got time off work to take my fiancée out for a special pre-nuptial lunch. We were as happy as 'kids out of school'. While waiting for our food I read her the Marriage Contract that I had put together.

It was complete with impressive gold and red seals with red ribbons attached to it that I received from my boss, Dr. George Woodward. We had a good laugh because I even promised to do dishes! Meridel loved it. We dreamed on about our lives together. I remember the entire elegant lunch cost a total of $10.95.

Finally the long awaited day dawned clear and bright. The ceremony was set to begin at 19:00 hours and all the guests arrived on time and were seated in the sanctuary. Grant and I met with Paul in his study. Grant had the rings and were ready and waiting. Calling his wife Kathy, in their parsonage home next door, Paul asked, "How are the final preparations going?"
...
"You mean she still hasn't done her hair? Make up? What about her what? NO I don't know where the bouquet is!"
Holding the receiver away from his ear he looked questioningly at us. "Jay, is her bouquet in your car?"
"I put it in the entrance hall of your home, Pastor," Grant said.
Slowly and distinctly Paul told his wife, "Kathy, the flowers are in the entrance! It is already ten minutes to seven!"
Being an experienced vicar's wife Kathy knew how to hold her ground when under pressure from her demanding husband.
"Kathy says they'll be there in a few minutes," Paul told us.

Walking single file we men took our places at the front of the sanctuary. Stoically we waited, and waited, and waited. By 19:30, sheepishly we retreated back into Paul's office. He called his wife again, and Kathy assured him that the bride would be ready 'shortly'. By 19:45, I truly believed that Meridel had gotten cold feet and, worse yet, maybe even gone back to India! Finally, she appeared!

Seeing her so radiant and confident in her soft organza wedding gown with elegant train was well worth the wait; every minute, every hour, every week, every month and every year we were apart!
Gracefully she strolled slowly down the aisle, to the familiar strains of Bach's "Jesu, Joy of Man's Desiring".

This girl was not in any hurry but savoring every moment.

Her oriental looking, floor length bouquet of magnolias complimented the soft exquisite folds of the gown around her body, gathered into a full train in the back. Her shining eyes were fixed on mine and even her flushed skin was radiant. The moment she took my hand we were immediately surrounded by love.

The ceremony was very meaningful and emotional for us both. After completing our vows we signed the registry in Paul's office. Our friends gathered around for hugs and kisses and, after photographs, we were off to our candle light dinner reception.

My friends were very quick to 'roast' me in true Canadian teasing style. Everyone enjoyed the beauty of the love that a bride and groom share. Special music along with the candlelit atmosphere made our private dining room take on the air of a palace.

Enjoying the younger crowd Mrs. Holmes blended in amazingly well. Toward the end of the evening she stood to bless Meridel and me on behalf of our parents by reading the Aaronic blessing.

Finally the guests bid us farewell and I helped my beautiful wife into the TR3 piling her train and extensive flowers on top of her.

Off we roared off to our honeymoon 'mansion' where I carried Meridel over the threshold. Thus we began our lives as husband and wife and we still remember that glorious moment.

The next day I was up at 6:00 am. Meridel made me breakfast and I was off to U of T because I had to present and defend my Master's thesis. I had sworn my classmate, Ken Reynolds, to secrecy about our wedding until I had at least finished my academic requirements.

But when I entered the lecture room my classmates broke out into applause and whistles. There on the black board in huge letters was written: "CONGRATULATIONS JAY and MERIDEL!"

Frankly, in that atmosphere I found it quite easy to present my indings and recommendations and to answer the questions of my faculty and classmates. The following year, 1969, I was presented with my hard earned Master's degree in Health Care Administration, Faculty of Medicine, University of Toronto.

Before my presentation that morning I had dropped Meridel off at the house of Mrs. Holmes. She even took a nap in my old room. We could feel love in her home and enjoyed the leisurely dinner she prepared for us that evening. It was almost as good as being home.

Over the weekend friends invited us out for meals. I had tickets for a live concert with soprano Dame Joan Sutherland in Toronto.

By Sunday noon, Meridel had our carefully packed bags waiting at the door to embark on a very special and romantic ten day honeymoon. We visited Montreal and Quebec City in French Canada, followed by a jaunt down the Eastern seaboard to Boston.

Full of joy we returned to our make-shift private haven which George, the Medical Director of the hospital had prepared for us in the Medical Library. The 'kitchen' consisted of one electric hot plate, a couple of pots and pans, plates and cups. We slept in two single brown metal hospital beds and shared the bathroom with several medical students who also lived there. Before Meridel entered the bathroom I had to make sure she was alone. Crazy stuff!

We were on a waiting list to qualify for an apartment when the married interns left. Meridel was amazingly patient and proved to be a good cook on that single hot plate. Or was it because I was a hungry young new husband? Just one month later, we were given the temporary use of a vacant apartment for married couples in the intern's residence. By the end of June I received my first pay check.

In July we moved out and rented a tiny, upstairs apartment under the eaves of an old brick home. The only room we could stand up in was the living room. The kitchen, bedroom and bathroom had drastically slanting ceilings. Fondly we remember the summer electrical storms when mighty clouds blackened the sky. Through many nights thunder cracked, lightning flashed and the rain poured down in torrents. Like small birds in their well hidden nest we snuggled together.

"I'm feeling a bit unusual," Meridel said one day in late June. "Could you ask someone to do a pregnancy test?"

"That's easy." I took her urine sample to the nearby GP clinic where I had done part of my thesis research.

The nurses did the routine test and assured me that they would let me know the results in a few hours. They were very friendly and tickled to give me the results for sure enough we were pregnant! I immediately phoned our apartment. "Hello, Mrs Meridel Rawlings?"
"Hello?"
"This is Mr Jay Rawlings and I have news for you!"
"And what would that be Mr. Rawlings?" she cooed.
"Mrs. Rawlings, you are going to have a baby... no, <u>we</u> are going to have a baby,"
"Oh... Mr. Rawlings," she responded very quietly with tears of joy in her voice.
"Put on your best dress. I am taking you out for a candlelight dinner tonight." Then we shared a short prayer of thanksgiving for this new life.

We calculated carefully and figured out we must have gotten pregnant on our wedding night! So Judy Johnson's warning was correct, "their bed did indeed make babies."
Meridel and I decided that summer was a perfect time for her to visit her parents and siblings for the promised reception. She longed to see them all for they had not been together for over two years prior Meridel's trip to India.
I drove her to the Canadian National Railway station in Toronto where she embarked on a three day, cross Canada journey, to Red Deer, Alberta. I arranged for my 'loved one' to have a comfortable sleeper car. Returning to the tiny apartment again, I was alone, but grateful knowing that this time our separation was only for three weeks.

Our plans were to meet in Victoria at my Mom and Dad's place in late July for the wedding reception we had promised them. The day I flew into Vancouver, James Rawlings picked me up in his Cessna 180 float plane. It was a warm, clear and calm summer evening. The scenery out over the Gulf Islands was breathtaking. During the short thirty minute flight he buzzed over my parent's home on Locarno Lane near the University of Victoria. James delighted in circling and dipping his wings. Seeing my Mom, Dad and Meridel frantically waving from the garden made my heart jump.

Looking down on the same patio where we had shared our breakfast and prayed just before she left for India, the circle was complete. Yes, it was a dream come true, a prayer answered. Two years before I had left home in trepidation and was returning with my graduate degree and a top position but, best of all, I was back in my hometown with my precious new wife, surrounded by many loved ones.

**At family wedding reception in Victoria, BC
for those who could not attend the wedding in Hamilton,
Ontario, Canada**

Later that week, Mom and Dad opened their home for an elegant afternoon wedding reception for my family and close friends, all eager to meet this mystery lady, Meridel. The love that we felt from each of the guests was quite overwhelming. Many brought carefully chosen wedding gifts of china, crystal and silver that grace our home to this very day. Meridel enjoyed being a bride for the second time.

My grandma, Miriam Cohen Rawlings had a deep and lasting effect upon her. Upon seeing her grandson's wife for the first time in her assisted living senior's home, Grandma took Meridel in her arms and embraced her for a long moment. She was a woman of few words. With a loving look she told Meridel, "I have prayed much for you both. I love you Meridel and am so happy for Jay."
It was the last time we saw her as she passed away six months later. Her gift to us were loving prayers for me, all those years since the death of her son, Vic, and her complete and loving acceptance of my bride Meridel.

Cousin James' wedding gift to us was a cruise in the family yacht through the Gulf Islands. What a "second honeymoon" it was!
We visited, joked, fished, and swam. Evening barbecues were always a surprise as our 'Captain' found us secluded beaches. The weather was perfect, the sunsets eternal. I was so glad to introduce Meridel to some of the places that James and I had explored and loved during our youth.

Then it was time to travel east through the fabulous Canadian Rockies to the wheat lands and oil rich Alberta, one of the wealthiest Canadian provinces. Soon I would meet Meridel's family for the first time.
Billy and Sheila drove us in their car, and we took our time going through the mountains. Mom loved to tell everyone, "JV and Meridel invited us along on their honeymoon!"

Being an only child I looked forward to meeting Meridel's Mom and Dad and her five siblings. As the eldest daughter of six children there were lots of new faces for me to meet. I was very glad to finally greet my two new brothers, Donovan Oriel and Roderick, a marvelous baritone.

And of course I loved meeting my three new sisters, Janice, Patricia and Nancy. Each one is a professional in nursing and/or education.

I had shared her photos during the time that Meridel was in India. Our parents 'got on' famously. My mom loved to sit and listen to Meridel's dad playing the piano. It seemed he could play anything, from classical to blues to boogie-woogie and jazz and down home spirituals. The family's love towards Meridel and me was overwhelming. It was obvious that she was a heroine, especially in the eyes of her mother, two sets of grandparents and little sisters.

"Wedding" number three was again unique from the other two. This time we were 'married' in the small wooden chapel just down the street from the family home.
Meridel's paternal grandfather, a pioneer pastor and preacher in Alberta, performed what we called "a dedication ceremony." Her Aunt Rita nee Austin, a Toronto girl, sang in her rich contralto, "Where ever you go, I will go..." from the Book of Ruth. This song turned out to be prophetic.

Of course, it wasn't actually a wedding because all of the official documents had been signed in April. But this service was created to honor and respect Meridel's parents and family who had missed our vows exchanged in Hamilton. Everyone was happy because Meridel, after all, was the first daughter and granddaughter to be married. Her Mom and Dad hosted the family and friends at a large candlelight reception and sit down dinner in the city's most fashionable hotel. Adding her personal touch, Meridel took time to hand write little place cards. She chose verses from the Song of Songs for each guest. Again, we were amazed with the gifts given. I always tell people that we were married three times, just to make sure! One of our minister friends Harald Bredesen once said, "The people that I marry, stay married, and the people that I bury stay buried."

Meridel's two youngest sisters made us promise that they could come to visit us the following summer. We agreed heartily.

With tearful farewells, we flew back to Toronto and then on to Hamilton where new job responsibilities awaited me. We soon found a very spacious second floor apartment on a quiet, tree-lined street in an older but elegant residential area of "steel town." The garage had at one time been stables for four horses and one stall was perfect for our little car. Our apartment was filled with light because of the floor length windows. The vistas into the trees gave the impression that we were nestled in the branches. We loved the 'old world feel' of the place, with polished oak floors and high ceilings. We also found a nearby furniture maker, who created two love-seats with matching chairs. Meridel made our drapes and with the polished hardwood floors, rugs and soft lights, our home became luxurious. We even had a small fireplace that I got working. On weekends we explored the fascinating southern Ontario countryside of farms and centuries old grey stone houses. Once we traveled to the Kitchener/Waterloo area to visit the famous Mennonite market. There we bought 'shoe-fly pie' and a vintage Mennonite hand crafted cradle. I sanded and sanded it and finally refinished it. I had to hurry because by this time Meridel's tummy was starting to show nicely.

To help out with all of our expenses she still worked for a few months as a nurse at the nearby St. Joseph's Hospital. Sister Mary Margaret, one of my classmates at U of T was the Administrator and she welcomed Meridel warmly to the staff. We also found a small congregation in nearby Stony Creek and settled in. We met lots of young people. The guys loved my sports car and, pretty soon they were all popping over to our home for visits.

My work at the hospital was very demanding and time consuming. I left home each morning at 7:45, working from 8:00 to 4:30, and many times I was away during the weekends because of required work related travel. We were planning to renovate and enlarge the hospital and I was on the Planning Team of senior hospital management. Along with our architect, we visited The Massachusetts General in Boston, The Mayo Clinic in Rochester Minnesota and The Cedars Sinai Medical Center in Los Angeles.

I was appointed to this august body because the departments that I was responsible for had the task of efficiently distributing items inside the hospital. I was head of such services as: patient information, food services, drugs, medical supplies, linens, inhalation therapy, beds and cleaning materials. I had to analyze each department and then come up with new and more efficient ways to deliver these services to the patients. Together, we worked to create a state of the art distribution system throughout the entire building. Needless to say, our lives were very busy. However, we had no idea how busy we'd get with the soon arrival of our baby and some medical challenges that he presented to us.

During that time I suffered severe migraine headaches. Sometimes they were so bad I had to go to bed in a darkened room for a couple of days. When they persisted, Meridel decided to pray for me as this affliction worried her. Since then I have not had any recurrence.
On the other hand, I realized she was troubled by a recurring nightmare that woke her up crying. One night she awoke both of us. "What is it?" I gently asked, trying to comfort her.
Clutching the sheets she cried, "I have this horrible recurring dream, where I am being chased by a naked man with an erection. I keep running, trying to escape, and just before he catches me I wake up, startled."
"That's it. We are not having this anymore!" I switched on the light, sat up and prayed, "Dear Lord. Thank you for taking away this evil and tormenting dream. Please heal Meridel like you healed me. Thank you, Amen."

I am grateful to tell you that this ugly tormenting dream has never, ever returned to bother her again. Praise God!

Timeless Secrets

"I am the LORD your God, I change not."
Malachi 3:6a

Change you can always count on. In just a few months we both had to deal with major changes. Big ones! I moved out of the interns residence to become Meridel's husband. Meridel returned from India.
We married. I became the bread winner of my family with a lot of new responsibilities and now I was an expectant father and Meridel was to be a mother. Change is one of the universal principles of life.
We drew comfort, knowing that the One we believed in was changeless.

"Trust in the LORD with all your heart, and lean not on your own under-standing; in all your ways acknowledge Him, and He shall direct your paths." Proverbs 3:5, 6

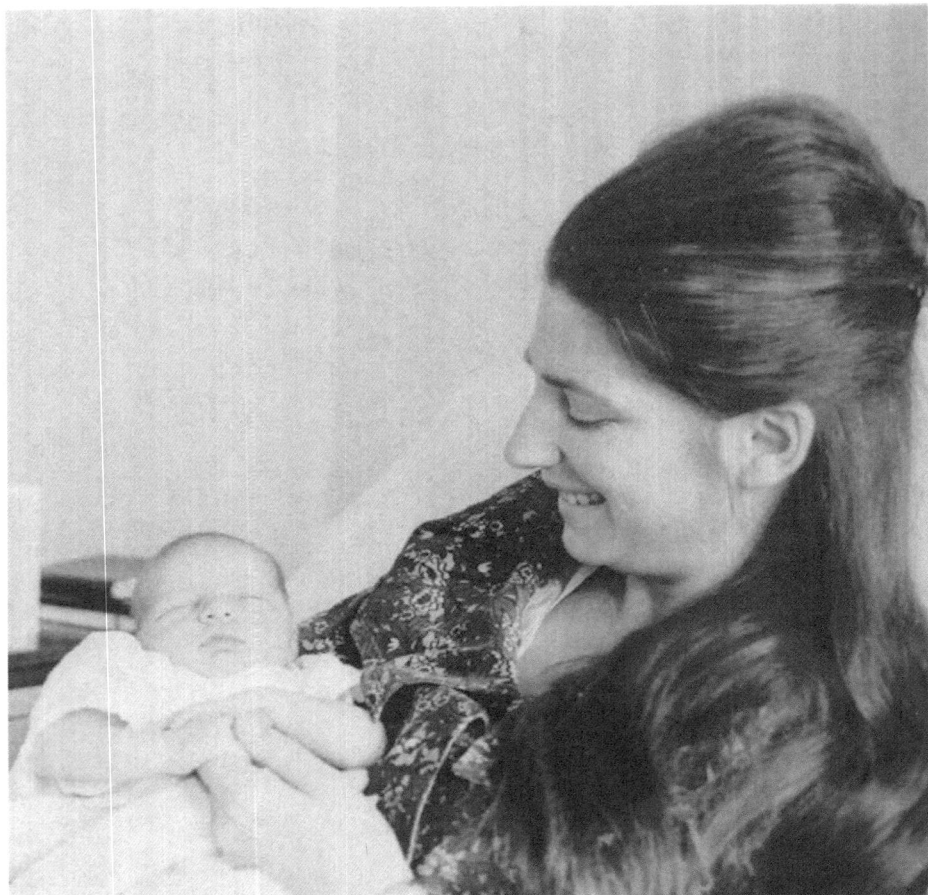

David, born January 20, 1969
Photo taken in February 1969 in our home in Hamilton,
Ontario, Canada

Chapter 13

A Gift on Loan

"Children are a heritage from the Lord, yet they are only ours in a secondary sense. They are on loan... We got this message very clearly when our five week old son needed emergency surgery... "

"This is the day!" Meridel's soft spoken words woke me up very early one cold, January morning. The weather was quickly turning into a blizzard.

"What day?" I mumbled, still half asleep. "I think it's Monday... January 20th."

"No, no," she said, "I mean the baby is coming today."

"Let's go!" Suddenly wide awake I jumped out of bed. "I'm taking you to the hospital right now."

"No, No," she smiled, "It's too soon darling. We have to wait for the pains to get stronger and closer together".

Calling our obstetrician, he told me, "Don't panic, Jay. Babies have been born before. But you can bring Meridel to the Admissions Department to get her processed."

It was also Inauguration Day in the USA. We watched President Nixon sworn into office on a small black and white TV at Meridel's bedside. By mid afternoon the contractions became stronger and faster. Nurses, keeping a watchful eye on her told her around 7:00 p.m. that she still was not ready yet. Since this was her first child, it was a tough delivery but finally, at 10:30 p.m. a beaming nurse handed me a bundled baby. "Congratulations, Mr. Rawlings, you have a baby boy!" As I looked into the tiny face of John David's face he yawned and we all laughed. I felt overwhelmed by the miracle I now held in my arms.

Two years before, New Delhi doctors had examined Meridel under general anesthetic. They told her that her womb was scarred with what they thought had been, 'uterine tuberculoses'. Their verdict: "You will never be able to have children."

Aren't you glad when the Lord overrules what man says and thinks? I certainly am! Our baby John David is living proof that with God all things are possible to those that believe!

When they placed the baby on Meridel's breast he began to nurse right away. After several days we took John David home and began our new routine. Measuring 24 inches long at birth, he needed filling out and nursed hungrily. However, five weeks later Meridel sensed that something was wrong. He wouldn't nurse properly and got very fussy and restless, and began to 'projectile' vomit. As a nurse, she immediately knew what was wrong because her older brother and younger sister had a hereditary condition known as *'pyloric stenosis'*. Twenty seven years earlier another infant brother had died from the same condition when he was four weeks old. This symptom of projectile vomiting occurs when the pyloric value at the exit of the stomach fails to grow in proportion with the child. The food stays in the stomach and is blocked from passing to the small intestine. The ingested milk is ejected out of the baby's body with unusually strong force - a horrifying experience for new parents.

Immediately, we called our family doctor but he was not convinced and asked us to bring the baby to his clinic. The moment we rushed into his examining room David vomited all over him. Still he was not convinced. Taking matters into her own hands Meridel had David, who by now was dehydrated, admitted to the hospital through the Emergency Department. Because of the family's genetic history, he was immediately taken to pediatric surgery. He came out of the operating room with part of his head shaved for an IV. To maintain his fluid levels a drip irrigation was placed into a vein in his scalp. He looked terrible, we felt so helpless but he was sleeping peacefully. "He surely will recover!" the pediatric surgeon assured us.

Because of his traumatic illness, the operation, subsequent hospitalization and lack of regular sucking, Meridel was not able to breastfeed any more. When John David was recovered he was ravenous so I searched for the thickest, richest canned milk to add to his formula, especially before we went to sleep at night.

He emptied his bottle in no time and hardly burped. Once he was on the mend you can imagine how we all slept. This wee lad put on four pounds in four weeks and hasn't looked back since. Soon he was sitting up in his high chair, demanding food; his crew cut blond hair made him look like a mini-wrestler.

Our baby was our treasure and gratefulness filled out hearts.
Life was full with loved ones, careers, friends, activities, and the youth group. But there still seemed to be something missing. I kept going back in my mind to the idea of being filled with the Holy Spirit. Meridel had shared her experiences with me but never pushed. Watching her closely, I notice how she lived fully and freely, unconcerned about what people thought of her. Her one goal in life was to please the Lord. She loved to sing in the Spirit and dance with David in her arms. She was some girl! I loved her so much and I knew that God saw her and loved her.
I also knew she was praying for me but she never let on.

Timeless Secrets

"Behold children are a heritage from the Lord,
the fruit of the womb is a reward. Like arrows in the hand of a warrior
so are the children of one's youth.
Happy is the man whose quiver is full of them."
Psalm 127:3

When a couple enters into marriage they make themselves available to love, serve and sacrifice for the next generation. This response in caring for our children is one of the principle ways we love God and build his kingdom. Children are a heritage from the Lord; they are only ours in a secondary sense. They are on loan. God gives children to parents as a man entrusts his fortune to his heirs. Jesus instructs never to despise or abuse one of these little ones and holds up their faith as an example for adults.

"Whoever receives one little child like this in My name, receives Me.
But whoever causes one of these little ones who believe in Me to sin,
it would be better for him if a millstone were hung around his neck and
he were drowned in the depth of the sea." Matthew 18:5,6.

We are often surprised and overwhelmed by the turn of events in life. We all need an anchor to hold us fast in the storms that will surely come.

"When you pass through the waters, I will be with you; and through the
rivers, they shall not overflow you. When you walk through the fire you
shall not be burned nor shall the flames scorch you. For I am the LORD,
your God, the Holy One of Israel your Savior." Isaiah 43:2.3.

Chapter 14

Searching in Suburbia

"With stammering lips and another tongue He will speak to this people... This is the rest with which You may cause the weary to rest and this is the refreshing." Isaiah. 28:11, 13*

The next months were full of activity. In the rolling hills of Dundas we found a special house for rent. What joy it was to furnish it, set up the sun deck adjacent to the swimming pool and care for the Shetland ponies, acquired with the property. It was a time of adjustment for us as newlyweds. We loved each other with all of our hearts and yet we had to learn how to live together. For me, having grown up as a single child, I had to learn how to substitute my wants and desires to the overall good of our growing marriage relationship and family needs. This is God's program to redirect the 'self' life. That principle in fact, never ends. Marriage is a lifetime process of giving and receiving. Mostly giving!

Meridel's life continued to be a real example to me. Growing up as one of six children her priorities were not clothes, purses, shoes or earthly possessions. She gets excited about relationships, especially with family. She doesn't worry about money. What is important to her are principles, such as good character, faith, prayer, honesty, integrity and purpose. Somehow she has a direct line above.
Mine was 'long distance'. *Is it the infilling of the Holy Spirit?* I kept asking myself. Wanting this for my life I didn't want to speak in other tongues. I realize now that actually I was a very inflexible person, painfully resistant to change.

Not so with Meridel. If she thought that God spoke to her to do something, she responded immediately.

---

* Isaiah 28:12 - *menuchah*, in Hebrew. **Strong's #4496**: derived from '*nuach*', a verb meaning 'To rest, soothe, settle down, comfort.'

She was, and still is, very generous and giving. I know now that we have been blessed because of this pattern of giving that she lives by each day.

In contrast, I worked very hard for every cent, and didn't part with it as easily as she did. I was still rigid and afraid to "let go and let God."

Then, one day Meridel received an invitation in the mail to attend the annual July Camp meeting of her American friends Ruth and Susan in Ashland, Virginia. I didn't want any part of it so when we discussed it I said, "No. Why would I want to meet the women who told you not to marry me?" However a few weeks later we went to a musical concert where Merv and Merla Watson shared their excellent musical talents and Israeli-sounding music. Following the concert I bought a book from the display table called, "They Speak in Other Tongues" by John and Elisabeth Sherrill.[28]

Immediately it spoke truth into my mind and heart. I realized that I had been very hard on Meridel. I could see the hunger of her heart but did very little to try and help her spiritually. I began to realize that the experience of being filled with God's Spirit was something real and way beyond my feeble mind and understanding. In private I kept reading and searching.

One day I saw an advertisement in the Toronto Star where a Corvette car dealer was having a sale. I asked Meridel about taking a run up to Toronto to check it out. Immediately she agreed. I was surprised. When we arrived, the car lot was already buzzing with activity. A salesman showed us several models and then we saw my "dream car." It was an amber gold colored classic Sting Ray design with black leather interior. It had only one previous owner, low mileage and was in mint condition. The price was right. Meridel could tell I was very interested but it had to be a joint decision. She whispered in my ear, "Go ahead, and let's get it!" That cinched it!

---

[28] *They Speak in Other Tongues*, John and Elisabeth Sherrill, Chosen Books. Baker Publishing Group.

They took my beloved Triumph TR3 as a trade-in. We easily arranged the financing, and drove home in our new car. I was like someone moving in a dream.

I could hardly believe it, because everything happened so quickly! The young people from our youth group loved the car and immediately told me all the things that could be done to it to make it 'cool'. I refused all offers with one exception. I gave permission to paint it in one of the youth group father's auto repair and body shop. Together, the teens and I chose a metallic burgundy color.

This became a major project for the guys. The young ladies in the youth group spent time visiting Meridel and playing with David while we 'men' worked on the car. Finally it was ready. It had been hand painted and hand polished three times. By now it just gleamed.

I rationalized that because my wife had been so generous in encouraging me to get the car, what could I lose by taking her to visit some strange people at this camp meeting, despite my reservations? Meridel never mentioned the camp, but one day, I announced, "How would you like to drive down to Virginia in our new car?" I didn't really care to meet Meridel's friends, but I loved my wife and knew this would make her happy. I didn't know what I was getting into. In fact, neither of us did!

Timeless Secrets

"Trust in the LORD, and do good; dwell in the land, and feed on His faithfulness. Delight yourself also in the LORD and He shall give you the desires of your <u>heart</u>." **Psalm 37:3,4**

Often we don't know what to do in life when confronted with a new reality. This is especially true in spiritual matters when we sense that we could lose control. The problem is really one of trust. Can I trust that there maybe is a better plan out there for me than I had thoughtfully calculated? The fact is, God has a perfect plan for every life. I have experienced how He can reduce us in order to get our attention and along the way help us to become teachable, but only so that He can add to us. He opens up the realms of His potential, His possibility and His creativity to us. But He will never overstep our will. Again, it is a matter of trust. It's a hard step to take for any who have not had a healthy relationship with one or both parents and do not know how to trust authorities. Do we run away, or do we openly face the Highest Authority?

> **Strong's Concordance #3820 states:** Heart refers to: intellect, awareness, mind, inner person, inner feelings, deepest thoughts, inner self. As in English, the Hebrew concept of *"Lev"* or heart encompasses both the physical organ and a person's inner yearnings. Perhaps the noblest occurrence of *"Lev"* is Deuteronomy 6:5 commending Israel to love the LORD, with all your heart. Jesus also laid great emphasis on this truth.

"The first of all the commandments is; Hear, O Israel, the LORD our God the LORD is one. And you shall love the LORD your God with all your heart, with all your soul, with your entire heart, mind and with all you strength, and your neighbor as yourself." Mark 12:29, 30.

Chapter 15

Old Red Eyes

"The good news about this place is that it's private. The bad news is that there is no running water or toilet... Just chalk it all up to good training!"

Like any sports car a Corvette is a two-seater. It was definitely not designed for a family. Meridel was great about the cramped quarters. She figured out a way to fix up a little bed for David right behind the driver's seat. Then there was just enough room behind her seat for his real cloth diapers, (the era before pampers), clothing, toys and his formula.

On the way to Virginia, we paused often to stretch and relax. One place I had always wanted to visit was Williamsport, Pennsylvania, home of Little League Baseball. (LLB) I began playing at the age of ten. So we stopped and enjoyed a picnic overlooking the carefully tended but empty stadium where the Little League World Series is held each year. We also visited their museum. This special organization has brought fun and challenge, while teaching sportsmanship to millions of kids worldwide. As well LLB has given entertainment to parents, friends and spectators alike at live games and via many international TV networks.

We took our time getting to Virginia and when we finally drove into the dusty lane of the campground it was early evening. Outside it was still hot, humid and very sticky. As we parked near the entrance many people carrying Bibles were on their way to the outdoor 'tabernacle' for the evening service.
"Hi y'all." The young, fair-haired woman who greeted us had cool, calculating blue-green eyes.
"Susan!" Meridel jumped out to greet her. "Jay, I want you to meet..."
"Hi, I'm Susie." Ignoring Meridel she came to my window and shook my hand warmly. "So this is the little baby, how cute," she grinned.

"You've had a long journey and you're all tired," she stated. "Why don't I show you to your cabin and ya'll can get a good night's sleep?"

She led us back out onto the main road and after 200 meters turned into a low lying field of tall grass. The rutted dirt way ended in front of a old ramshackle cottage. We could hear frogs croaking loudly. Opening the door, Susie showed us into a run down two room dwelling with a sagging roof. She flicked on the single light bulb hanging from a cord in the middle of a sparsely furnished room. She and her colleague Ruth had tried brightening up the place with some paint and photo treasures from their world travels.
"The good news about this place, she said, is that it's private. The bad news is that there is no running water or toilet, but its good for us to learn how to make do, isn't it?" Susie waited for my response and when I said nothing she smiled. "Just chalk it all up to good training!" *Good training for what?* I thought.
Giggling, she left with, "See you for pancakes and eggs in the cafeteria at 7:30 in the morning."

When the screen door slammed shut behind her, a sense of finality hit me. I felt trapped. We were definitely not used to living without running water or a toilet, especially with a baby.
Meridel cheerily said, "Don't worry. I've got food for David and some crackers and cheese for us. I have a bottle of water for drinking and brushing teeth."

After settling the baby into our double bed that sagged in the middle we ate our dry crackers in silence. As we lay down, I clung onto the side of the bed so as not to roll toward the middle. Meridel did the same. Immediately we began to sweat. There was no air conditioner, not even a fan nor any outside air movement. I could smell the mold. Unconsciously our breathing became shallow and both had the feeling that the walls were imploding. Over the incessant racket of crickets and frogs, singing wafted in on the hot humid night air, followed by the impassioned shouting of a preacher at the 'service' somewhere off in the distance.
Meridel and David almost immediately fell asleep. In the darkness, humidity and strange surroundings I had trouble settling down and kept

tossing and turning. Finally, I dozed of and began dreaming but soon woke up because something made my skin crawl. *What is this? Did I have a dream? Is a night vision?* Like in a horror movie I saw two beady red eyes staring directly at me. *What is this?*

On the one hand I wanted to run, but I had to protect my family. Was this to be a test or a duel to the death? *Those satanic eyes want me to run and hide*, I knew. Praying, I turned to God and stood my ground.

I knew I had to make a decision to totally follow God with all my heart or not. Somehow I knew I was about to make one of the most important decisions of my life: serving God or myself?

Exhausted from the internal struggle, I fell into a fitful sleep.

The next morning we arrived at the cafeteria just before 07:30 where we met Ruth Heflin. She was an impressive person, large of stature and confident, yet jolly and kind in her manner. There I was, unshaven and disheveled, without my morning shower. Still shaken by the night vision I did my best to appear confident. We made small talk until she introduced us to her father, Pastor Wallace Heflin Sr. He was sitting at the end of one of the tables wearing an open neck white shirt. I could see his huge shoulders and chest; he looked like an old prize fighter. His knurled yet gentle hands cradled a mug of coffee. He grinned and laughed as he talked. Everyone around him at the table listened carefully to his faith stories between mouthfuls of breakfast.

He looked up and when he saw us said, "Well, I heard that you arrived last night! Did you have a good sleep?"

"Oh yes," I lied, trying to be gracious to the man who had built the camp 'by faith,' with his bare hands, and a motley crew of volunteers. Later I learned that these volunteers consisted of old ladies, divorced moms with children, the odd carpenter and plumber and lots of teenagers. Immediately the little girls fell all over David, squabbling over who would 'carry' him next. He loved their attention.

After breakfast we were invited to 'Morning Service' and made our way to the outdoor auditorium. I noticed a lot of old stuff lying around, *Why don't they just clean up all this junk?* I thought.

The 'junk,' I later learned was what people had donated to the camp to help build it 'by faith.' Like in the Bible story, the Children of Israel brought their gifts to Moses so that the original tabernacle or meeting place with God could be built, so in like manner here lay the 'offerings'.

Then I saw the big sign hanging over the entrance to the "Tabernacle Calvary Pentecostal Summer Camp Meeting. Welcome!" We were given front row seats. Folding chairs, old theatre seats, and home-made benches were all laid out in concentric rings. Thread bare carpets covered a dirt floor and dust rose in columns when the saints got up to dance and praise God. Some overstuffed armchairs were randomly placed for the oldest members of the congregation to be comfortably seated.

David was whisked away to play. We settled onto our metal folding chairs just as Sister Edith Heflin, Ruth's mother, arrived and took her seat on the raised platform. She was always the morning Bible teacher. Ruth's brother, Wallace Heflin Jr. or 'Sonny' as he was known in those days, took the microphone and called everyone to take their seats.

I was fascinated by the orderly disorder. Playing the electric organ Ruth began singing in a very loud voice, "Oh how I love Jesus," and everyone joined in. The singing was upbeat and enthusiastic. I had never seen anything like this before. A few more people, both young and old, joined her on the platform to sing. The chorus changed and pretty soon people came to the front to 'dance before the Lord.' Many sang, while others raised their hands and shouted in tongues, diverse languages given by the Holy Spirit.

Meridel and I watched intently. We were fascinated, trying to take everything in. We also tried to join in but I was nervous. Another part of me was intrigued by the shining faces of the people who were obviously caught up in the joy of it all. This was the kind of religious experience we had only read about.

When it was time for the morning offering they handed out plastic ice cream buckets. Fumbling in my wallet I put $10 into the container. Like the other guests we didn't have to pay for the camp - everything was free: the food, the accommodations, and the Bible teaching.

However, everyone was encouraged to give what they could in the 'offerings' in every service. Somehow, all the needs were met.
This was the first time I saw such an approach and it reminded me of the Book of Acts where the apostles and early believers had 'everything in common.'

Then Sister Edith Heflin started to teach. She stood for a while and then, tiring, sat with her Bible open on her lap. She was teaching from the Book of Revelation. It was very interesting to hear her homespun insights that included personal experiences along with the scripture lesson. After about an hour, she moved her chair to the edge of the raised platform. She sat and closed her eyes while people in the audience came forward. In an orderly line they stood in front of her. Sister Heflin gently touched the people one by one on the forehead and gave them each a personal 'word from the Lord' by the Holy Spirit.

This really interested me. Meridel and I drew closer to see and hear what the Holy Spirit was saying through her to the people. Some actually fell backwards when she touched them. This was anticipated by 'catchers,' usually strong men, who caught and gently lowered the limp bodies to the floor. Young ladies discreetly covered the legs of the women who were 'out under the Power,' with prayer cloths.

Was this something like in the Bible when Solomon dedicated the Holy Temple in Jerusalem?
In 1 Kings 8:10,11 we read that the glory of the Lord came down on the priests and musicians and they all fell on their faces because of the powerful presence of the Living God. *Why do these people fall on their backs?* I wondered.
After everyone had been prayed for, Ruth came up to me and said, "Let mother pray for you." She could see I was quite reluctant but I inched forward slowly. I closed my eyes tightly and felt the light touch of Sister Heflin's hand just above my forehead. Before she could say anything, she drew in her breath and said, "Oh. Oh. Oh! I see something very strange. I see two red, beady eyes looking at you. This is the enemy. He wants your life. You must now make up your mind, to serve either God or Satan. This is the day. Choose life and be filled

with the Holy Spirit so that you and your family may live."

Staggering, I had a strange tingling feeling over my neck, shoulders, and back. This was a shock! I had told no one about what had happened to me the night before, not even Meridel. This could only be the Spirit of God. Was this the word of knowledge mentioned in 1 Corinthians 12:8 I read in the Bible? All the Prophets exhibited it in their lives, David escaped from King Saul warned by it and, in the Book of Corinthians, it was one of the mighty gifts given along with the fruit of the Spirit. I didn't know, but certainly this confirmed what I had seen in the night. I was in a tug of war and realized that the Spirit of God wanted my life but Satan also wanted it. Obviously I had choices to make.

"Thank you," I said to Sister Heflin.

"I have never seen anything like that before... those eyes!" She whispered.

"I know how horrible they are, I saw them in a dream last night." Then I said something I hadn't planned on, "I think I need to fast and pray until I am able to open up to this infilling of the Holy Spirit."

She smiled knowingly, "Let's pray for God to help you in this." Ruth laid her hand on my head and BAM! I was 'out under the Spirit power' for about 30 minutes. When I got up I felt that a new inner strength had come into me.

My desire and resolve to pursue my spiritual path had been strengthened. The Lord was helping me to place my will into His will. This requires childlike trust, and I was really taking it by 'faith' not by 'sight.' I did desire His purposes to come to pass in my life. How well I realized that my will was limited and subject to my own selfish purposes. I read about fasting, but I had never fasted a meal in my life. I began right then. During the next days, while Meridel and David went to the cafeteria, I stayed outside reading portions of the Bible. I started to be 'fed' spiritually like never before. I also learned how to yield to the Lord more than to my appetites. It was not easy for me because I loved to eat, but I realized that a dedicated life had much more to do with attitude than the cessation of food. It was a tangible way I could begin to get out of myself and approach the realms of a Holy God. As I decreased, the spiritual principle here is that He is to increase. If you think it's a joke, just try it! This is not for the faint hearted. After several days of drinking only water, I was getting desperate.

We decided to take a day trip to Jamestown, Virginia, where the first colonists settled in 1609. There we saw the famous Living Reality Museum of the first settlers to America. Walking through the village, we entered the recreated world of the 1600's. Where was my family then? Some were in Spain perhaps Romania and Scotland, and Meridel told me something of her ancestors arriving and settling along the St. Lawrence Seaway in the 1600's from Ireland, and her Swiss family sailing down the Rhine River to Rotterdam, traveling on to London they refused the Crown's offer of land in Ireland, and sailed on to New Amsterdam in 1765.

Everyone here was dressed in period costumes as in the days of the British Colonies. They looked and acted just like the early pioneers. I wondered if it took more courage for the pioneers to branch out into an unknown world from the Continent in times past than it does today? Courage has always been a character quality forged in the fires of affliction. Handcrafted items were sold in stalls, where artisans used similar tools to those used by the early settlers. Brick ovens in a bakery produced stone ground wheat bread. My mouth watered and my resolve wavered. Delicious smelling soups, stews, breads and cakes left me weakened, sitting on a bench. It all smelled so good. I was hungry... It had been five days now and not a morsel of bread had passed my lips. I took myself by the scruff of the neck and shook myself and said aloud, "I'm fasting!" I was embarking on the most important quest of my life, and I was seeking God! I resolved not to weaken and eat before my encounter with the Spirit of God. We got up and walked on, past a potter at work with a lump of unformed clay revolving on his wheel. Instantly I saw myself in that clay. You may think. "Isn't that a bit extreme?" Yes, I suppose it was, but please understand that I was sensing a transition coming and I was throwing myself out onto the mercy of God by denying myself daily bread.

Fasting was opening my will to the Almighty and weakening my sense of self sufficiency. Fasting was also changing my priorities. Instead of getting my natural strength from food, I gave it up in order to receive my spiritual life and gain strength from the Word of God. I had to de-crease so that He could increase. This is one of the many mysteries of a life of faith, and I assure you, it works. It also helped me to become more sensitive to the 'Still Small Voice'.

North America is known for its endless 'eateries'. There are drive-ins, fast food restaurants and enormous food courts in malls everywhere. This 'instant gratification' culture has become 'normal.' Eating is big business worldwide and keeps us dull and insensitive to the spiritual realm and blind to those who are starving all around us.

That evening, just before we returned to the Camp, we were driving along a secluded side road. Suddenly I stopped the car, stepped out quickly and took the pouch in which I kept my tobacco and Meerschaum pipe. I threw it into the thick forest undergrowth as far as I could.
"What are you doing?" Meridel loudly whispered, not wanting the baby to wake up.
"I have to give up my smoking habit," I told her. Even though I wasn't a heavy smoker I occasionally enjoyed my pipe in the evening after a hard day at work. I found the aromatic blue smoke comforting, but the camp folks were talking about the 'fire of the Holy Ghost.'
I remembered reading that aromatic incense was burned in the early morning and evening in the Temple in Jerusalem. Maybe I needed a little adjustment in my senses. Meridel had told me she wanted to learn to love the things God loved. Now, I decided that I did too.

Now, I felt there was nothing between me and the Lord. He had to be first and foremost in my life in all areas. That night, at the end of the service, everyone came forward for prayer. I was feeling weak and shaky after five days on water but I went forward with Meridel. Kneeling at the front on the worn carpet I closed my eyes to pray. Just then Ruth passed by me, stopped, came back and put her hand on my head and BAM! Again I fell to the floor and this time started speaking in a language I had not learned. Yes, I was fully conscious and aware of what was going on, but I was experiencing a new kind of rest that broke deep internal tension. I lay there praying in the Holy Spirit for sometime, in no hurry to get up. I was no longer afraid when I stood to my feet. Gradually I could speak a new language clearer and clearer.

It's hard to describe my feelings and emotions at that moment but there was a palpable release of my spirit, mind, and body to my Creator. I experienced a deep, quiet peace deep inside of me and no longer had a hang-up about speaking in other tongues. What a blessing!

Amazing things were also taking place inside of Meridel's life. Quickly she opened up, and found it easy to clap and raise her hands and even dance. One afternoon Meridel didn't show up in the tabernacle for a healing service. Before Ruth preached the sermon, I told her that
Meridel suffered from an ongoing illness sustained in India. For a year and a half now she was under the care of North America's number one parasitologist. "During her pregnancy some of the prescriptions were so strong she had to stay on bed rest because of possible heart damage," I told Ruth. "But, today she is in a crisis, passing blood and mucous, with cramps and internal burning along with nausea and vomiting." I was concerned.
After the service Ruth found Meridel fully clothed lying on a bed in one of the guest cabins. Pale, weak, cold and clammy her brow was wet and feverish to the touch. Ruth leaned over the bed. "I've come to pray for you Meridel." .

Meridel:
At that point in my life, I knew nothing about divine healing. Yes, I was a nurse and had worked with the infirm and intensely sick for six years including India and Nepal. But 'divine healing' was a mystery to me.
Looking at Ruth I said, "I didn't know that God could heal..."
Seemingly impatient Ruth waved my doubts aside and put her hand on my head. "Dear Lord Jesus, please come right now and heal Meridel. Thank you." It was a very simple prayer. "Now you can get up," she ordered, turned on her heel and left.

My emotions lay pretty close to the surface and I waged a war in my mind because I felt both Ruth and Susan accused me. Because I had chosen Jay, and not their way, I felt unaccepted by them.
Even though I fought against my negative thoughts of rejection by them I physically did not 'feel' different. But I had a choice and made a fundamental decision right then and there in that humble little cabin, to agree with the prayer. Believing that my God was able to heal me
I also had to work with Him.

Forcing myself to sit up I then put my feet on the floor. Still weak I then moved toward the door. Then I walked toward the sounds of rejoicing coming from the tabernacle and joined other worshipers at the front. I made myself move my feet in time to the upbeat choruses. The more I moved the better I felt, and I began to dance in small circles. The more I danced the stronger I got. I began to reach out with my arms. In my mind I was lifting up my wounded spirit to my God who I could trust above all others. I worshipped, first in my thoughts and then in my body. My legs carried me in ever widening circles. I soon discovered that I had danced right outside into an open field beside the old tabernacle. Then, it was as if wings were given to my feet. I spun all over the camp-ground for about an hour. I danced when there was no music to be heard. I was now dancing to another tune being played in my soul and spirit. I was dancing right out of illness that could have ended my life prematurely. It was miraculous. Most of all, I was simply astounded that the Almighty loved me enough to heal me. Yes, 'me,' Meridel. He loved me! It sealed something in me. God's personal care became real in a way I had not experienced before.

It was amazing! I had first encountered Him when I was four years old, and that experience changed my life. But this healing somehow brought His love right home to my internal organs. You can't live without a liver, and He had come and healed it and saved my life."

Jay:

With my own experiences and now Meridel's, then and there I sensed a new destiny for us as a family. Our accommodations now didn't seem so bad. Now able to put them in perspective I realized afresh that we were 'just passing through'. I must add though, on looking back, that the sagging bed was a good preparation for me. It was like a boot camp, preparing me for the thousands of beds I have slept on all over the globe these last forty seven years!

Meridel:

I began to realize that these peculiar people were doing their best. They had encountered the Living God, and the Bible says He doesn't come to the proud. He heard their prayers and had come and claimed their humble lives for His Kingdom. It was another world here. If they wanted to share the good news of Heaven with others who were we to criticize? But now, I wanted to address the deeply embedded strain that we felt with Ruth and Susan. If you recall, when I left India for Canada to marry Jay, I knew they disapproved and since then they made a point of making us feel that as a married couple we were less valuable to God than singles. Well, that was the way Ruth was raised, but it was hurtful to me and insulting to Jay.

Jay:

Jay and I were happily married. So in moments of privacy, we shut out the bewildering and complex personal relationships we discovered in this "religious world". We had many questions coming from professional medical backgrounds with a pervading sense of respect and responsibility. Those borders had been very clear, especially since lives were at stake. Patient care was serious business. Now a challenging adjustment was required to try to figure out the mechanics of the relationships going on between Ruth and Susan, and their followers. We sensed a lot of tension. Why? People were told what to do. These two women were unmistakably 'in charge' and firmly ruled those under them. If anyone had another opinion, or idea, they could be ridiculed, marginalized or even sent out of the fellowship. Their leadership style was in sharp contrast to our life experiences. Were they recruiting 'yes' people with no free will?"

Meridel and I discussed the subtle control being exerted over us. There were many times when we felt edgy, unsure, at odds, nervous and insecure. One was even made to feel guilty with no understanding of why. We often wondered, "What have I done?" They sometimes put us down in front of each other. It was demeaning and hurtful. Nothing seemed straight forward. Where was the trust and confidence? We were confused, especially because this order was supposed to be "a higher calling" in the context of God's love and service. Maybe we were just naive, or so we thought.

The human dynamics of this "Fellowship" has remained a delicate subject to some friends who shared these experiences with us. This is true even fifty years later. At the time any alternate suggestion to their leadership was seen as a threat, insurrection or outright rebellion.

Such qualities neither of us had ever be labeled with before. One of my Jewish Grandmothers once said so wisely, "It is not how we begin the race, it's how we end it that counts!" Truer words were never spoken.

In all due respect, Ruth was a messenger chosen to bring greater vision and faith to many. Often she succeeded. Sadly, though many of their Fellowship paid dearly in emotional terms for the control inherent in their leadership style. Often it is terribly painful to have to stand up for one's convictions, against those in spiritual authority. But confrontation is a part of growing up and is often required for progressing on to the next level in life. Actually, we can only discern the quality of a life lived by the fruit it produces; not by the power gifts. 1 Corinthians 13. However, we did stay in this autocratic system for some time until Jay was able to resist the continual abuse of our free will. Even God does not do that! So, we moved on.

"But the fruit of the Spirit is love, joy, peace, long suffering, kindness, goodness, faithfulness, gentleness, self-control. Against such there is no law." Galatians 5:22,23

After several more days it was time to head back to Canada. We were up early, packed and, after breakfast, said our farewells. We put all of our money in the offerings, but we were leaving far richer than when we arrived. Brother Heflin Sr. was there cheering us on. As we were pulling away, Sonny Heflin came up and handed me a flyer about his Holy Land trip in October.
"Why don't you join us on this tour to Israel? You will never be the same again."
"Yeah, sounds good," I responded, "but I'll have to save up my pennies, won't I?"
"See you then, slugger." He grinned,

That was a strange note on which to end our trip to the Camp. Or was it? Meridel leaned out of the window waving to the little barefooted girls and teens that were running after us down the dirt lane shouting good byes. What an experience!

Timeless Secrets

"The Spirit of the LORD God is upon Me, because the LORD has anointed Me to preach good tidings to the poor; He has sent Me to heal the broken hearted, proclaim liberty to the captives, the opening of the prison to them that are bound and to proclaim the acceptable year of the LORD." Isaiah 61:1,2a.

Don't kid yourself, there are two realms out there, one of darkness and one of light. Being confronted by the 'dark side' God got my attention! It was a wake-up call. Have you had any lately? I challenge you to be willing to begin to move toward 'The Light' in new ways and explore this unending realm of Life. In order to survive in this world of increasing darkness we must learn to yield more of ourselves to the most powerful force of all, the Holy Spirit of the Living God. The spiritual experiences that we both received were documented in Scripture. This fact gave us courage to know that we were within the safety net of the Word of God. This is something we must never forget. If you can't find a certain teaching in the Bible, have nothing to do with it!

Everything of Satan is Evil. The dark side can lure us with its seemingly beauty. It doesn't have to be ugly or repulsive. This dimension in the spiritual realm is all about pride, deception, control, hatred, murder and death. Everything of the Kingdom of God is Life, joy and peace. Jesus brought mercy, love and victory down by walking and living the Word in order for mankind to understand the heart of Father God. Daily I was learning to walk through my world but hopefully now in the wisdom and kindness of the Holy Spirit. I worked at being faithful to the instructions I received. I did my homework. The battleground is always the mind first. We are exhorted to bring into captivity every thought to the obedience of the Messiah. Every thought! Now if you want a challenge for your life, there it is! But first, if you are sincere and call out for help, the Almighty will answer. This is the miracle and my life is living proof of what I am saying.

I think the most important secret of survival is to live a life of <u>being filled</u> with God's Spirit daily, moment by moment. That is His plan for you. You were created in Love. Ask Him right now to come to you and He will. Keep asking! If you need help, seek guidance and instruction from a trusted, mature leader. Do it! You will not be sorry.

"I will put My Spirit within you and cause you to walk in my statutes and you will keep My judgments and do them." Ezekiel 36:28

"And it shall come to pass afterward, that I will pour out My Spirit upon all flesh; your sons and your daughters shall prophesy, your old men shall dream dreams, your young men shall see visions and also on my menservants and maid servants I will pour out My Spirit in those days." Joel 2:28, 29

Chapter 16

Welcome Home?

"Let God fight your battles for you by holding your peace and going your way. This is opposite to human nature that always wants to justify self…"

Pulling into our driveway in Hamilton, Ontario, Canada, we were welcomed by our entire youth group standing on both sides of our driveway and waving to us. Amidst the many young hands reaching out for David, I saw a hastily drawn 'Welcome Home' sign. I couldn't help but compare this little group to the Virginian kids running behind our car at the camp as we left a few days ago. The similarity was striking, while the settings and cultures were quite different.

Immediately, Meridel put on the kettle and quickly thawed the frozen cookies in the oven. Spreading out blankets on the lawn we enjoyed the moment in the cool and serene evening. We told our eager listeners all that had happened to us in Virginia and they were intrigued. The kids hung on to our every word. All young people love a challenge. Boredom it seems, is the greatest disease of all.

In private they came to us, one by one, unanimously saying, "I want this experience too!" During the next several days we prayed for many of those precious young adults to be 'filled with the Holy Spirit.' The Lord answered prayer!

Meridel:
'We both put a lot of energy into encouraging our youth group to ask questions, break out of their limited backgrounds and learn from every life experience. Jay and I taught them to serve others less fortunate. We visited old folks' homes and busied ourselves with street missions and helping the needy. We taught them to pray for the under privileged, the weak and the sick.

We let them ask us any question, no holds barred. Consequently we had great times together. Their queries flowed freely without any thought of embarrassment in an atmosphere of trust.

Later that summer, my two youngest sisters, fifteen year old Patricia and thirteen year old Nancy Lynn visited us. They chose to endure a long and arduous three day bus trip across Canada from Alberta to Ontario just to get to us. Having left home at seventeen to begin nurse's training my little sisters were just three and five at the time. Those years of separation only served to increase how they idealized me. I sincerely wanted and needed some catch-up time with them. Immediately upon arrival David had their full attention 24/7. Both girls were in great need of comfort and fun after having to endure living with an alcoholic father all their lives. Things were not as bad as when I was a girl at home, but they had been traumatized. Along with many of our youth group they too asked for us to pray for them to received the infilling of the Holy Spirit. One evening in of our living room, they sang duets for us. Since they were tiny tots their voices have resonated perfectly together. In that atmosphere of worship it was very natural for us to pray together. The Spirit of God answered our prayers and filled their hungry hearts. That began their walk with the Comforter, another name for the Holy Spirit. Today, more than 47 years later they are skilled professional community leaders in health care and education.

That summer my sisters helped us make the move to our country home. We spent our mornings outside on the lovely lawns with David romping around on all fours chasing our Siamese cats. Pat played guitar and often together we worshipped the Lord in song. Meanwhile, David, who was in their charge, crawled all over and found his way to the bright red geraniums,. They sang and he happily sat there eating the blossoms and dirt! Yes, now that we had even more space, our county home was 'grand central station' for our teens.
Our door was always open.

Young people have traumas, and most of them are sustained right in their own homes. How perfect it is if they can receive vital healing and deliverance in their tender formative years.

Only our Father in Heaven can see our gifts and true potential.

We love to encourage all people to give Him permission to move upon their lives. A life worth living is the undeniable result. We felt that giving time and energy to the young people, including Pat and Nancy, was one of the most important ways we could spend our time.

Looking back, there are no regrets, except we didn't have enough 'one on one time' for all the kids under our care.

One of the first things we had to do upon our return to Hamilton was to keep my appointment at the Toronto General Hospital.

I had been an outpatient there for fifteen months under the care of North America's top parasitologist. This was arranged by CUSO as a result of her contracting amoeba in India. He was keeping a close eye on me and, to date, there had been no apparent progress after all of his treatments. But now, after examining me, he exclaimed excitedly, "What has happened to you?"

"I was prayed for and God healed me," I told him, beaming.

Smiling, he threw his hands up in the air and excitedly exclaimed, "The God!"

It is not uncommon for a Jew to exclaim thus because in Hebrew the term for God is *Ha Shem* or "The Name!" My short, balding Jewish professor who had escaped from Nazi Germany, still spoke with a heavy German accent. Smiling from ear to ear he said, "I can't find any trace of the disease! *Baruch ha Shem*."[29]

I continue to enjoy the profound effects of healing prayer unto this day. Let us give honor to whom honor is due: to the Lover of our souls, our Savior, Healer and the Rock of our Salvation. Hallelujah!

Jay:

We were growing in faith, energized and excited to know that in fact, 'with God nothing is impossible to him who believes'.[30]

---

[29] "Blessed be the Name", Hebrew for "Praise God!"
[30] Jeremiah 32:17; Luke 1:37

The teens loved feeling 'effective' and knew their prayers were being answered. Sharing the Scriptures about the infilling of God's Holy Spirit became our focus of study with questions and answers. We saw the teens grow in their interest and appetite for a closer relationship with the Lord. They wanted to move on in faith so that their lives could make a difference. When they told their parents of their new experiences, some became very upset. Much to our astonishment we were completely misunderstood.

Several weeks later the Pastor and elders of the church called us 'on the carpet'. The Pastor did not mince words. According to him, we had overstepped our privileges. He and two board members of the church who were also parents of some of our youth were there with him. They asked us to explain our actions. We were being accused of 'confusing' their young people with this 'Pentecostal doctrine' of 'speaking in other tongues.'
Completely taken off guard Meridel and I looked at each other. Naively, we were unaware that this issue of the infilling of the Holy Spirit and speaking in other tongues was generally forbidden in their congregation. Now we were facing the fiery furnace of differences of doctrinal interpretation.

They told us that their official denominational policy concerning this issue was, 'Seek not, Forbid not'. In other words do not seek this experience, but if the Holy Spirit visits you, do not stop it! It sounded 'politically correct' but for us it wouldn't work in practice. We knew beyond a shadow of a doubt that the Bible says something very different. Deuteronomy 4:29 promises that when *"we seek God with all of our heart, we will find Him."*

As Meridel and I stood there, the silence was deafening. Confused, I asked, "Why would anyone refuse a blessing from heaven? Especially, when it concerns their own eager and sincere teenagers?" God clearly worked in our lives and in the hearts of our young people. None of us could deny the work of God's Spirit, but the Pastor and elders sitting before us had to abide by the doctrinal line of their authorities.

Trying to ease the tension in the room the Pastor said, "We, as the Board, have decided to ask you both to step down from your responsibilities with the Youth Group and with your Sunday School class for six months." Taking a deep breath, he continued, "We have decided on this action so we can observe you both to see if, indeed, there is love working in your lives to balance out your experience of the Spirit." They were not impressed by the gifts but needed to see fruit. Although it was Scriptural this seemed rather judgmental.

Meridel:

Doing his duty the thin, nervous Pastor did so in an unemotional, monotonous voice. His piercing, dark eyes seemed to dart at us without meeting our gaze. He played hardball and left no loopholes. It was clear that he was not going to put up with any doctrinal irregularities. The fact that twenty- three millionaires were part of the congregation made me wonder if money had something to do with his action. Inwardly I countered every negative word spoken against us, thinking, *None of the fathers and mothers in the Bible were ever told by the Almighty to take less than all He had provided for them to live by... so why should we?*

Swallowing hard, Jay cleared his throat and said, "Well gentlemen, if that is how you feel, we will comply."
But the more I thought of what was taking place, the more my indignation grew. It was the injustice to the kids that bothered me most.
It's like we've been fired! I thought. *This place has many influential multi-millionaires and they are just making sure that nothing irregular happens to upset the 'status quo'.*

Jay:

In spite of our misgivings Meridel and I both knew that we had to comply. But what about our lovely group of young people? They were so eager to learn and excited to see their prayers answered.
The final blow came from a board member who, as an afterthought stated, "Oh, yes, one other thing! We will not permit our young people to visit your home on Tuesday nights or any time during this probation period."

"We love them and only want the best for them," Meridel protested. "But don't worry gentlemen." She cleared her throat. "We will comply with your wishes. We won't be bothering your kids anymore because God is calling us out of Canada."

In an effort to pour oil upon the troubled waters, I added, "We are very sorry to hear that we have caused you difficulties and concern. However, I'm sure you don't expect us to apologize for the thrilling spiritual growth we've all seen in the lives of our youth group?"

Meridel:

No response was forthcoming. Jay's words hit a 'religious brick wall.' It was just like a ball served in a squash court it bounced right back. The meeting was over. Keeping my eyes lowered we tiptoed out of the office, out of the building, and out of the neighborhood, never to return.

Jay:

Needless to say it was a rather cool parting. Once we were back in the car I asked Meridel, " I'm puzzled. Tell me, where did your statement ' we are leaving Canada' come from?'"

"I don't know? It just flowed out of my mouth. I didn't even think about it!" She explained.

Only later did I realize that she had a prophetic understanding of our future. I was soon to learn more about this gift the Lord has given to her. In fact I am still learning to respect this gift some 50 years later. Meridel is a seer according to the old Biblical terminology, and in the Christian world she would be considered 'prophetic.' This God given gift has both challenged and blessed us over and over again, all through our marriage, family life and ministry. Yes, people have even tried to 'buy' her in order to manipulate the 'gift,' but more of that in Volume 2 of this Timeless Secrets series, called "Miracles among the Nations".

Looking back, I was naive to assume that Christian leaders would not be thrilled to have their young people filled with the love of God through His Holy Spirit, simply because their definition of God's ways are limited by their man made doctrine. Have they missed a key part of

the exciting life God gives to us when we decide to let Him have full control as the

Executive Director of the universe and in our individual lives? He alone
knows the end from the beginning. But an undeniable paradox comes in
here because now the youth group kids loved Jesus more than ever
before in their lives. This became evident after their encounter with the
Holy Spirit. Everyone could see that now they were more effective in
reaching out to others in hospitals, retirement homes and at school.
They sang and loved as never before. It was heart warming to see the
generations coming together. The kids were torn by the curfew set by
their parents and church leadership that actually made them even more
desperate for spiritual food. Now they would come to visit us secretly
almost every day because nearly all had cars. I cautioned them. "We have
to honor your parent's and the pastor's decision." Nevertheless they
came and we tried our best to answer their many questions, albeit briefly.

Next, I began searching for a mentor, or some wise spiritual person to talk
to about our situation. Rejection hurts. It chips away at one's self-esteem.
I had never been rejected like this. Especially because we felt that we had
done nothing wrong we were disturbed by the sense of guilt hovering
over us. In desperation, I opened the *Hamilton Spectator* and turned to
the church page. Finding someone named Pastor David Mainse I quickly
called and made an appointment to meet with him and his wife.

David answered and warmly invited us to their home located on the
upper level of the city of Hamilton, called 'the Mountain'. We had no idea
what to expect and we were instantly comforted by his wife, Norma
Jean's warm greeting at the door. She led the way into their family room
attached to the kitchen. Her voice was mellow and calming. Her soft laugh
broke the sense of 'strangeness' we were feeling.
As we sat around the coffee table, she served us warm home made
muffins and mugs of coffee. David came in and greeted us. What a
relief it was just to have good fun with such kind and easy going folks that
morning.
David excitedly told us about their new weekly fifteen minute TV show,
called "Crossroads".

Looking back, I will never forget David as Pastor, standing tall, his love-ly face beaming, as he plucked his big bass with the praise group musicians in Bethel Gospel Tabernacle on Hamilton Mountain. We loved their expressive music, and joy surged through us in finding true friends who encouraged us.

He is the kind of Christian leader we were delighted to find at last. Norma Jean is the essence of human kindness.

We were thirsty, so thirsty for this example of genuine goodness.

Meridel and I are forever grateful for their love and prayers at a pivotal time in our lives. We have remained friends for more than forty years. Even our children are close.

Timeless Secrets

"He said, and whoever will not receive you nor hear your words, when you depart from that house or city shake off the dust from your feet."
Matthew 10:14

Read on to discover one of the most important timeless secrets of all! You cannot please everyone all the time! I suggest that when you come to a closed door, or if the door is slammed in your face, simply move on. The only successful way to do this is learning to close the door behind you before you try to advance. Jesus strongly rebuked the religious elite of his day. He stood up for mercy and truth, but it cost him big time. Jesus countered the politically and religiously 'correct' crowd.

Never ever, under any circumstances speak against the work of the Holy Spirit. The Bible clearly warns us on this issue. This is one of the most vital truths of all because the Word of God says that all sins can be forgiven except blasphemy against the Holy Spirit.

Our Father in Heaven speaks. He speaks out loud or by the 'still small voice.' Jesus speaks, and endorses the Father; we have the New Testament record as proof. But who speaks for the Holy Spirit and His work on earth? None, except you and I. He is totally dependent on our endorsement of His amazing work of teaching, guiding, comforting, delivering and blessing people.

However, if He is spoken against or misrepresented, the damage is irreparable. Jesus warned His disciples when the multitudes cursed Him and accused Him of casting out demons by the power of Satan. He said, *"How can Satan cast out Satan? If a kingdom is divided against itself, that kingdom cannot stand... Assuredly, I say to you, all sins will be forgiven the sons of men and whatever blasphemies they may utter, but he who blasphemes against the Holy Spirit never has forgiveness, but is subject to eternal condemnation - because they said, (to Jesus) he has an unclean spirit."* Mark 3:23, 24, 28-30 NKJ

It is a given that we all will encounter trying situations in life. One of the most difficult responses for anyone to make is to let God fight your battles for you by holding your peace and going your way. This is opposite to human nature that always wants to justify self. I am speaking specifically about a situation when you know that you have done nothing wrong. It is only natural to want to return an 'eye for an eye,' to get even, or to have the last word. But it never works. Man is very clumsy at revenge. Wait, and let God work to vindicate you.
I remembered my mother's good advice, "The least said the easiest mended."

Today, as the father of four sons and eight grandchildren I am positive that the most important treasure I could impart to them is to desire the Kingdom of God and His 'wisdom'.
Proverbs 7:4 and 9:10 instruct us to, *"Say to wisdom, you are my sister and call understanding your nearest kin."*
If men actually read and lived by the treasures of Biblical morality, wisdom and knowledge given in the tiny book of Proverbs, the world would be a completely different place. Just try reading a chapter a day. As you do it then ask the Lord to open the new doors He has already prepared before you.

"Happy is the man who finds wisdom and the man who gains understanding. For her proceeds are better than the profits of silver and her gain than fine gold." Proverbs 3:13, 14

Chapter 17

Go Among the Nations

"You called me too," I cried. "Why would You not let me go with Jay?" …. No answers came…"

Meridel:

Here our story picks up from Chapter One. Wow, who would believe that daring to listen and obey the voice of God could bring so much change in just one month? I wondered if Abraham started out after just thirty days of 'prep' on his way to the Promised land? But I see our spiritual life something like our natural life. We are conceived in secret and yet we are not 'born' until we reach the 9th month. How long is God's gestation period in any life before it awakens to a spiritual birth? No one knows exactly where it all begins. How can we measure the value of the prayers of our Godly ancestors? Prayer is 'living out' an ongoing conversation with our Heavenly Father. The more we learn about faith and following the less we can take credit for anything. His plans are not our plans; His ways are not our ways. For example the Book of Psalms is as alive today as it was when it was written 3,000 years ago. It is as much a book of praise as it is prayer and is completely relevant today. That is why the Word of God is called 'the living Word.'

Jay:

Saturday morning, October 18, 1969 we were to leave Hamilton to commence our 'journey of a lifetime'. By now, our home was completely empty. My second cousin Jean and her husband, Norm, insisted that we spend our last night in Canada with them. Norm, a hard working brick layer, couldn't for the life of him understand why I gave up my position, which held so much promise of financial security. Taking off his plaid cap, and scratching his bald head he said, "Really, Jay, I just can't believe you are doing this! You have such a good future in the hospital world."

Before leaving Canada to Israel in September, 1969

Actually, Norm raised a valid point. I discovered, some thirty five years later, that a few of my classmates were earning six figure salaries or more a year as executives of the largest hospitals and healthcare services across Canada. But our course was set. The compass was pointing east.

Our trip to New York started out rather auspiciously. We kissed and hugged Jean and Norm, midst a few 'wee tears' and so we launched out from southern Ontario. Steve, a young man from our youth group, volunteered to drive the three of us to JFK Airport in New York. He borrowed his father's luxurious new Cadillac for the trip. The lesson we learned by being shown this favor simply proves that if we 'let go and let God' He is able to accomplish wonderful things.

The Cadillac was owned by one of the most influential elders in the church who put us on probation concerning their youth group. This turn of events was quite ironic because, in spite of the elegant transportation we enjoyed, I had only a few dollars in my wallet. After having paid all of our bills we had just enough for gasoline, food expenses and an overnight stay along the way to the airport in New York. This situation has never changed over the past forty five years . The Lord's provision is simply enough for this day, not more, not less.

A mighty challenge loomed upon this new horizon. Meridel and I were painfully aware of our financial vulnerability. Even though we had only paid for one air ticket to Israel and around the world, Meridel also packed her and David's suitcase including summer clothes.
We launched out 'by faith'. Although we had declared to everyone our intentions to follow the Lord, we always sensed that we should only tell Him about our needs, which He knew of anyway!
So we said nothing about our financial straits.

Meridel:
It was a sleepless night, my mind was working overtime and there were no answers. Jay was exhausted from the whole ordeal of the past month. He had chosen to let go and walk away from his dreams in exchange for a life of faith, which we knew little about.
Unlike Abraham's 'household' of flocks and servants, this man set out with two small suitcases, a baby carrier, the sad wife and a nine month-old first born son. We were a curiosity, an oddity, and very much alone.

Soon I heard Jay's deep rhythmic breathing that comes to the exhausted. David snuggled down beside me and never stirred.
Both lay in 'perfect peace,' something I knew little or nothing about that night. Crying out the pain tears streamed in rivulets down my face. When the dam of pent up longing broke my nightie and pillow became soaked. Every part of me hurt and I tried to convert my pain into prayer. I have always believed that I am being heard when I pray, which for me is simply pouring out my thoughts and emotions.

"LORD," I silently cried out, trying not to make any noise and wake Jay. "You called me too... why would You not let me go with Jay?" Sobbing, my body shook with emotion. Like an old record player whose needle gets stuck my mind kept running in circles. No answers came...

The deep stillness of the night was soft and yielding, as if it were listening to my cries. Serene silver light from the full moon blanketed us. Visible and invisible shadows that had once filled our room melted as the moon rose in the sky. Slowly the tension eased away. I don't remember giving in to the relief of sleep, it just came over me as kindly as the gentle moon light. The only shadow that remained in the room was the one covering my soul.

"Meridel..." Jay whispered as he shook my shoulder gently to awaken me. Bright sunshine hurt my tired eyes that were red from lack of sleep. My eyelids were embarrassingly puffy from too much crying. Today was the fateful day... October 20, 1969! We had waited for this day with great anticipation. For the last thirty days we both worked day and night to be ready to leave our homeland. Jay had staked his whole life on the belief that the living God told him that we would be leaving. But... still I had no ticket!

There were no butterflies in my stomach now, only an emotional numbness that comes when one can't cry anymore. I couldn't even think about the fact that I might have to turn back. Jay and I didn't talk about it. His cheery spirit, along with David's irresistible smile and baby talk, helped me brighten up. Our tiny son's life was on the line too. What a message to me it was! Didn't I also have an *Abba*, a Daddy in heaven? Didn't He know my need even before I asked? He was my Shepherd. I shall not want! That day, those words were of little comfort because I was so filled with want and longing.

Jay:

Steve dropped us at the huge John F. Kennedy Airport concourse in New York City. We blessed him for his kindness and I emptied out my wallet to make sure he had enough money to get back to Canada.

Next, we found our tour group assembling before the SAS check-in counter. As we got into the lineup of more than 50 people, our tour leader, Wallace Heflin, Jr. came up and said as kindly as he could, "Well, Slugger, how wonderful to see you three here!" Despite his smile he seemed surprised. "You understand, of course that I had to cancel Meridel's ticket as well as David's because you didn't send us any deposit payment?"

"I know." I glanced at Meridel. "But we still believe for a miracle for their tickets."

Looking a bit dumbfounded by my boldness, or was it foolishness, Wallace said, "I'll agree with you in prayer for the tickets."

"Thanks, now we'll just sit over here out of the way and... pray." I gently guided Meridel and David to the side.

As a Pastor and man of faith Wallace was sympathetic to our predicament but he couldn't do much for us so close to departure time. We all knew that we needed a kind of parting of the Red Sea miracle. Remember, this was happening in an era before 'e-tickets.' We needed complicated 'round the world' fares which could not be issued at the airport in 1969. I didn't even have a credit card to arrange the last minute payment. In spite of our predicament we tried to remain hopeful.

Some of the tour members who became aware of our situation came over to us with words of encouragement. Logically speaking, it seemed impossible. We were on our own. Again that awful sense of aloneness and anxiousness increased. The final members of the group checked in. Watching their suitcases disappear down the baggage conveyor belt had a certain sense of finality to it.
All we could do was pray!

When two businessmen walked into the check-in area they called our tour leader and began conferring in a quiet counter. Meanwhile, Meridel was trying to comfort nine-month old-David who was fussy, tired and needing his afternoon nap. A few minutes later, the tour leader walked over to me.

Motioning me to come to the side he said in a hushed tone, as not to wake David, "Jay, something just happened that is hard to explain. A lady from St. Louis can't make the tour due to the sudden illness of her mother. She wants a refund but her 'round the world' ticket is written to exactly the same cities as yours. It's quite amazing! The owner of the tour company is here from Chicago with this news. Also, the manager of SAS Airlines in New York is here. These two men are the only ones authorized to change the passenger name on the cancelled ticket and substitute Meridel's name. All you have to do is pay them the $1,800 and Meridel can go. They can also issue an infant ticket, on the spot, for John David, as he can sit on your lap. This will cost a further ten percent. So if you can come up with $1,980 right now, you can join the tour group. Can you do it?"

With anticipation and faith rising, I said, "Well, let me talk it over with Meridel."

After explaining the situation to her, all she said was, "God called me too." Then we heard over the loud speaker above us, "Would Mr. Jay Rawlings please pick up the white service telephone?"

I looked around, wondering if it was the Lord speaking. Quickly I went to a nearby counter and picked up the receiver of the ringing phone. "Hello," I answered.

"Mr. Rawlings?"

"Yes, that's me."

"Wait on the line, please," the operator said. "You have a long distance call from Canada."

"Who could that be?" I wondered, waiting for the call to be put through.

"JV? (my nickname). Is that you?" Mom asked. "Son..." was all Dad said.

"Yes Mom." Relief flooded my voice. "But how did you know where to find me?"

"Well, we called the JFK Airport and told them our son was leaving on SAS Airlines," Mom said. "And that we just had to wish him and his wife, 'Bon Voyage,' and they put me through. But do you need anything?"

After a few seconds of silence I said, "We really appreciate your thoughtfulness." I took a deep breath. "I may have to send Meridel and David to you for a while, until they can come to me."

"What?" Mom exclaimed. "What's the matter? Don't you have enough money for their tickets?"

I was silent and then confessed, "That's right, Mom, I don't."

"Well," she ordered, "Get off the phone and get their tickets NOW. You cannot go without her." I could hardly believe my ears. Her next statement took me by complete surprise. "Money is no problem. We want to send you whatever you need. How do we do it?"

"Well," I said, "I think your timing is perfect!"

"What? What, do you mean?"

When I explained the situation we were she said in a breaking voice, "Oh, quickly! Tell us where to wire the money. We will do it right now."

"Oh, thank you! This is amazing!" Shouting excitedly into the phone drew the attention of some people. While I was still on the phone a business man in a striped grey suit approached me. Jack Chappell, one of the tour member and a successful Virginian executive, instantly assessed the situation. After speaking with the tour operators, Jack said, "I can write you a check on the spot for your tickets."

"Really?" I was dumbfounded.

"Yes, consider it done," he smiled. "Just have your parents wire the money to my bank account."

He proceeded to write a personal check for $1,980 - enough to purchase Meridel and David's miracle tickets.

My mind was almost spinning out of control. Turning back to the phone I said, "Mom, Dad, could you wire funds for our tickets to a gentleman here in the States who is writing a check as I speak?"

"Yes, just get us the details, Jay," Dad now said.

"How can I ever thank you Dad? This is an answer to our prayers... in fact it is a miracle."

"Now son, you know I'm not a believing man. Don't go telling everyone it was us!" It was his way of cautioning me not to get carried away. Mom was crying. "It is so hard to say good bye. Look after wee David and love each other," were her parting instructions as we signed off.

Immediately I joined Rev Heflin the tour leader and Jack, along with the heads of SAS and the tour company. All the arrangements were completed in about twenty minutes. The waiting check-in attendants quickly processed us, and tagged our bags. Mysteriously, mechanical repairs delayed our flight one hour, giving us time to run to the departure gate, board the plane and find our seats. We settled down in the huge aircraft feeling excited and very, very grateful. No one but the Lord God of Israel could have engineered all of those many last minute details ! The wonder of it all is that He had chosen to work through ordinary people like the head of the airlines, the lady who cancelled her tour, the tour operator, Mom and Dad and Jack.

That was it! It was done! We were on our way.

Then, as if putting the icing on the cake, another tour member, Harold McDougal, an American serving in the Philippines, put two brand new $20 US bills in my hand.

"Thanks Harold," I said, reading his name tag. Grinning, I put the bills into my empty wallet.

That was an extra blessing because for the next three weeks all of our expenses were paid on the tour. While writing about our launch to Israel over forty-five years ago, I realize that those forty dollars have multiplied over and over, countless times, as we learned to trust Him along the way. You will read about some of these remarkable miracles of how God supplied in the next volumes in this series.

Timeless Secrets

"But this I say: He who sows sparingly will also reap sparingly,
and he who sows bountifully will also reap bountifully.
So let each one give as he purposes in his heart,
not grudgingly or of necessity;
for God loves a <u>cheerful</u> giver."
2 Corinthians: 9: 6,7

Finally there are some amazing secrets in this chapter that I want to share with you as we conclude Volume 1. For example, I have discovered that the Lord wants to meet both the natural and spiritual needs of any sincere follower. The key is the universal principle of sowing and reaping. What a man sows he is going to reap, whether it is attitude, potatoes, grain, time, acts of loving kindness, or money.

Without even realizing it, our last months were filled with sowing the 'truth' of faith in the invisible God into our lives first and then those in our family, congregation and hospital community. It just happened naturally, as we tried to walk and live in obedience to a different drum. This pattern has been our portion over the years and I believe this is how the Lord wants it to happen - spiritual blessings happen naturally.

Next, about money! Tithing is a way of sowing. The tithing principle is tried and true; it always releases funds to anyone who faithfully pays his tithe by giving 10% or more of their gross income to the Lord's work. Do you realize that by doing this, you are making the Almighty your Senior Financial Partner? 'Doing' is the key word here, because you are then actually sowing into His Kingdom or to the poor of it all around you. He will reciprocate and see to it that you will reap the benefit, in good time. Start to give your tithes and offerings with joy and generosity, without fail. It is a 'blessed' way of life. All I know is that it works. You cannot out give God.

We would never have been able to complete the forty five years of work and all of the projects that we were called to do without this principle being fully operative in our lives. It would have been impossible to accomplish the speaking, writing, traveling, film production, TV shows, and Internet sites, purchasing of TV time, publishing and supporting other worthy causes and people without God giving us the increase via tithing.

Meridel also faithfully tithes of our personal funds and, in so doing, we've never lacked when it came to renting homes, educating our sons in international schools and universities and paying mortgages to build a home. This is astounding when you consider that we are not part of an established system. We had no back up support, other than from ordinary individuals who were inspired by our work and donated to the furtherance of it. These people are our heroes! Why? First, they are lovers of God who comprehend the value of what we do for His kingdom on earth and His people. Secondly, they were obedient to His voice and thirdly because they live out the principle of sowing and reaping.

Dear reader, as you consider the Scripture below on tithing, please note, this is the only time in the Bible when the Lord asks us to 'try' Him and to 'prove' Him on any matter. Trusting with obedience is the underlying requirement of tithing. We tithe to God, but we give to man. There is a difference. God gives the increase back and yes, He uses people.

Malachi 3:10 says, "Bring all the tithes into the storehouse that there may be food in my house. And prove Me now in this", Says the Lord of hosts, "If I will not open for you the windows of Heaven and pour out for you such a blessing that there will not be room enough to receive it."

Tithes, as I mentioned, can be paid in many ways according to scripture. Here are some examples from the Hebrew Bible. One can give tithe to the poor, to widows, to the fatherless, to the storehouse where you receive your spiritual food or on occasion one can even use it to create a feast and to invite ones neighbors to attend.

---

[31] Crudens Concordance on "tithes", page 694

In ancient Israel tithe was paid in ones produce of the tiniest spices such as mint and cumin or olives, olive oil, grain, fruit or kind such as livestock. Even firewood was required to be tithed. [31]

"And all the tithe of the land whether of the seed of the land or of the fruit of the trees, is the Lord's. It is holy to the Lord!" Leviticus 27:30

The Cohanim (the Priestly family) and the Levites were supported entirely by their local community as they performed their priestly functions. How? By their tithing and freewill offerings. In North America the emphasis is almost completely on returning the 'tithe' to ones local church. In the New Testament neither Jesus nor his apostles have commanded anything in this affair of tithing.

I encourage you <u>to begin to try it</u>. I know that in a marriage often a couple fails to pay tithe because of one of the partner's negative attitude or uninformed opinion. One, perhaps sees it as throwing money away. Yet, if you will agree together and do this faithfully, you will bless yourself out of debt. When the economy of your world gets shaky, because we all go through down times, you will survive. God always has a better idea. Give your best to the Lord and He will show you what to do and how to find ways that will pull you through. If you have been faithful and honest with your time, energy and tithe money, you are not going to be alone and destitute in the hard times. He will be with you.

"He who has pity on the poor lends to the Lord. And He will pay back what he has given." Proverbs 19:17

Expect financial well being to follow when you tithe. Realize that tithing is not only a part of the Mosaic Law where the tenth already belongs to God but it is a timeless covenant of privilege to exercise in joyous giving...not as a grudging legal requirement.

On the way to Israel, October 1969
At the Tivoli Fountain in Rome

David with friend in Egypt at the Nile River,
on the way to Israel

Chapter 18

My People Forever

For You have made Your people Israel;
Your very own people forever.
2 Samuel 7:24

I believe one of the most direct ways in which one can be blessed is to love what God loves. It is clear from the entire Biblical record that God has chosen His People, Israel, to be an example people to the rest of the world. It is not because they are better but simply because God chose to use them as an example to the world, giving blessings for obedience and discipline for disobedience.

As the SAS airliner roared, full throttle, eastward down the JFK airport runway, my thoughts were of thankfulness for His mighty provision. We were, however, hurtling towards a completely new reality: our encounter with Israel. It was departure day from all that was familiar. The memories of our last month's activities in Canada began to fade and soon seemed worlds away as the plane slowly banked. From my window, flashes of sunlight, now low on the horizon, glinted off the glass clad buildings of the New York skyline.

Yes, we sat amazed at the way the Lord had launched us so dramatically, yet honestly I felt panic rising. As the plane gained altitude my previous securities dissolved. What had I done? I had just given up a very lucrative job and promising career in a world I was familiar with. Now, I was taking my young family into the unknown. Israel, to me, was only a dream and Jerusalem, the intriguing Holy City, mentioned eight hundred times in the Bible was a mystery. The stark reality was that from now on, I had no income, no backing. It was just Meridel, David, me and the Lord. Honestly, I'd like to say I had great faith at that moment, but it felt more like great fear.

Up until this point in my life, I had not learned the *Timeless Secret* of tithing nor embraced the trust factor required to start and to keep on putting aside 10% of my income for the Lord. Soon I was to learn that with obedience comes faith and confidence.

Someone said that fear is the opposite of faith and that faith grows through hearing... in this case hearing the Word of God as Romans 10:17 tells us. After dinner, as we all settled down to sleep while traversing the North Atlantic, I took out my pocket Bible, clicked on my overhead light and started to read about Abraham of old who had left his father's house and in obedience taken his family on a journey. He didn't know where he was going either, but the Lord who called him did. That helped to calm me down but still it was a daunting adventure.
My step-dad had taught me the principle of being a good provider for my family, thus it was deeply ingrained in me. Now I was being forced to look to my Heavenly Father as my source. *Is this faith or presumption,* I wondered?

En route to Israel we had brief stopovers in Denmark, Italy, Egypt, Cyprus and Lebanon. I was quietly grateful for the new experiences of learning about different cultures, languages and customs. Meridel took it all in her stride having been a world traveler as a single woman. David was the picture of health bouncing on her lap or riding high on my back in his baby carrier. He drew smiles everywhere we went with his outgoing 9 month old personality.

Finally, we landed at Lod (now Ben Gurion) Airport in Israel. It was a beautiful sunny, clear and warm day but we were not prepared for what was about to happen to us. The moment our feet hit the hot tarmac we both had a powerful sense that we had come 'home!' We could not rationalize this feeling, yet it was there ever so strong. I had never been to Israel before but this new sense of 'home coming' was unmistakable. There is an expression in scripture, "my heart leapt." That is what happened to both of us almost simultaneously. It was a 'supernatural knowing.'

This was Meridel's second trip to Israel and her resonance with the land was even stronger now than on her first visit. As we walked from the plane into the terminal we both fought against our tears . *What is this feeling?* I wondered, gradually realizing that this unshakable sense of 'belonging' in my spirit was a personal witness and confirmation of the truth given to Abraham four thousand years ago. This foundational promise was concerning the land of Israel. It was given by God's Spirit to Abraham and to his descendants. This sacred oath has two parts: an everlasting covenant with His people and an everlasting possession, His land. As in any contract it also had a built in time element. This one is... forever.

I realized then that Israel's prophetic destiny gave the Hebrew prophets the unique privilege of penning the mind and message of God for man and the nations. This is Israel's greatest gift to mankind - the Bible. The Hebrew word *Tanach* is an acronym of the Hebrew letters, *TNK - Torah* - the first 5 books of Moses, *Nevi'im*, the Prophets and lastly the *Ketuvim*, the Writings including Psalms, Proverbs and the minor Prophets. All these comprise the Jewish Bible.

Something happened the moment we physically placed our feet onto this Land of Promise! We were somehow touching the living, foundational and everlasting Abrahamic Covenant. Our soul and spirit witnessed that we had returned to the physical place where these promises were first given over the land and over the chosen people. The call that Abraham received was unique, thus completely original. When he finally arrived in Bethel, I wonder if he was overwhelmed by a sense of the Almighty's pleasure? Was it possible that 4,000 years later, we were also experiencing something similar? How did he know he was in the right place? We know from scripture that he heard the still small voice. He had a divine "witness" and a name change.

No matter what politicians say this ancient covenant is still in effect today because it is an irrevocable pledge that God Himself watches over and keeps His word concerning the Promised Land and His Chosen People.

In Genesis 17:5-8 we read what God spoke to Abraham to begin this unique relationship: *"No longer shall your name be Abram, but your name shall be Abraham; for I have made you a father of many nations. I will make you exceedingly fruitful; and I will make nations of you and kings shall come from you. And I will establish My covenant between Me and you and your descendants after you in their generations, for an everlasting covenant to be God to you and your descendants after you. Also I give to you and your descendants after you the land in which you are a stranger, all the land of Canaan, as an everlasting possession and I will be their God."*

Blessed be the Lord God of Israel from everlasting to everlasting!
1 Chronicles 16:36

I was intrigued by this unmistakable awareness that we were now witnessing! Clearly it was something of immense value from the past as well as something very much alive in the present moment. Yes, in the here and now we could feel it. Otherworldly, yes! Hard to comprehend intellectually, yes! Palpable, yes! I was beginning to grasp it, but couldn't explain it. All I knew was that the concept of "covenant" is one of the most foundational in Scripture. The Hebrew word for covenant, *Brit* appears several hundred times in the Jewish scriptures or *Tanach*. Now, in this instance, we are referring to an everlasting covenant or *Brit Olam*.

> Strong's # 5703, *"Olam"* means - forever, ever, or "ad" in Hebrew meaning everlastingness, perpetuity, eternity, evermore, forever; time passing on and on, for all time forward, continually, without end.

That, to me is a very long time!

I saw that such a covenant, agreement or contract could be between individuals, a ruling king and his subjects, or between God and His people. In Genesis chapter 17, the Almighty was pledging, without precondition, an unbreakable oath that He would be the "One and Only God" to Abraham and His offspring <u>forever</u>.

The Promised Land was to be the stage upon which this Divine drama would unfold. As we know, throughout history, this drama has involved all of humanity past and present and indeed for the future. God makes it clear, that no matter what Abraham or his progeny, through Isaac, did, He would keep His part of the bargain, FOREVER!

Why was this covenant established? That is the question of the ages! Abraham had been called out of an idolatrous family and nation. The world was then and still is filled with man-made gods, but Abraham's God was different. He called Himself, 'the Most High God.' That means 'the One and Only; like no other' and who is incomparable. This promise to Abraham is actually the foundation stone of Israel's eternal relationship to God and reveals the Almighty's loving nature or character. When Abraham showed his willingness to offer his son Isaac, then the covenant was set forever. I discovered that all other Bible promises are based on this one. It is a truth confirmed by King David and by the Lord Himself that Israel will be a nation forever.

"Thus says the Lord, Who gives the sun for a light by day, the ordinances of the moon and the stars for a light by night, who disturbs the sea, and its waves roar, The Lord of Hosts is His name. If those ordinances depart from Me, says the Lord, Then the seed of Israel shall also cease, from being a nation before me forever." Jeremiah 31:35,36

As we made our way from the airport terminal, I glanced up at the bright Israeli sun, set in the cobalt blue sky. Yup, the sun was still shining. This is a daily confirmation that Israel is here to stay. I was comforted in that moment and shared these thoughts later with Meridel amidst a few "wee tears" as I realized we were in the midst of a revelation that would change us forever.

Upon arrival in Jerusalem our tour guide took us immediately to the Mount of Olives for an overview of the Holy City. The ancient walls of Jerusalem lay before us. I felt I could reach out and touch the Golden Gate, known in Hebrew as the Mercy Gate. Jews and Christians believe Messiah will walk through this gate when He enters the Holy City. Graves of the faithful lay at our feet on the Mount of Olives, sleeping in the dust until resurrection day. What stories these souls could tell us! The reality was breath taking!

Sight-seeing in Israel, October 1969

We had stepped into ancient yet modern history welded together right before our eyes. This was 1969, just two years after the Six Day War. At the time the atmosphere in the Holy Land was one of pride, confidence and euphoria. The Israeli people had hope and expectation for their future. Since 1967, Jerusalem was now in the hands of the Jewish people. It was the first time in over 2,000 years that the Holy City was united under Jewish sovereignty.

In a miraculous way it had been quickly wrestled out of the hands of the Gentiles or the invading Arab armies of Syria, Egypt, and Jordan fulfilling the prophecy of Jesus in Luke 21: 24 which says, Jerusalem will be trampled by Gentiles until the times of the Gentiles are fulfilled.

But now the battle was to be ratcheted up a notch. According to Islam, Christians and Jews are called the "people of the Book" and all are worthy of death at the end of days if they do not convert to Islam. It was clear to me that the "jesus" of Islam is not the Jesus of the Bible. There was so much to learn.

Little David loved his vantage point, sitting in his carrier high up on my back. Frankly he was quickly gaining weight and by this time was quite a 'load.' He made friends everywhere we went. I remember several evenings later, as we were walking to our hotel just inside the New Gate, we passed by an army truck packed with Israeli soldiers waiting for their orders. We were soon encircled. They spoke only Hebrew but wanted to gently touch David's blond hair and squeeze his rosy red cheeks. Those teenagers looked so robust, healthy, and very handsome.

They were the 'vibrant new nation of Israel' born out of the ashes of the Holocaust. I thought immediately of the words of the prophet Ezekiel which he received from the Spirit of God. In obedience and faith he wrote: *"Prophesy breath... and breath came into them, and they lived and stood upon their feet, an exceedingly great army."* Ezekiel 37:10

Now the Bible literally came alive to us. Every day was an unfolding adventure. We went north to visit the Sea of Galilee, the Lebanese Border area, and the Golan Heights. Our last afternoon in that area, Meridel and I spent time sitting on the shores of the Kineret, thus named because the Sea of Galilee is shaped like a harp, *kinor* in Hebrew. Drinking in the beauty we also enjoyed the warm sunshine and the cool water. We shared our hearts with each other while small waves lapped at our feet. She didn't want to go anywhere. She was ready to stop, leave the tour and stay forever in Israel.

As for me, I was astounded that God had chosen this minuscule parcel of real estate for Himself. We discovered that the Sea of Galilee was like a heart shaped jewel. It is a liquid oasis in the midst of a desert area on earth. It is tiny in comparison to the Canadian Great Lakes or the Caspian Sea. I could see from one end of it to the other and across it easily. Yet, from here the words of Jesus were sown into the nations. His teachings have been carried far and wide by the wind of God's Spirit. Now a mighty harvest has grown up from His life giving words... worldwide! Here we sat, two thousand years later, witnesses to the truth of the prophets of Israel and of the Son of Man, Jesus. It was a timeless moment. The Word of God was and always is alive! Daily it is accomplishing what it was sent to do; to bring life out of death!

By the end of our two weeks in Israel, we had become accustomed to the sights, sounds, aromas and unique spiritual dimension that surround the Holy land. The peoples are colorful, vibrant, friendly and expressive. We loved to stop at roadside kiosks and eat hummus, falafel with salads stuffed inside fresh pita bread, and to finish up with strong Turkish coffee. We particularly enjoyed the novelty of so many small shops and the variety of shopkeepers we met.
Everyone had a story to tell.

Meridel was 'gung-ho' as we say. She reminded me about her first visit to Israel in 1965. As a single young woman, she took time to visit the Chagall windows at Hadassah Hospital Medical Centre.
It was then, during a quiet moment in the chapel where the stained glass masterpieces are mounted she vowed to the Lord, "I could live here forever!" That statement was prophetic.
Now five years later as a married couple, we could never have imagined all that did transpire to bring us to this moment. Little did we realize that our future was to be forever intertwined with the Eternal city of Jerusalem?

We did get a slight inkling, though, of what was to come. Just before we were to leave Israel, the Lord gave us this word in prayer:

"I have brought you to My home. One day it will also be your home! I am calling you here. Now, go and travel among the nations. Go to My people and call them to come home to the "promised land. You will travel, and travel, and travel. You will be in some places a day; other places a week; other places a month and in other places a year. Fear not. If you will listen to My voice and heed it, I will be with you and provide for you wherever you go. Remember, in the hard times, I will bring you back home! Go in peace!"

There it was again. The Lord's still small voice had given us our next set of instructions. They were clear yet vague. They were just vague enough for us to have to launch out 'by faith.' We didn't know where to go or what to do exactly. We had air tickets to the next destination and that was all we knew.

I remember praying with Meridel about our future in a cold hotel room in the Sisters of Zion Convent located just inside the walls of the Old City of Jerusalem, "Oh Lord, not our will but Your will be done in our lives."
We both sensed that the 'round the world' plane tickets we had so miraculously been given held the key to the route that we were to follow. Mind you, being human, we briefly considered cashing them in and staying in Israel. But once the Lord had told us to "go to His people among the nations" we discarded that idea. *Is this how one learns to "follow the Lord?* we wondered. It seemed a steep learning curve.

Meridel:

Jay, David and I walked down to the Western Wall, making our way through the busy and colorful Arab market. Now that Jerusalem has been united since 1967, Jews could pray at their holiest site denied them for the previous nineteen years. From 1948 until June 6th 1967, the Western Wall, considered the 'most holy' of Jewish sites, was barred to all Jews. When the Jordanian army was in control, they systematically decimated the Jewish Quarter. Synagogues and homes were burned.

Gravestones were used as latrines, garbage dumps, and stables. Now since '67 while under Jewish control, Israel cleaned up and restored the ruins of both churches and mosques in the area. They allowed Christians and Muslims to freely worship in their own sanctuaries.

We were enjoying our 'family time' in Jerusalem but as we approached the wall, we both had a sense of expectation. For what? We were not sure. I was happy to see the plaza was free of crushing crowds and relatively quiet this warm sunny November afternoon. Jay and David entered the men's side and I the woman's. The intensity of prayer could be felt as I joined my sisters, many of whom were supplicating with tears. With my forehead resting against the warm Jerusalem stone, I found myself relaxing into its soft smooth living warmth. Immediately I sensed, 'God is in this place.'

Four thousand years ago, Jacob uttered similar words.
"Surely the Lord is in this place, and I did not know it. How awesome is this place! This is none other than the house of God, and this is the gate of heaven!" Genesis 28:16,17

I understood that the Western Wall is a natural, historical and spiritual treasure whose spiritual dimensions go all the way back to Abraham and his willingness to sacrifice Isaac on Mt. Moriah. It serves as a constant reminder of God's promises to Israel. It is the remains of a significant part of the foundational retaining wall of the Temple of Herod the Great, which stood in the time of Jesus. It is one of the mysteries of history that the Romans left the retaining walls in place that we see today. Herod's Temple was built on the remains of the humble temple of the returned Jewish captives from Babylon led by Ezra and Nehemiah. They in turn, under the constant threat of war built their simple temple over the ruins of King Solomon's Great Temple.

We sensed another dimension of the plan of God: He is 'The God of Mercy' as He is known in the First Covenant. Mercy in Hebrew is *rachamim* whose root is *rechem* - womb. I was so aware of the Almighty's 'heart of mercy' at work birthing within the fabric of the nation of Israel and in the lives of Israeli's His Plan.

It is a plan for national redemption through the Messiah! God's plans are good and are continually unfolding. His prophetic plan, in gestation for so long, is now appearing for those who have eyes to see.

Of course, He has heard the prayers of His People all down through the millennia and here we were standing in the reality of answered prayer. The nation now reborn is thriving, birthed out of the graveyard of history. No other people have this heritage. They have been resurrected out of the ashes of the Holocaust. Actually the Jewish people have suffered untold persecutions and death throughout history. His people are now alive in their
ancient homeland and speaking their revived biblical language. This has never happened before to any other people. Daily prayers offered faithfully from ancient times have been answered.

"Now, it shall come to pass in the latter days that the Mount of the Lord's House shall be established on the top of the mountains, and shall be exalted above the hills; and all nations shall flow to it. Many people shall come and say, "Come, and let us go up to the mountain of the Lord, to the House of the God of Jacob; He will teach us of His ways, and we shall walk in His paths. For out of Zion shall go forth the law and the word of the Lord from Jerusalem." Isaiah 2:2,3

Standing in this holy place, I felt like a child reconnected to the umbilical cord. Jerusalem speaks of the source of my own existence and all that I love. To me Jerusalem represents the 'mother heart' of God. Jerusalem is also the altar of God on earth. This, I believe, is what separates Jerusalem from all other cities in the world.

"I am zealous for Zion with great zeal. I will return to Zion and dwell in the midst of Jerusalem. Jerusalem shall be called the city of Truth. I have chosen Jerusalem, the mountain of the Lord of Hosts, the holy mountain." Zechariah 8: 2a,3

I placed my requests into a crevice in her stones and quietly read Psalm 122:

"I was glad when they said to me; Let us go into the house of the Lord. Our feet have been standing within your gates O Jerusalem! Jerusalem is built as a city that is compact together; where the tribes go up, the tribes of the Lord. To the Testimony of Israel, To give thanks to the name of the Lord. For thrones are set there for judgment. The thrones of the house of David. Pray for the peace of Jerusalem: 'May they prosper who loves you. Peace be within your walls, Prosperity within your palaces.' For the sake of my brethren and companions, I will now say 'Peace be within you.' Because of the house of the Lord our God I will seek your good."

Jay:

As we strolled back to our hotel I said, "This journey is an extraordinary school. Somehow we have been given the chance to study here by our Master Teacher, the Spirit of God. How remarkable. Israel is the Bible's 'show and tell' and His people are exemplary custodians of it. It's an education and I feel unworthy of the honor.

But I believe, if we are teachable and trustworthy to pass on what we learn to others then we can ask the Holy One to mentor us and to give us of His good treasure day by day. I believe He holds many secrets. I want us to be willing to learn continually. There is so much to glean about His people and His land. The best way to do this is by serving them and by encouraging others to do likewise."

Meridel:

I whole heartily agreed. "It's like we've been snatched up, out of one life, to begin another," I said. "But remember the words, "If you love Me, love my People." I don't think we have a clue with our natural minds what we are being challenged to do. Our spirits are soaring because we are in this place where heaven and earth meet.

Actually we are on a treasure hunt, yes but we should realize that ultimately the Holy One of Israel is the real treasure."

Jay was very supportive of me and together we chose to try to learn as quickly as possible. We also made a covenant with each other to with-hold nothing. We must now discuss everything together.

Our challenge was to be completely honest and open with each other. Actually this is a good practice in any marriage. It is a *Timeless Secret* that has to be worked on daily. Somehow I knew we had to agree together before we launched out into any new venture or direction. We have held onto that principle for the last nearly fifty years, and it works.

Jay:

Yes, we both felt sad to have to leave Israel. Our plane tickets showed India as our next destination. Most of the tour members had gone back to the USA and only a small group was left. Gathering together we talked and prayed about our ongoing journey to the Indian subcontinent. From India, some of our group were to go on to Hong Kong and then directly back to the States.

Our schedule was different - after India we were also to travel to Hong Kong and the basic plan for the three of us was then to go to the Philippines. After that we didn't know yet. It was a walk, or should I say 'a journey of faith'.

Our next book in this series "*Timeless Secrets*, Volume 2 **Miracles among the Nations**" starts with our arrival in India. We found the unexpected and we needed "miracles" just to survive.

It is an adventure you don't want to miss!

Timeless Secrets

I will bless them that bless thee.
I will curse Him that curses thee.
Genesis 12:3

I believe one of the most direct ways in which one can be blessed is to love what God loves. It is clear from the entire Biblical record that God has chosen His People, Israel, to be an example people to the rest of the world. It is not because they are better; but simply because God chose to use them as an example to the world, giving blessings for obedience and discipline for disobedience. His character of unconditional love in action is revealed in his dealings with Israel, the only Jewish nation on earth. Who else but the Jewish people keep the biblical Feasts of the Lord, the Sabbaths, and a Hebrew calendar? They gave the rest of the world the Word, the covenants and promises and the Messiah. What is your response to the nation and people of Israel today? It is your choice! Here is the Creator's amazing principle which, if you look back through history has been fulfilled to the letter. Those nations and people groups, who blessed Israel, flourished. Those who cursed Israel disappeared.

Genesis 12:3 is a bench mark scripture that has blessed the humble and obedient. Beware! It has also caused the demise of the high and mighty that refused to bless. History bears record to this truth. Every anti-Semite throughout history has experienced the harsh reality of this Divine principle of judgment.

As we conclude the *Timeless Secrets* section in this volume, I would like to leave you with something you can hang onto easily to ensure blessing for your life and the lives of your loved ones.

If you will study the words 'everlasting' and 'covenant' in Scripture, you will find in the Bible that from Abraham, to the Patriarchs, through Israel, to the Messiah and up to the present, the theme of God's eternal covenants is central to Scripture.

This is where you can take a biblical stance in support of Israel. It is your choice to endorse His promises and to act upon them. If you do, you will be blessed. Especially if you choose to also honor the everlasting covenants,' by standing with Israel, you will experience abundant blessings coming into your life. Why? Because Zechariah 2:8b says that the people of Israel are 'the apple of His eye'. "Apple" is Hebrew for pupil of the eye.[32] The prophets of Israel were called and given the task of seeing God's plan and recording it. They are the people the Almighty uniquely created to 'see' and to 'pen' His plans for all of mankind. Pause and think of that! Selah!

"Remember His covenant forever, the word He commanded to a thousand generations...[33] and confirmed it to Israel for an everlasting covenant." 1 Chronicles 16:15, 17

"And the King will answer and say to them, 'assuredly I say to you, inasmuch as you did it to one of the least of these My brethren, you did it to Me.'" Matthew 25:40

*"Entreat me not to leave you,
or to turn back from following after you:
for where ever you go, I will go;
and wherever you lodge, I will lodge;
your people shall be my people
and your God, my God."*

Ruth 1:16

---

[32] The pupil holds the lens of the eye. Israel was given the task of 'seeing and recording' God's plan for all mankind and it is forbidden to hinder this plan.
[33] "A thousand generations" in Hebrew literally means 'eternity'.

To Be Continued...

Dear Reader:

The book you have in your hand, *Love My People,* Volume 1 is the first in a series known as Timeless Secrets, Volumes 1-8.
Faith is an incredible journey, sometimes stranger than fiction.
We invite you to continue reading and hope these books will be a blessing and an encouragement to you.

Timeless Secrets Series

Volume 2

Miracles among the Nations, takes you from Israel to India, on to Hong Kong, the Philippines, Asia, South America with a short trip to the former Soviet Union sandwiched in between. In each place Meridel and I discover that 'faith' can be learned. Ours is a unique school of listening and daring to 'be obedient to' the whispered instructions of the still small voice. Beginning in the Philippines, we experienced powerful blessings and tremendous revival. One of the secrets: each player on the team laid aside personal agendas for the common goal of touching that nation with what we called a "Spiritual Fiesta." Through these celebrations inside the Catholic Church, hundreds of priests and thousands of nuns where filled with the Holy Spirit! What a joy it is to bring you into our lifetime of adventures being led by the Holy Spirit. Along the way we learn many timeless lessons and we are delighted to pass them on to you. Our hope is that these secrets will be keys to His blessings in your life. Utilize our useful survival tips during those stressful times of life that we all going through now and in the future.

We share with you how we watched the Living God bring national revival into the traditional Catholic church of the Philippines and then out into many countries of South East Asia. First, we learned to have faith for ourselves. Later we learned how to have faith to travel the world.

That brought us to have faith to run a campground for 500 kids free of charge in Ecuador, South America. We watched as the Lord helped us to believe for the food to feed 1,500 meals a day near Quito. He used the most ordinary and down to earth local people. It was very heart warming yet challenging. So we sent out a "Macedonian call" back to the Philippines for help. Several of the dedicated young men and women we worked with in Manila responded immediately and came to help us. With the camp overflowing with children, the Filipinos humble, dedicated service was greatly appreciated by all.
We learned to believe God to heal the Ecuadorians sick bodies, refurbish their souls, and teach them to worship and in the midst of it all to pray for Israel.

The Spirit of God kept us 'current' in what was happening at that time in Israel. A band of children stood together with us. We received words and visions and intercession for the Yom Kippur War in Israel before it was even on the news. We were also greatly challenged to reach out to bless the entire region of South America by visiting many Jewish communities there. All this was in preparation for our next set of instructions.

Meridel and I were called to leave Ecuador to take up a brand new challenge. With our two young sons and one on the way we visited many of the Jewish Communities in Latin America. Our work was to warn them of impending danger by ever present "hunters" better known as terrorists. From time immemorial violent evil forces have continually tried to destroy God's people in the midst of their divine destiny. In this matter we were not prepared for the serious warnings we were given from on High to deliver to the Jewish communities in Argentina and Brazil. History has proven that they turned out to be shockingly accurate.

Volume 3

The Ingathering of My People leads us into an entirely new adventure. You will thrill to read how God gave us His instructions with practical ways to bless Israel. We began in earnest to visit the Jewish Communities in Europe teaching Christian people along the way.

We visited countries with histories of persecuting Jews; Italy, Spain, France, Holland, Poland, Ukraine, Yugoslavia and the USSR. In each place the Jewish people were targeted by anti-Semitic hunters. A mighty move of God was initiated among Christian people worldwide who continue to this day as 'fishers' helping in what has become a large modern day in-gathering of the Jewish people back to their nation of Israel.

For almost five decades we have traversed over 100 nations to warn the Jewish Communities of the real danger and tragedy of the 'hunters'. Historically they have pushed Jews towards their homeland, Israel. Our focus was always to raise up a body of believers in each place to understand God's Eternal Covenants with the people of Israel.

Volume 4

Fishers and Hunters. Jeremiah 16:16 describe Fishers and Hunters, the name of Meridel's first book. The fishers are Christians who help the Jews return home, and the Hunters (see Jeremiah 16:14-16) are fanatic Muslims who seek the total destruction of all Jews everywhere on the planet. This day is upon us, and the hour is already late.

Volume 5

Apples of Gold finds us moving from the French Riviera to Israel. After years of visiting Jewish communities, we practiced what we preached by gathering up our 3 small sons and returning to live in Zion. We are happy to still be here. Navigating our way through the many trials of new immigrants was a challenge. The boys had to come to grips with Hebrew school in Haifa and later in Jerusalem.

Israel Vision Studios were created and Jay began a brand new career as a documentarist. Our first film *Apples of Gold* drew the attention of the decision makers of Israel. We were invited to give a private showing first to President Navon in the Presidential mansion, February 1980. Days later the world premier was held in the prestigious Israel Museum in Jerusalem. The Israeli Foreign Ministry placed this documentary in their Embassies and Consulates worldwide.

That was the first of the 120 documentaries and hundreds of TV shows created in our studios. Apples of Gold was produced in concert with 100 Huntley Street TV of Canada.

Volume 6

Shoulder to Shoulder, is the untold story of the founding of the International Christian Embassy in Jerusalem. It centers on the establishment of this amazing ministry. In September of 1980, along with Merv and Merla Watson and Jan Willem van der Hoeven, Meridel and I, along with a hand full of others became the co-founders of the International Christian Embassy - Jerusalem. I was head of media and carefully documented the amazing birth of this organization. Today the ICEJ is perhaps the largest Christian Zionist organization in the world doing great good for Israel and her many peoples globally.

Volume 7

Let My People Go - Gates of Brass takes you behind the Iron Curtain into Soviet Russia. We were able to create a major film Gates of Brass based upon live interviews with Jewish Refuseniks (those Russian and Ukrainian Jews *refused* visas to Israel by the Soviet authorities) locked inside of the Soviet Union. What we did was absolutely forbidden. The KGB did their best to stop us but to no avail. We give all the glory of the Holy One. This film, produced by World Vistas/Israel Vision, won the First Production Award from The Canadian Film and Television Association.

The Jewish Community world wide used this film to educate and stir people into action. Consequently Jewish activists and Christian supporters joined together (often after viewing the film) and went into the streets and marched in front of Soviet Embassies worldwide crying out "Let My People Go".

Let us never forget that the Lord has answered the daily "Amida" prayers of centuries of faithful Jewish people crying out for "the ingathering of the exiles." The pleas of the suffering refuseniks were also heard from within the USSR. Slowly the Iron Curtain started to crumble.

Christians prayed and gave generously for flights and buses to bring them home. When the two peoples Jews and Christians found a way to agree together for a common purpose, then miracles took place. Over 1,000,000 former Soviet Jews were released home to Israel between 1991 and 2005.

Volume 8

Fruit that Remains gives you a peek behind the scenes of a media family living in Jerusalem. We recount a further set of amazing opportunities afforded us in Israel. Walk with us as we produce over 100 documentaries and 30 promotional DVD's for worthy causes about modern Israel. All of our productions give a Biblical perspective on unfolding events in the "land of Promise". By God's grace we created hundreds of TV talk shows, which were broadcast worldwide giving prophetic understanding to an extensive international audience in English, German, Finnish and Norwegian, concerning Israel living out her historic and Biblical cause.

Always expanding, our Blog now reaches more than a hundred countries with up to date insider information about Israel. Our sons have all gone on in media work, and the best is yet to come.

Fasten your seat belts, there is a lot more and we would be delighted if you would join us for the ride.

Jay and Meridel Rawlings

About the Authors

Jay Rawlings, BSC, DHA, PhD

Jay is a Canadian Israeli dual citizen who has worked and lived in Israel since 1969. Jay has produced, directed and written over one hundred thirty documentaries on various aspects of Israel that have educated a global audience. Several of his awards winning productions were placed in Israeli Embassies and Consulates worldwide. Israel Vision, the Rawlings weekly TV program and blog giving a Biblical perspective on Israel's historic cause, is broadcast worldwide and available on the Internet. As some of the first "fishers" the Rawlings visited Jewish Communities worldwide calling them home to their Promised Land where the Jewish people have a unique prophetic destiny. For nearly five decades the Rawlings media input has focused primarily on the People and Land of Israel documenting the fulfillment of the everlasting Covenants and promises of the God of Israel in and through His people.

Meridel Rawlings, RN, BA, MA, PhD

Meridel works as a researcher, writer, speaker, TV host, psychologist and therapist to the abused. She was a public health nurse with aboriginal tribes in India and later with Mother Theresa's Missionaries of Charity saving the lives of desperate Tibetan refugees in Darjeeling.

Fishers and Hunters, her best selling book, has seen multiple printings. It takes the reader into Jewish Communities world wide telling them of the need to return to the safety of Israel in accordance with scripture. The majority of the stories were lived out by the Rawlings family. Today the need for 'fishers, is more urgent than ever before with the impact of the 'hunters' rising up on a global scale. These radical Islamists and their doctrine of "jihad" are determined to destroy Jews, Christians, moderate Muslims and minorities. This epidemic is growing day by day.
As a survivor of sexual child abuse herself, she has for decades championed the cause for freedom for victims of abuse. She has produced a Power point, Small Talk, 'for children of all ages.' This cutting edge presentation gives tools needed to address difficult subjects; and equip children and people of all ages, not to "Put up or shut up!"

The Power of One is a DVD tracing her counseling work 'one on one' with clients in Europe and North America for the last thirty years. You will watch her counsel and teach during live sessions that bring dramatic change.

Meridel speaks out on vital family issues and abuse. Her highly acclaimed TV segment, Still Small Voice and newsletter impact people of all ages and add a unique and practical perspective on life.

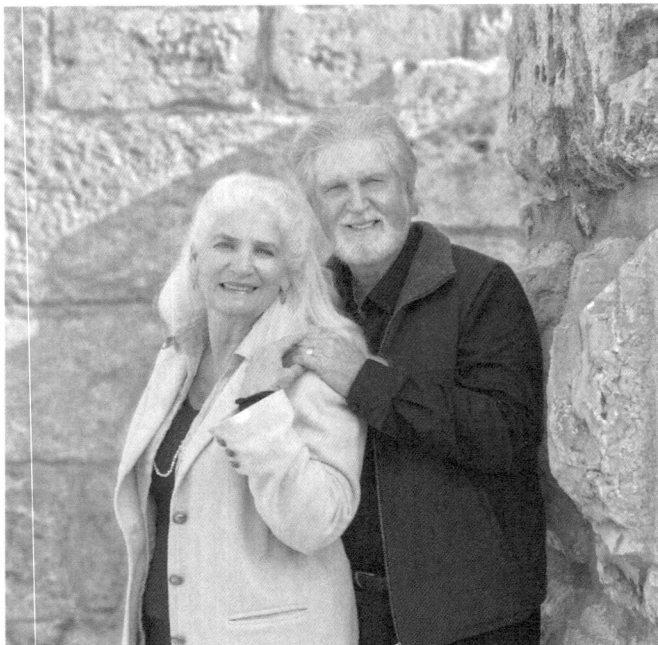

Jay and Meridel reside in Jerusalem, Israel.
Married 48 years, they raised four sons and now have eight grandchildren.

Media Resources

Books

1. Fishers and Hunters
2. Honor Thy Father?
3. Gates of Brass
4. Prophets Among the Nations
5. Blow a Trumpet in Zion
6. Israel, Islam and the Intifada
7. Choosing Life - Sexual Abuse Seminar Workbook
8. Erasing the Indelible Stain

Documentaries

(Available on You Tube, Israelvision.com, online and some are in DVD format. This is a current list but not exhaustive. Some items may be not yet been posted online or are out of stock. Most productions are 28:30 min in length and are broadcast quality)

1. Apples of Gold
2. Anatomy of Child Self Sacrifice
3. One Jerusalem Rally
4. WHY 2 K?
5. A Way in the Wilderness
6. Choosing Life
7. Music for Messiah
8. Redeemed, Part 1 & 2
9. The Word of the Lord from Jerusalem
10. Israeli Leaders Speak, Parts 1, 2,& 3
11. Streams in the Desert
12. Canadians in Israel
13. Hora Dance Troupe- Jerusalem We're Not Leaving You
14. Gates of Brass
15. How we got the Word
16. Five Deceptions of Islam
17. Homes in the Desert - Exodus Nord
18. Israel and the Coming World Crisis Parts 1, 2 & 3
19. Fire on Carmel
20. Messianic Praise and Worship from Israel
21. God's Key to World Redemption Parts 1, 2, 3 & 4
22. The Samaritans – Covenant Keepers
23. An Environmental Peace Plan

24. The Russians are Coming
25. The Terror Factor
26. West Bank Settlements, - Holy Land or Holy War?
27. Helping Jews Home
28. From Hebron to Jerusalem
29. Fishers of Men
30. What's New in Old Jerusalem?
31. Study in Jerusalem - Jerusalem University College
32. Between a Rock and a Hard Place
33. Oil in Israel
34. Israel at 50 Parts 1 & 2
35. A Lion of Judah – Teddy Kollek
36. Two Olive Trees – Israeli Prime Ministers Shamir & Peres
37. Love Your Neighbor
38. Temple Mount Faithful
39. Reviving the Stones
40. Rooted in the Land
41. Christian Revival for Israel's Survival
42. An Oasis for the Exiles
43. Tents of Mercy
44. Israel's Flying Carpet
45. One Jerusalem Rally
46. Jerusalem – Cup of Trembling
47. Fact of Fantasy – Middle East Analysis
48. Below the Red Line - Israel's Water Challenge
49. The Deadly Peace Game
50. The Violence of Lebanon – Past and Present
51. Golan Heights - A Peace Gamble
52. Creation Dance - Everything is Open - Miracles for the Handicapped
53. Empowerment Through Tradition - Bedouin Women
54. Peace, Peace and There is No Peace
55. The Crusades – Faith or Folly
56. Blessed is He that Watches
57. They Shall Come with Singing
58. Remembering the Past: Shaping the Future - Yad VaShem
59. Grandpa Jack's Farm
60. Operation Second Exodus – ICEJ
61. Assaf Ha Rofeh – A Hospital with a Heart
62. Zvi Givati – A Friend Indeed
63. Quest for the Hero Heart, Part 1 & 2

64. A Canadian Apology to the Survivors of the St Louis
65. Mount Moriah Trust - Part 1 & 2
66. Healing for the Family
67. Fountain of Tears - Part 1, 2 & 3
68. Kehilat Mevasseret Zion - A Unique Synagogue
69. Catch the Vision - Israel Vision TV promo
70. Home for Bible Translators Parts 1 & 2
71. Love My People- Israel Vision Update
72. The Power of One
73. Gilad Shalit - A Call for the Release of a Kidnapped Israeli Soldier
74. The Israeli Dance Troupe with Adi Gordon Rawlings - 'A Man Shall Arise'.
75. Fourth Jerusalem Assembly - Jewish & Christian Zionists Speak Out
76. Pastor Umar Mulinde of Uganda: The Heart of a Lion, parts 1-6
77. Israel, Iran and the Bible - Where Are We Today on God's Time Clock?
78. Israel, Syria and the Bible.
79. Israel, the Nations and the Future?
80. Human Trafficking in Nepal - C.A.N. Change Action Nepal. "You can make a Difference" against human trafficking
81. An Enduring Canadian Legacy - Part 1. Lambert Love, Pioneer Hotelier
82. An Enduring Canadian Legacy Part 2 - Keys to Success -The Bill and Audrey Martin Story
83. The Heart of God - At Work in the Holy Land Today
84. Abandoned No More - Operation Rescue of African Refugees
85. Exodus '47 Ship - 70th Anniversary
86. General Allenby Remembered - 100th Anniversary
87. US Embassy Moves to Jerusalem
88. Olive Harvest
89. Lifetime Achievement Award - Dr Jay Rawlings - World Jewish Congress and The Knesset Christian Allies Caucus
90. Israel at 70 (in production)

Power Points Productions (some in English, German or Finnish)

a. The Deadly Peace Game
b. Israel - the Most Unique Nation on Earth
c. Israel - Iran and the Bible
d. Israel - Syria and the Bible
e. Israel - the Nations and the Future?
f. Israel and the Coming World Crisis
g. Israel - Fact or Fantasy
h. Israel - World Terror, ISIS and Revival
i. Christian Zionism
j. Passover Seder (illustrated)

Sexual Abuse Seminars
◊ *Part 1 The Anatomy of the Disease* - DVD
◊ *Part 2 Global Implications* - DVD

Meridel's teachings are balanced with insight and wisdom that comes from years of experience and study. She weaves Biblical understanding into her years of practice in the field of counseling. "Enlightening, encouraging and enabling," describes Meridel's way of dealing with the 'secret' of abuse. Today, with the explosion of sexual abuse worldwide, her teachings are a must for all people.

Family Healing Seminars - 3 to 5 days, are life changing.
Attendees study from her interactive Choosing Life workbook. Meridel always makes time for children first, who are among her most enthusiastic listeners.

Newsletters
Sign up to receive Jay's **Israel Vision Newsletter** and Meridel's popular, inspiring yet personal **Still Small Voice** newsletter. Both give insight into the Land and People of the Bible as well as teaching you how to hear and obey the Still Small Voice. Sign up on line, www.israelvision.tv www.stillsmallvoice.tv

We are a faith-based operation wholly depending on the freewill offerings of our viewers, friends and partners. Thank you.

Donations
For tax-exempt donations to Israel Vision media work: send checks made out to Jerusalem Vistas / Israel Vision or donate on line via Pay Pal at our websites and blog. (Tax deductions available in Canada, USA, UK, Germany and Israel.

CONTACT INFORMATION

Jerusalem Vistas/Israel Vision
P.O. Box 40101
Mevasseret Zion 9080500
Israel

Office telephone: +972 2 533 0382

Email: jvistas@gmail.com

Websites:
www.israelvision.tv
www.israelvisiontv.blogspot.com
www.stillsmallvoice.tv